Celebrating the Pagan Soul

CELEBRATING
the
PAGAN SOUL

*Our Own Stories
of Inspiration and Community*

Compiled and Edited by
Laura A. Wildman, High Priestess

CITADEL PRESS
Kensington Publishing Corp.
www.kensingtonbooks.com

CITADEL PRESS BOOKS are published by

Kensington Publishing Corp.
850 Third Avenue
New York, NY 10022

All Kensington titles, imprints, and distributed lines are available at special quantity discounts for bulk purchases for sales promotions, premiums, fundraising, educational, or institutional use. Special book excerpts or customized printings can also be created to fit specific needs. For details, write or phone the office of the Kensington special sales manager: Kensington Publishing Corp., 850 Third Avenue, New York, NY 10022, attn: Special Sales Department; phone 1-800-221-2647.

First printing: May 2005

10 9 8 7 6 5 4 3 2 1

Printed in the United States of America

Library of Congress Control Number: 2004116403

ISBN 0-8065-2624-6

To Saundra A. Katz-Feinberg

(1949–2004)

Her life was an epic tale that left us wishing for more

and

to my children, Orlando, Kin Srey, and Xena,

whose stories have just begun

CONTENTS

3. FIRE: Magical Transformation—from Wow! to Oops!   109

4. WATER: The Seasons and the Cycles of Life   147

THE CYCLES OF LIFE

Acknowledgments

his book could not have been created without the many individuals from the Pagan community who willingly shared private moments, personal epiphanies, and humorous gaffs. I received numerous amazing and wonderful stories—so many that choosing which to put into this book was extremely difficult. I wish there had been space to print them all. To all who offered their beautiful moments, I give a deeply felt thank you.

Thank you to my friends, Mary Grace Farley, Judy Harrow, and Susan Taplinger, who helped me edit some of these works, giving helpful comments and support.

To my many friends whose love supported and sustained me during the difficult hours of compiling and completion.

To my siblings: David, Douglas, Ken, Judy, their spouses and children. We may not always see eye to eye on everything, but whether we are debating or sharing laughter, we are always family. And to my parents, Paul and Victoria, whose love for their children and extended family is inspirational.

To the members of Apple and Oak Coven; your continued presence in my life nurtures my soul.

Thank you to Jennie Dunham, my literary agent, and Bob Shuman of Citadel for holding my hand throughout the process, giving helpful suggestions, and cheering me onto completion.

To my beloved husband, Tom. Ours is a love story that continues to captivate my heart. And to our beautiful children, just the thought of you makes me smile.

And to the God and Goddess, who guide my steps. Even when the lessons are difficult to understand, I am still grateful for the gifts offered each wonderful day.

INTRODUCTION

itches and Pagans have a unique way of experiencing the world. Our Gods and Goddesses are not separate from creation. They are an active part of our everyday lives. Magic is real and through it we believe we can, and do, create change, altering our lives—sometimes with unexpected results. This book is a celebration of the Pagan experience, an intimate glimpse into the fascinating, and usually private, lives of Pagans. It is a collection to savor, filled with personal experiences, magical stories, and tales of transformations, memories, and insights. It includes a sharing from individuals whose names are well known within the Pagan Community as well as those whose smiles appear only on the fringes of magical circles.

It has been said by the statisticians who keep track of these things, that Paganism is one of the fastest growing religions in the United States. The Wiccan Tradition, in its various flavors of practice, is the largest and therefore most well known of the modern Pagan faiths in the United States. But while all Witches are Pagans, not all Pagans are Witches. The title Pagan covers a plethora of religious traditions including, just to name a few, practices such as: Ásatrú, Druid, Heathen, Santerian, Voodon, Witches who are not Wiccan, and Reconstructionist religions which attempt to reproduce, as best as can be actualized, the rites and practices of ancient Pagan cultures.

Whether Witch, Shaman or generic Pagan, they are all considered to be members of the Pagan Community. This makes our Community a delightful diverse mix, consisting of a wide range of social and economic backgrounds, beliefs, ages and races. Each member contributes his and her own unique spice to the hearty Pagan soup. In order to give the reader a good overview of perspectives, I tried to scoop up as many tidbits as possible from the stock.

While I've never met a Pagan who didn't have a magical story, when I began this project I wondered if people would be willing to expose these personal moments. A sharing over the light of a campfire with friends of like mind about the night the Goddess stepped down from the moon and claimed the teller as Her priestess is vastly different from putting that experience down on paper to be published for public scrutiny. To my joy, although I did receive a couple of polite refusals to my request, the vast majority of those I contacted were not only willing, but also eager to contribute.

As I began to collect submissions, an additional potential emerged. Contributors and myself began to see this volume not only as a vehicle to share magical insights and Pagan lives, but also as an opportunity to disclose moments in our magical history—a format to record for future generations personal memories of treasured teachers who helped to forge the beginning of the Pagan movement, to tell of the struggles we have faced as we strived for recognition as a religious faith, and a sharing of moments that transformed both the Community and the world. For me these pieces are the most precious. As our Community ages, we are losing our Elders, those individuals who helped to form the Neo-Pagan movement. With their death, we lose portions of our past. Our collective memories often prove to be faulty, as we inadvertently, or intentionally, rewrite history to reflect current ideals. For those teachers and the students who loved them, I give a heart-filled thank-you for being given the honor of allowing your memories to be shared with the public. To all who submitted pieces, I give my deepest of thanks. It took courage to come forward and risk the offering of a self.

While many of the tales within these pages are inspirational, humorous and joyful, this is not a feel-good book. The wheel of life contains moments of tragedy and loss as well as joy. As Pagans, we embrace the fullness of the cycle. Here you will find pieces that will touch your emotions and others that will be more thought provoking than motivational. The common factor between all the stories in this book is that they are all true experiences.

The book has been split into five chapters, loosely associated with the five elements: earth, air, fire, water and Spirit.

Earth, is our Community. As our first author points out, whether it is the physical embrace of friends or a whisper spoken in our ears by our Gods, we are never truly alone. The Community is the deep roots which sustain and nurture. The Community can provide for its members a place of stability from which to grow. It is the space where we can share ourselves, our experiences of joy, anger, disappointment and healing. It is our coven, our tribe, and our family. It is the generations that came before and those who will come long after we have turned to dust. Be it through birth, friends, classes in an occult store or chance meeting that provided the key, the finding of Community is often called, the "coming home."

Once the path is made clear, the next step is to learn the ways. The second chapter is Air, the breezes that bring clarity. Here we gain understanding through our teachers, mentors, students and inner guides. The gaining of knowledge is not always easy. "Are you willing to suffer to learn?" is a question heard at some initiations to the mysteries. This does not mean physical pain. It is the ache of stretching beyond personal boundaries to connect with the Divine forces. It is the emotional pain of looking within and facing inner demons or touching old festering wounds, seeing them with clearness so that the healing process can begin. Learning can also be as gentle and inspiring as a story told by an elder that holds layers of meaning for the student. Or the guidance of a teacher who helps the student to make a connection that illuminates new areas for self-discovery. As the story, *The Mandala*, explains: "The expanse of knowledge is unlimited. There is always another petal, another area to explore."

Magical Transformation is the heart of Fire. Magic takes many forms, from the ceremony that touches the emotions to the manipulating of energy to create change. The chapter begins with Oriethyia's poem, "Magic Is Not Easy." It is the intent, the will, the heart that directs the magical energy. Everything is connected. Change begets change. One touch of the delicate web will affect the other strands. For this reason magic, and the forces that preside over the elements, should always be approached with respect or, as the wise words from Penny Novack in *Youthful Hubris Meets Elements*, "I highly recommend one remember one's manners when dealing with Beings Who move vast forces."

Water is deep, fluid and changing, as are the continuing movements of the seasons and the cycles of life. It represents the fourth chapter in the book, and it is split into two sections. The first contains stories focused on the wheel of life, rites of passage from birth to grave. "These rites," as is mentioned in the introduction to *Growing Pains*, "help to transition both the individual who is experiencing the transformation and those whose lives are affected by the change." The second offers stories that are entwined with Sabbats, our seasonal holidays, and celebrations.

"Have you seen the face of God?" is the question that begins the last chapter, Spirit: The God and Goddess in Our Lives. The Gods and Goddesses are with us, in us and around us. She can be seen within the face of a drunk woman who dances in abandoned joy. He is found in the song of a warrior's battle cry. They manifest in our dreams, offering warning or support during points of transition, or journey to us on the back of dark storm clouds. Our deities are not inaccessible, can sometimes have a sense of humor and often will manifest in unexpected ways.

Enjoy *Celebrating the Pagan Soul.* I hope these stories touch you as they did me.

1

EARTH

*Community—the Roots That Nourish,
the Families We Create, the Coming Home*

In the last twenty years, alongside the often noted resurgence of "occult" and "magical" groups, a diverse and decentralized religious movement has sprung up. . . . While these religious groups all differ in regard to tradition, scope, structure, organization, ritual, and the names for their deities, they do regard one another as part of the same religious and philosophical movement. They have a common name for themselves: Pagans or Neo-Pagans.

—Margot Adler, *Drawing Down the Moon*

✒ A Witch Is Seldom Alone
Cat Chapin-Bishop

I put on my coat and head for the door. I think of going up into the pasture to meditate, but I decide I need to walk. Closing the door behind me, I am swallowed by the dark. It is the waning moon after Halloween, and only the stars give light. The road is an ashy ribbon; my feet are the only sounds. The stars are jewels hung in the bare branches of the wild cherry tree.

I let the rhythm of my stride lull me into a half-dream, until I feel a creeping between my shoulder blades. There is the vivid sense of something behind me, and if this were a trance journey, I know I would see Him when I turn to look.

I turn. I see only darkness. Once more, I resume my walk along the country road.

I didn't become a Witch in order to join a coven of thirteen. Does anyone? Despite the forms of modern Wicca, surely for most of us who name ourselves Witch, the original attraction is to the old, archetypal figure of the old wise woman, living alone in a little hut at the edge of the woods. Certainly that was the figure I grew up with in my imagination. And as joyful and meaningful as my contacts with other Pagans and Witches have been, it has been as a Witch alone that I have experienced most of what is meaningful to me in my religion.

The high pasture is to my east, where the shoulder of the mountain looms behind it. I can see my neighbor's house now, and across the road a streamlet has cut itself a silver runnel in the turf, up there by the crossroad. This is the place I once heard something like a woman singing, and yet not. Looking up now, I watch a shooting star mark the spot.

3

*I walk on and stop thinking. I feel wind cutting my face, open-
ing my eyes until they seem clearer and more awake than usual,
although I am almost blind here in the shadows.*

I think about this sometimes, now that I'm a High Priestess
of a fairly bustling coven. When do I ever walk into my house
without a half-dozen messages on the answering machine? The
standard response to a ringing telephone in our house is a
groan. But again, almost never do I pick up the receiver without finding that the caller is someone I really want to talk to. I
love my Pagan friends and my coveners, and they feed my
spirit. The work we do together is meaningful and rich, such as
healing magic for a child with cancer and more healing magic
for a dying elder, to ease her or his passage. This week one of
us has lost a job; last week I was asked to bless an expectant
mother's pregnancy. The study coven will meet at my house
tomorrow, and there's a sabbat to plan for next week. This is
the work of the Witch, and I honestly do love it. It gives me
everything I need, spiritually . . . except, of course, for solitude.

*Soon I pass another house, a warm cluster of lamp-lit windows
where I am not expected. I feel like someone in a story, and that
house looks kindly to me. Though I would like to stop and bask in its
light, I know that even here, among my neighbors, the people who
live there might feel uneasy if they see me standing, watching from
the darkness. I move on, leaving their lights behind.*

When I was a new Witch, living in Vermont with my baby
daughter and her father, solitary visions were all I had. Working
from books and magazines, I taught myself to seek the Goddess and God in meditations and trance journey. I taught
myself to see my own aura, and, by trial and error, to cast a
simple spell. When I finally found those first few other souls
who felt as I felt, and believed as I believed, I became drunk

with the excitement of it. So much of my early work as a Witch had been in silence and without validation, that coming into my first Pagan circle was like coming indoors from the frost and the silence of winter's coldest night. I wept the first time I heard Pagan music played on a friend's guitar.

I grew, and I learned, more and more quickly with the support of loving friends. The night I was initiated as a Witch was a cold one, just past Samhain, and there was snow spitting at me from the high Vermont hills where we had gathered. When we came inside after the ritual, to food, music, and laughter, I began to feel for the first time what so many of us have described: having found my people, coming home at last. And that Beltane night a year or so later, when I first drew down the moon in a coven of my own, something in me cracked wide open. So much of the bitterness, shame, and foolishness I'd hoarded in me for a lifetime came spilling out. I didn't become someone else, but, in a sense, by letting Her flow through me, I became myself for the first time.

As I pass the graveyard, where neighbors a hundred years dead keep their silence in the night, another star falls above me, like a blessing or a tear.

It wasn't exactly gratitude that made me become a teacher of the Craft, and it wasn't exactly a plan. More like the way my Witchcraft grew, or the unwinding of the road beneath my feet. I found myself questioning safe assumptions that had held my life pressed neatly together, like the twin halves of a walnut shell. As I said, my relationship to the Goddess cracked something in me wide open, and when the changes were done, I found myself living in a different state, divorced, remarried, and beginning to teach what I had learned. Or to try to teach. Truthfully, I think that all I can offer as a High Priestess is one-half of the experience I had: the welcoming and fire-lit part.

The lonely road students have to discover for themselves. And they do—but, in the meantime, Witchcraft for me has become mostly a matter of details: making sure everyone gets directions to the ritual site, that the ritual starts on time, and that every student learns to ground as well as raise the power. This is meaningful work, but hardly ecstatic.

I hear a noise now, just behind me. This time, as I turn, I see I have a companion: a black darker than the shadows, and a white bright enough for even my eyes to see. It is a skunk. As I move quietly on, he keeps pace beside me, like a tame cat or small dog. In a while, he turns aside, busy with errands of his own.

"If you see the Lord Herne, tell Him I miss Him," I call out softly. The skunk does not answer me, and again I am alone, my only company the cutting edge of Vermont wind and the sound of my own feet.

There is a saying among Buddhists, "Before enlightenment, chop wood and carry water. After enlightenment, chop wood and carry water." And Witchcraft, even more than Buddhism, is a religion of the here and now of life. Having been to the mountaintop, of course I must return to the valley and share what I have seen. But there has to be a balance. If I only teach and act as my coven's administrator, my spirit will die, and my spiritual teaching will be a dead teaching. And so I read, write, teach, lead, and focus energy within the group, and that is good. But I never cease to hunger for those moments of transcendence, even when they leave me quivering and afraid. I need the Gods to lift me out of myself sometimes, not just in drawing down, but in other, more private and mysterious ways. I make what openings I can. I go to some gatherings without my child or my coven, so I can greet my Gods outside my roles of mom and teacher. I walk my dog alone in the woods, and I try to listen to what I hear in the quiet. And I go, from time to time, to a Quaker meeting, where I can feel the presence of community and Spirit without being center stage. These times are harder to arrange than you might suppose.

But my hunger is part of my spiritual journey, too. Without community, I had so little focus or purpose in my life. And without my time alone, or at least my hunger for it, what would remain of mystery in me? I didn't put this longing into me. I like to believe that They did, and that They have a reason for it.

Suddenly, I hear it: another sound . . . hooves? Hard, vigorous, in the road ahead. I hardly dare to breathe, though the sound is gone almost as soon as I hear it. The wind falls still. Rusted apples from a ruined tree squelch beneath my feet. A pasture slopes away from me, halfway down to the valley floor below. And now I hear it truly: hooves. One set, heavy, running. A large animal, quite near. My heart beats fast. Not a cow—much too swift and no one pastures cows near here. A horse? Again, there are none near. Could it be a deer? It must be! But so large! A great deer . . .

The sound of hooves is gone as suddenly as it came. I watch until I am very cold, but I neither see nor hear anything more. I turn at last for home—and now I feel it once again, that creep behind my back. Always, always, what I seek and what I long for is just behind me, just beyond sight. I walk alone, looking for my Gods in the shape of a tree trunk, the sound of hooves, and the feel of wind. I can't tell if my hunger is emptiness or fullness. Am I blind? Or do I live in visions?

So I walk home again. Wood smoke and the brilliant yellow lights of home enfold me. I take off my coat, put away my athame, and reach for my pen, ready to write down all that I have seen, or not seen, while I wandered alone in the dark.

Tunbridge, Vermont

∾ Thoughts from the Median Strip
Margot Adler

A few years ago, I had one of those experiences that crystallize inchoate feelings. In December 2001, I was asked to do a report on some people who stood on the median strip of the West Side Highway in Manhattan and cheered the rescue workers on: the firefighters, the metalworkers, and others who went back and forth from Ground Zero. I had heard vague stories about some of these folks, and I had a picture in my head of some patriotic characters waving flags and such. There hadn't been too much written about them and I wondered who they were. I knew that, personally, as a Cold War red-diaper baby, I was not about to wear a flag lapel pin, even after all this, but I thought I would have a look.

Then I got a call from a science reporter at NPR who said he knew one of the leaders of this disparate group that gathered on the highway intersection of West and Christopher Streets. His name was Barry McQuade and he was a gay man, and what's more he was HIV positive and had been so for twenty years, and he had been "adopted" by a local fire department. I thought this was pretty unusual in itself—you don't ordinarily think of firefighters being sympathetic to gays . . . so at nine o'clock that night, I went off to meet Barry in front of a Chelsea neighborhood fire department on West 19th Street.

Barry was carrying a very large American flag that he had picked up from somewhere. It had worn, fraying edges. He had tacked the flag to a pole. He said he was known as the "flag man" at Christopher and West Streets, where the people gathered to cheer. He said he was a good twirler, a skill he learned in the Gay Pride Parade. He pulled up the sleeve of his jacket to show me a tattoo he had just had made: it was a red AIDS ribbon that had POS, for HIV positive, written on it. He showed me around the firehouse, where the guys all knew him. For two and a half weeks after the events of 9/11, he cooked for them, answered phones, and helped neighborhood organizations respond to needs. He had no expertise, he said, but the skills he learned caring for his dying brothers gave him the knowledge of how to help.

The fire station, like all the firehouses around the city following 9/11, looked like a Tibetan shrine, or one of our Pagan altars, with candles burning, pots of flowers, poems etched in stone and written on paper, walls of children's artwork responding to the 9/11 events, and, of course, pictures of the five firemen that this company lost. Notices of dozens of memorial services were posted on a bulletin board. After he gave me a tour of the firehouse and greeted some of the guys, we left for Christopher and West Streets.

It was ten p.m. The median strip on the highway had someone there most of the time. There were two or three black teens that Barry described as homeless, who guarded the signs, the bags of posters, and the cooler of water and sodas. One was riding around on a bicycle, but didn't really want to talk. There was a huge door that Barry found on the street and that he had painted. It faced the highway with the words: "Hero Highway." And there was a sign that faced the other way that said, "Point Thank You." There were about a dozen people on the median strip: An Irish American couple in their sixties (whose politics I would probably disagree with) holding signs that said, "Thank you, Heroes." There was a young woman named Diane who jumped up and down with red, white, and blue pompoms, and a woman named Claire who had all these pins on her Yankee hat—representing police and fire departments all over the country that while on their way to and from the site stopped on the strip to have a word with the cheerers. "I've been pinned," she laughed.

As cars passed, particularly trucks with debris or busses filled

with the next shift of replacements, the group cheered, whis-
tled, waved, and the vehicles honked their horns in response.
Many of these people told me that when volunteers were not
needed at the site, they came to the median strip because it
was something they could do. A policeman stopped to say hello
and thank them. Barry told me a woman once told him that
the people who cheered had saved her husband's life. Because
he had been working for so many hours at Ground Zero, he
couldn't see straight as he was driving home. He was just about
to close his eyes at the wheel when he saw the people with the
signs and flags cheering, and it gave him enough energy to go
home. A guy named Steve, who is a neuroscientist—he only
came down very occasionally—said to me, "I am doing all kinds
of things I have never done in my life. I am cheering police,
wearing a flag, buying cigarettes for relief workers, when I don't
believe in smoking."

Maybe it was different in New York City—being in the cross
hairs so to speak. Being in a city that felt like a target. But a lot
of us went through convulsive and life-changing emotions. For
me, my whole fifty-five years of life was defined by being an outsider in my own country. I was the child of socialists. My father
was a Marxist. My mother was a bohemian. I was a Jew, a New
Yorker, a woman, a Pagan, a Witch, all things that made me
"the other" in America. When John F. Kennedy was killed, I
couldn't really mourn: my family was so afraid that we would
become a target, because my mother belonged to the Fair Play
for Cuba Committee . . . and Lee Harvey Oswald was a
member. I always stood silent in my public high school during
the Pledge of Allegiance, and I fantasized that I was the daughter of a Soviet diplomat. It was a fantasy, but the feeling of
being an outsider in my own country was real. Although I fell
in love with an American soldier in Vietnam, I also, for a few
days, harbored a deserter during the war and believed quite

frankly that we were supporting the wrong side. During the 1960s, I came very close to joining the Communist Party, I was arrested in the Free Speech Movement and went to jail, was a civil rights worker in Mississippi, cut sugarcane in Cuba with the Venceremos Brigade, and was gassed in demonstrations in Chicago, Washington, D.C., and Berkeley.

For years, I also felt some of the desperation that fuels violence. While I don't know if I could ever *do* violence, I was so alienated from my own country in the late 1960s that I was sympathetic to the Weather Underground. And, more recently, my own deep frustration about the chances of saving the earth from environmental destruction led me to feel a certain sympathy toward the Unabomber and those who take drastic—even destructive actions.

And there I was, as always, in the city that was never loved by America: it was too diverse, too European, too sexually out there, too dressed in black, too un-American in some way, and suddenly, we in New York were the heart of America. And we were a target not only because we are the business capital, but because we are seen as a kind of symbol that all fundamentalists from Osama Bin Ladin to Jerry Fallwell hate. I was on a highway with people who are often the "others" in America—black homeless teens and gay men with AIDS—and they were waving American flags and cheering the rescue workers on, and suddenly I found myself overwhelmed by emotion—a feeling that I was no longer a stranger in my own land. I felt stirrings of kinship I could barely recognize—as if I had become a true citizen of my country for the very first time.

And I was not alone. As I talked to my husband in the morning at breakfast, I realized that my whole family was changing its self-definition. We were no longer quite so much outsiders; we were part of a living community that felt under attack. And we questioned those new feelings daily.

Having given up that sense of being apart, of being a

stranger in a strange land, an identity that I had held on to so fiercely for five decades, doesn't lessen my concerns about America's political direction or its leaders, or my qualms about military tribunals, racial profiling, or attacks on civil liberties, but it does change my relationship to America—it has healed it in some odd way. I do not think I will ever wear a flag pin, and I still believe that the U.S. Constitution is a better and more powerful symbol to fight for than a piece of cloth that's red, white and blue, but there is this new feeling and identity. As we approached the new year of 2002, we were enmeshed in our city, our community, and our country in a new and powerful way, and that change was larger than any we could have ever imagined.

New York City

Note to "Thoughts from the Median Strip": This article was written less than three months after the 9/11 attacks on the World Trade Center brought New Yorkers of all classes and races together in community. My own identification with my city and country was deep and genuine. But in the years since I wrote this essay, many politicians have exploited the tragedy of 9/11 for their own gain. Most New Yorkers, myself included, once again feel like aliens. Once again we are outsiders, separated from much of America by our ideals and beliefs.

∾ Through Loneliness
Judy Harrow

It was the community meeting at the end of a weekend Pagan gathering—time for feedback, which usually means time for a freewheeling gripe session. This one was more acrimonious than most, although I don't remember what we were arguing about. It was years ago.

In the middle of some agitated disagreement, an elderly gentleman with a slight foreign accent stood and shouted over the voices, "Don't you try to tell me what's what. I was Pagan before you were born!"

Huh? Nobody around here was Pagan before I was born. The Pagan movement in my area was jump-started by emigrants from England who arrived during my teen years. What in the world was this old guy talking about?

After the meeting, a few of us went up to him and asked.

He'd been born and raised in Germany, where nineteenth-century artistic romanticism raised interest in native folklore. By the twentieth century, this had developed into an early neo-Pagan movement. As a teen, he joined a Pagan youth group that had been started by an enthusiastic and popular high school teacher.

Then the Nazi regime took power. It tried to co-opt and pervert native German neo-Paganism. Shamefully, some of the leaders collaborated. Others resisted. Some perished in the camps. And some, like this man, escaped.

He made his way here, to the United States, became a citizen, and married an American woman. By then, many Americans had come to associate German Paganism with Nazism, so he kept his faith in secret. All those years, observing as best he could, he did not even tell his own wife about his religion.

They had a son. He, too, had no idea of his father's long-held beliefs. The boy grew up and went to college. While there, he and a group of friends on campus discovered the Craft. One day, the young man went home to face Mom and Dad, to level with them about his new religious commitment.

In time, the old couple renewed their marriage vows in a Pagan ritual. Their son acted as Priest. May all who keep the faith through hardship and through years of lonely silence eventually come to such a moment!

Metropolitan New York

✎ Sharing a Common Flame

Laura Wildman-Hanlon

The lights were slightly dimmed, and the candles and incense on the altar were lit as we began to make our way into the ritual space. A group of singers were softly singing Yuletide songs, "The Holly and the Ivy," "The Animal's Yule," "Deck the Halls," and others familiar to the crowd. Many joined in with the singing, lulled by a sense of comfort and familiarity.

Clutching song sheets and an unlit candle, we formed a large circle around the perimeter of the room. With a moment of silence, all were encouraged to look around and see the many smiling faces. The circle of smiles said, "See, we are not strangers here. We are just friends who haven't yet met."

The overhead lights were then shut off, causing the glow on the altar in the middle of the room to become the center of attention. There were eight candles on the altar, each representing a sabbat, a point in the seasonal wheel. Beginning with last Yule, moving to Imbolc, Ostara, Beltane, and around the seasonal year events and celebrational activities associated with each holiday were recalled by the participants. For example, for Ostara participants spoke about hunting for colored eggs and the marriage of friends within the Pagan community. The remembrance of each sabbat ended with the extinguishing of its corresponding candle and the statement, "But tonight it is winter solstice, and we're in the dark." With each holiday remembered and its candle extinguished, the room became darker, and darker, until all that lit the space was the solitary center candle representing the current solstice. When that, too, was extinguished, the group, all sitting in a windowless room, was plunged into complete blackness.

Total silence echoed through the space for what felt like an eternity but was, in fact, not more than a minute. Suddenly, a match was struck in one corner of the circle, and a single candle held by a short older man wearing a yarmulke stretched its light across the room.

"Shalom!" he greeted the celebrants.

You could see a few puzzled expressions among the participants.

"This time of year," he continued, "those of us of Jewish faith celebrate Hanukah. Let me tell you about the miracle that occurred at our temple of Solomon—of the oil lamp that shed its light within the temple walls for eight days!" Then he told his story. It was completed with the phrase, "Now it is Winter Solstice, and we're in the dark," and then he extinguished his flame. The room was once again plunged into blackness.

Across the circle, another light was lit to reveal a woman holding a candle in one hand, and a staff in the other. She was dressed in a simple white robe that was covered with a plain, dark hooded cape.

"This is the eve of the battle between the Holly King, king of night, and his brother the Oak King, ruler of light," she said. "Let me tell you the story of why the mistletoe is sacred to us Druids and the twice-yearly battle between the brothers of night and day." When she had finished, she too plunged the room back into darkness.

Another light was quickly struck in yet a different section of the room.

"As Isis gave birth to Horus, and many other Goddesses give birth to their Sun Gods, so does Mary give birth to Jesus." And so the Christmas story was also told.

Another light. "Gutten tag, let me tell you about the Yule Log . . ."

Yet another, "Saturnalia, is our Roman holiday . . ."

The African American celebration of Kwanza, Native American tales, English and Scandinavian stories, and even a rendition of the modern classic *'Twas the Night Before Christmas*, was

shared. Each story started with the lighting of a candle and finished with a quick breath and darkness. Over a dozen different
celebrational allegories of the season were shared.

The last to speak was Kurt Talking Stone. "Greetings to all
beings upon Turtle Island," he welcomed us. "The longest
nights brought my people together as a community. All the
campfires in all the lodges were extinguished with the excep-
tion of one, the central fire pit in the middle of the village.
The tribe would gather around this fire. As an extended family,
they would sleep by it. They would eat by it. They would sing by
it. They would share the burden of cold and dark together. All
the members of the tribe would tend this central flame, ensur-
ing that it would not go out and leave them to bitter winter.
For three or more days they would do this. Then a warrior was
chosen from among the tribe. He would take a torch, light it
from this central fire, and run from lodge to lodge, relighting
each camp from this shared common flame, taken from this
communal fire, which all the people had spent time and energy
tending. In the darkness of winter, we are all one tribe, sharing
a common flame." And the light went out once again.

Silence was strained after the flurry of stories. When the tension in the room could be felt, a voice whispered.

"In the darkness of winter, we are all one tribe, sharing a
common flame. Slide your hand along the floor until you
touch another person in the gloom. You may sit now in the
cold and in the dark, but see, you are not alone. There are
others beside you. They are your friends, they are your community. They come from many different worlds; they have
many different perspectives about life. But tonight we all have
joined together. All of us share one common thought at this
time of year: we hope and pray for the growing light, the
returning of the Sun."

The striking of a single match after our eyes had become
accustomed to the blackness blinded us for a brief moment.

When our sight returned, we found standing in the center of the room a young boy, wearing a white and gold robe, his face and hands covered in gold glitter, and a crown of oak leaves on his head. Holding his candle up high, he loudly proclaimed, "Light is returning!"

With shared tears of joy, the flame from his light was passed around the room from candle to candle, binding us together as a community, while we joyfully sang Charlie Murphy's: *Light is Returning*.

Together, we went from light into the darkness, and darkness back into the light. The diverse stories of the winter season, with the glowing light that accompanied each tale, brought to heart that our group was larger and more intricately beautiful than we may have originally realized. In the dark, we had to reach out into the unknown in order to touch it . . . to connect with it. It was through this experience that the true meaning of the passing of the flame around the circle would be completely understood.

So it is with our beautiful community. You have to trust that out there, in the unknown, there are others of like mind . . . stretch out your fingers in the dark until you find your community. Once touched, its light will be brighter than can ever have been dreamed.

Western Massachusetts

ᕒ Community Is a Verb
Thom Fowler

Community is not an accident. Community, like love, is a verb. It is something you *do*, not something you *have*.

The Pagan Community, like the Gay Community, doesn't look or act like a single-minded group of people. So why is it called a Community? Because there are people, events, businesses, groups, organizations, and institutions that provide touch points for interaction in and involvement with . . . well, the Community! It is a Community because "it," as a general idea, is a space that can contain you and nourish and nurture you.

In the summer of 2003, I spent a week at a Pagan retreat center in Geyserville, California, called Isis Oasis with Francesca De Grandis, my friend, initiator and teacher. Isis Oasis is a temple to the Egyptian cosmic mother Goddess, Isis, and a retreat center all rolled up into one. We arrived at the site during the last day of a retreat sponsored by a non-Pagan writer's group. Since Francesca and I are also writers, Loreon Vigne, the proprietor of Isis Oasis and a priestess of Isis, felt that Seshat, the Goddess of the written word, would be an appropriate goddess around which to build the weekly public ritual. I'm never averse to getting divine inspiration before I sit down to write. Allowing the Goddess to inspire what I do is a service to the Community.

Francesca is one of those multihyphenate types. She is a Witch, a writer, *and* a humorist. Hanging out with her is fun if not a lesson in practicality. During a walk around the retreat site, she found a jack rabbit that had been freshly crushed by a vehicle. When she returned, she told me about the rabbit.

"Oh, how tragic," I replied.

"The whole body is crushed, but the feet and the ears look okay," she said in a matter-of-fact way that sounded more like she was directing a salvage operation and I was already supposed to understand that. And then she asked, as easily as if she was suggesting I go to the farmer's market for some organic greens, if I would go back, find the rabbit, cut off the good parts, and preserve them for her.

Because it was just one of those days and because I knew from being her student that there is always more to what Francesca asks me to do than what is apparent, I decided to stretch myself. I said, "Okay." When I was in junior high school I lived in a town called the Valley of Enchantment in the San Bernardino Mountains. While it wasn't exactly a rural, agricultural community, there were self-styled "mountain people" who were living a somewhat more rugged life simply by virtue of living in the mountains. My neighbors decided to raise rabbits. It was through them that I learned how to skin and clean a rabbit carcass. Francesca and I weren't going to use the animal for food, but being shamans, we would work with the animal for magic and spiritual healing.

It was a serious, perhaps even *grave* favor she was asking of me, but the way she asked struck me in an ironically funny, B-movie horror flick way. Because I knew from that point forward, the first thing I would think whenever I see roadkill is, "What part of this can I use?"

The only knife I could find, and I probably shouldn't be telling you this, was a dull, serrated kitchen knife from the guesthouse at Isis Oasis. (Ewwwww!) I'm not telling you which one. But I did wash and sterilize it, because to do so was an act of taking care of the capital "C" community.

I pulled the carcass to the side of the road where I hacked and sawed at the legs and ears. A good pair of poultry shears would have done the job faster and easier. Luckily, the leg bones were crushed so I only had to sever the skin and tendons. It is much less savory tearing at a crushed animal while fur, bones, and blood go flying about than buying a properly butchered bunny at the grocery store.

I brought back the feet and ears and we said a prayer in the Native American tradition to guide the rabbit spirit back to the Great Spirit. The rabbit was killed by a human for no purpose; it was even an unconscious act, what the military might call "collateral damage." Our ceremony helped repair the sense of disconnection between us and the rest of the living world. My spirit and your spirit are intricately woven into the spirit of nature and the cosmos and tending any part of the Goddess's Garden through ritual or ceremony, however brief or improvised, also touches the deepest, most mysterious parts of ourselves. Some people call this holistic healing or deep ecology, and the practice of permaculture, based on similar ideas of cultivating the well-being of the whole, has recently seen an increase in popularity since first being introduced in the late 1970s.

I was working on a Third Road–style self-initiation for several months before this retreat. The Third Road tradition of Witchcraft was developed by Francesca out of her own Craft practices. Walking the Third Road is a gradual surrender to power that honors your uniqueness, which results in a radical repossession of one's self. It shares a portion of its mythology and practices with traditions such as Reclaiming and other fey-blooded traditions first taught by the shamans Victor and Cora Anderson, but has its own distinct character. At its core is the Craft. While I hadn't planned on doing it that weekend, the conditions were right for it. I spent a few days creating the rite, which Francesca helped me polish.

I was at Isis Oasis with Francesca, who was the only person there I knew and was a part of my life, but I felt like I was surrounded by my Community. I was being held and nurtured in a space that allowed me to be my Pagan self and act out my personal mythology and make the magic of my life. Loreon and Zarita, who help take care of Isis Oasis, Francesca, all the people who have walked this path, myself, and now you, the reader, are in this Community because we are supporting each other's journeys of being Pagan and living with and loving in the Old Ways with the God and Goddess and the Old Gods and the wild spirits of nature and the cosmos. Thanks for being there!

During that same period, my Burning Man camp, *You Are That Pig*, was finishing up the details on our miniature golf course. Burning Man is a week-long fringe art and performance festival held each year the first week of September in the Nevada desert. The hallmark of the festival is that there are no spectators, only participants, and there is no commerce or trade, only giving. Our contribution that year was a miniature golf course. We didn't have any luck finding putters and a search of the thrift stores in the San Francisco area yielded a harvest of exactly two. Francesca told me about the Salvation Army complex near Isis Oasis. This time I hit paydirt. We went there and found a load of cast-off golf equipment. I acquired thirteen putters for which I only had to pay five dollars because I told the guy who was pricing the stuff that they were for an art project. Isn't it nice to *get a discount* as an artist rather than *being discounted* as an artist?

Isis Oasis and Burning Man—there aren't too many places where I get to be queer, Pagan, freakish, cosmic and costumey without any judgmental or inquisitive stares. These are places that celebrate diversity of expression. Every time I try to integrate with mainstream society, I get evicted. I did all the things you are supposed to do. I went to college, developed a career, got a corporate office job, and even got out of poverty to become middle class. But it is an uneasy and uncomfortable fit, like a shoe that is just too tight or a turtleneck that itches. More times than I can count, I've been politely asked to move along.

I shuffle the Tarot cards and ask the Goddess what she is trying to do for me. I draw the Fool. The Fool stands outside order—the order of urban planning, of suburban subdivisions, of job interviews and hierarchy, of laws and contracts, of industrialization and finance, of dogma, tradition, and habit. The wisdom of the Fool card characterizes my need to take risks, to walk without thinking, and to trust that the Goddess is leading me into places where only I need to go and where only she can take me.

In order to train and explore my mysticism and work my healing magic for myself and the larger capital "C" community, I have had to return to the edges of what is possible so that I can re-enter the order of our society and speak to it in a new old way and teach it new old things and bring it new old places. Without my Communities, this journey wouldn't be possible. I would become roadkill like the jack rabbit whose foot still rests on my altar. But unlike that foot, which ties together ritual and spiritual power, my own Foolishness is treated as childish irresponsibility by the larger culture. My journey forces me to find creative ways to live and work inside our cultural matrix—a matrix which is so contrary to what I feel in my bones and blood and spirit.

Without my precious Community, I am just another novelty item, a spectacle, a curiosity, having the parts of me separated from the whole mystery of myself, dried and displayed, lifeless and inert, holding neither power nor wisdom.

The culture I was born into is poison to me. The Community I have chosen to guide me and support me on my healing journey is mother's milk.

Geyserville, California

✎ A Generic "Coming Home" Tale
Spellweaver

I call this story a "generic tale" because it varies little from those told by the vast majority of people who found their spiritual home within the Pagan Community. The years may have changed small aspects of the story; the first book for many seekers has shifted from Drawing Down the Moon *or the* Spiral Dance *to one written by Silver RavenWolf or a site on the Internet, but the essence remains the same.*

It begins with an acknowledgment that he or she is different from those around them. A search begins for something that is unidentifiable, a need for a connection to something that seems elusive. Then one day there is a chance finding of a book, or an unexpected meeting with an interesting individual, that gives that something a name. This word opens up a whole new world. The seeker finds that he or she is not alone; there are many who share similar beliefs.

The first experience of meeting others of like mind might be a small private ritual with friends or a large public gathering. Either way, there is a rush of emotions as the realization hits that the search has ended, they have come home.

I grew up in a small town in western Massachusetts. This was before the farmer's fields gave way to the tendrils of suburbia. I remember spending hours reading mythology and fairy tales while sitting atop the old apple tree in my backyard. From this perch, I watched the yearly cycles: the production of buds, leaves, flowers, and finally apples. When the fruit dropped to the ground, it decomposed into the soil. Its nutrients were taken up with the water into the tree's roots completing a cycle. It was magical. This old tree gave me more than flowers and fruit, it gave me the seed to my spirituality; the bud of a religion that only after many years would I understand had a name: Paganism . . . Wicca.

Adolescence often found me alone and wandering the woods and fields. I knew that the earth and sky were speaking to me. I could feel the energy buzzing around me, vibrating like contented bees. As I walked through the woods, I never felt solitary. There was always this feeling that around the next bend, or behind a tall tree, something else tread. Something was watching and quietly waiting. Having a Christian background, I wondered if it was God.

So, I tried participating in a born-again Christian group. But the more I read about the angry God of the sky, the more I realized that His myths didn't speak to me. This was not what called to me from the mountains, trees, and rivers. I turned to the library. There, I found books on magic and witchcraft but, in the early 1970s, it seemed they were all demon focused. Wicca and neo-Paganism, while churning and developing in conclaves throughout the country, had not yet reached my part of the world in a form that could easily be recognized. The concepts that I found in these books of working with energy, the animating forces that connect all life, rang true, but Satan was no better than his counterpart. I rejected it.

In high school, I began creating rituals to better understand and connect with these forces. Under an old pine tree whose sweeping branches touched the earth while its pinnacle met the sky, I made offerings to the Lady of the woods and gave honor to the seasons. I used the lessons from my sweet apple tree, the stories of fairy lands, and the myths of the mighty Gods and Goddesses, to guide me. When I left for college, I kept my beliefs to myself, locked safe inside.

Life continued on and many years passed, but the feelings, though sometimes quieted under the static of everyday living, never left. Then one day, over coffee conversation with one of my friends, for some reason I began to talk about my beliefs. I told her my belief that the earth and all on it are alive and that all life is interconnected in an intricate web; one touch could affect the whole; that energy could be used as a tool, to be moved and directed to create change; and that while I considered myself deeply spiritual, I did not relate to any of the Abrahamic religions.

She laughed and said, "Of course not, you're a Witch!"

That word took me aback. All the negative connotations flared up. "No, I'm not interested in Satan," I shot back.

"No. I mean you're Wiccan. You know, earth-based spirituality, Paganism, Goddess worship," she simply replied.

The next time I saw her, she handed me the book *The Spiral Dance* by Starhawk. I read it cover to cover in one night. Here was everything I held as truth. Here was the voice that called to me from the woods since I was a child. It had a name. There were others in the world that also heard this song and shared in these beliefs. I cried in relief. I cried with joy.

One year later, on a chilly May evening, I arrived at my first Pagan gathering. Shaking with excitement, I followed the sounds of the drums echoing through the night air to the ritual fire. The faces of the men and women around the circle glowed from the heat of the flames. The air crackled with energy. Dancers, in a variety of non-wear, leaped and danced to the beats. Voices joined in with the drums, sending sounds of passion and joy up with the smoke.

I felt the Goddess and God around me. They were in those who moved with me in sacred motion. They were in the air and the flames. They were in my blood and bones. They were the life forces that pulsed through all. The wind gently blew and for a moment I was back atop my beautiful apple tree riding the branches as they swayed with the breeze. The earth was alive in a continuous spiral of life.

A warmth rose from the ground and up through my body. It filled my heart until it felt like it would burst. I opened my mouth and the primitive howl, held captive all these years, burst forth. It joined with the community of other voices, carried up to the star-filled sky. Joy rained down and washed over me in waves of emotion. I had come home . . . I was home.

Goshen, Massachusetts

❧ How I Became a Witch

Brook Willowbark

In 1967, I went to my first love-in on Boston Common and met the Hippies. Soon afterward, I started working for a downtown bookstore, which I loved. The owner opened a paperback books and posters area in the basement and put me in charge of it. I did pretty well, thank you.

About that time I was also given a copy of Timothy Leary, Ralph Metzner, and Richard Alpert's *The Psychedelic Experience* and was told that when I was ready, my first dose of LSD would be bought for me. I took my first trip in the classic way it was supposed to be done: in a controlled environment, with an experienced Guide. I stood looking at the tiny pink pill in my palm thinking about the dire warnings in the press that I could easily become insane or accidentally commit suicide. But I needed my life to change. I felt that, as much fun as I was having, somehow I was just spinning my wheels, and some greater path lay just out of my sight. It was worth the risk.

Life changed, and life didn't. I still worked, paid my bills, occasionally balanced my checkbook, bought veggies, protested the War, swept the floor, made coffee, sang Beatles tunes, and rolled posters. But something had changed that I wasn't aware of. It was as if a neon sign had been placed on my forehead that only certain people could see.

One fine spring day, two people came down the stairs into the bookshop and set off every alarm in my psyche. First, I saw a little, bent, old woman with a hooked nose. *Well,* I thought, *if ever there was a classic witch, there she is!* But then her companion came into view—a much younger very black man well over six feet tall with a pompadour hairdo. Somehow, the two of them together terrified me. They began to look at the stacks. I kept my head down and kept rolling James Dean posters. After a while, she and her companion headed straight for me.

"I'm looking for a book my coven recommended to me," she said.

Her coven, I thought. *Great. Let's try to keep her religion out of this.*

"It's called *Stranger in a Strange Land,*" she said.

My enthusiasm took hold. "That's a great book!" I said. Our distributor couldn't keep up with the demand, and we had been out of stock for over a week. I told her so and offered to go into the back and see if the stock person had found it. But no, it still had not come in. As I headed back to the front of the store, a very clear message came to me. It said that if I wanted my life to remain safe, I would get someone else to go talk to these people and find something upstairs to do for a while. Yet, something else in my deepest self yearned to go forward, even if it meant going off some kind of cliff. With a lump in my throat, I stepped back behind the counter.

"It's still not in yet," I told her. "But it's a great book, and if you can find it elsewhere, you should do so."

She looked at me thoughtfully. "My name is Witch Leslie," she said, "and this is Brother Ruby Heart. Our coven meets on Thursday nights at this address." She gave me a slip of paper. "You should come." Then she left.

I was absolutely flummoxed. Was I still in the twentieth century? I thought all the kooks lived in New York. Having no intention whatsoever of going to her coven meeting, I threw the slip of paper away rather quickly. Life went on.

And yet, over the next year or so the oddest thing began to happen. Three times strangers came up to me—at work, on the street, and on the subway—with variations of "Hello. I'm a Witch. Here's my phone number. Please call me." I began to become really frightened. Had I been marked as Sacrifice Du Jour? I had long since given up on Christianity and had studied several other religions, but none felt right. I liked Alan Watts' explanations of Hinduism and Buddhism, but I wasn't interested in disengaging from a world that didn't seem all suffering to me. Finally, a flaky acquaintance of mine came up to me one day and said there was someone she really wanted me to meet. "He's a warlock! I invited him over to your house for supper next Saturday."

I knew I was trapped. Obviously, I was not going to be let off the hook until these people had had the chance to make their say. So, okay, I'd listen as politely as I could, say "No thanks" politely and firmly, as if I were dealing with the Mafia, and send them on their way. I made spaghetti.

On Saturday evening, she appeared on the front porch with a middle-aged man who had piercing blue eyes and a forked beard. It was a very tense supper. We retired to the living room with coffee and dessert. I sat very close to my boyfriend. The man broke the awkward silence.

I felt as though I had asked questions as a child and been shut down so many times that I had forgotten about them and had agreed to walk the path as those around me did. But now someone was speaking to these questions in a straightforward and logical manner. No one had proof of religious truth. All propositions had to be tested, at least in the heart. He began to go into the physics of magic. I realized that these people didn't want me as a blood sacrifice, they wanted *me!* I felt profoundly split in two. One side of me still firmly intended to get away from these nut cakes just as fast as I could. *You're a scientifically educated American. You have every economic and educational advantage. You can't possibly fall for this! Witchcraft!? Be real!* The other said, *If you were a young reporter, and a spaceship landed in front of you and the door opened, would you walk away? If you turn your back on a chance like this, the rest of your life will be mediocre. Is that your choice?*

After a week or so, when it was clear that my doubting head and my fearful body hadn't a chance against my heart, which felt at home with this role, and my spirit, which essentially told me that if I walked away from this, we would cease to be on speaking terms, I officially asked to be taught.

I was asked why I wanted to learn, and then he wanted to know if I had the talent. "Not everybody does." He brought me out into the backyard on a sunny day and asked me to dissolve a cloud that he pointed at. I had never heard of such a thing, but after some instruction on how to focus on the clouds and visualize them dissipating, I did as he described, and to my surprise, it worked. I did three in a row of his choice, and that satisfied that requirement.

He next advised me to get not only a Tarot deck, but also an unset moonstone. He said that the moonstone, when charged by the power of the full moon, acts as a battery giving power to the deck. I was to take the stone and place it under my tongue, against the two great veins, and meditate on the full moon. The stone, filled with both the energy of the moon and of the Witch, is then placed on the Tarot deck, empowering the deck.

It was July, and the hedge of roses was in full bloom, scenting the night air. I set up a lawn chair, sat down, put the moonstone under my tongue, and gazed at the moon. I must have been out there an hour or more, but at some point I blinked, and there before me was the Goddess Isis, kneeling with her wings spread before the Moon. I blinked several times, but She did not disappear. I was mesmerized with love and devotion. Then I blinked again and both She and the Moon were gone, though the sky was still filled with the opal light. Very softly on my head I felt two hands, and my whole being held very still. It lasted no more than a minute, and when I blinked again, there was the moon in the sky, seeming smaller and further away, and I knew that whatever happened to me had passed.

Since that night I have called myself a Witch; I have learned a great deal, and I still feel abysmally ignorant. The Craft has grown and changed, and become a legitimate religion on the world stage, one with much to give and with a great future.

I hope I can find some way to contribute to its success, and I have never regretted my choice for an instant.

The wild woods of New Hampshire

❧ Where the Wild Ones Were
Susan Taplinger

On a cold March afternoon in the late 1970s, two fifteen-year-old girls from New Jersey set out on a quest to find a mysterious place called the Magickal Childe. I was the first of these two; the second was my unsuspecting friend, Caroline. Neither of us had ever been to an occult shop, but we were buzzing with adrenaline at the prospect of actually finding one.

My fascination with the occult had begun two years earlier when, at a garage sale, I unearthed a tiny Dell purse-book titled *Everyday Witchcraft*—a bargain at 10 cents. On the cover was a photograph of a fluffy white cat lounging beside a tall pink candle. Inside were spells for protection, love, revenge, and beauty. The book taught that Witches typically greet each other with the words "More Power to You" (a phrase that, to this day, I have yet to hear a Witch utter).

My next big find was *Helping Yourself with White Witchcraft*, by Al G. Manning. Manning ran the ESP Laboratory in Los Angeles. Following the instructions in the book, I soon developed a daily practice of chanting and energy exercises.

I would sit at my little makeshift altar (nothing more than a tray pilfered from my mother's bedroom and candlesticks borrowed from the china cabinet), light my candles, and chant, "Spirit of the Great White Light, burn away my psychic night." This incantation was meant to cleanse the room and purify my own energy. Manning explained that as soon as you started to do psychic work, unseen forces would try to stop you. This concept frightened me and made sitting down to chant an act of conquering fear in itself.

Other times, I would sit cross-legged, visualizing the chakras, wheels of light beginning at the base of my spine, and ending somewhere above my head. I would intone a different note of the musical scale for each, trying to sense the energy rising as I did so.

So far, my occult pursuits were hidden from the adults in my life, except when I had to explain my reasons for closeting myself in my bedroom every evening to summon the cosmic forces of the universe. Otherwise, my practice was solitary and detached. Now, however, I was ready to step brazenly into a new, mysterious world populated by Witches and Warlocks.

When we arrived at the Magickal Childe, I stood gazing in at the storefront window. It was crammed with sinister-looking props: skulls, black candles, knives, and all sorts of objects I didn't recognize. This froze me momentarily. *Good* Witches didn't traffic in such evil-looking things, did they? After some hesitation, and with more than a little trepidation, I entered the store, pulling poor Caroline in after me.

A pretty woman with long flaxen hair stood by the counter. I approached her timidly and asked, "Uh . . . do you practice white Witchcraft or black Witchcraft?" She sighed a great sigh that seemed to say, "You *worthless* little brat! Do I look like Glinda from the *Wizard of Oz*?" Out loud she said in a withering tone, "Witchcraft is a RE-LI-GION. The magic is secondary." Deflated and chastened, I slouched away to continue my exploration of the store, peering fascinated at the rows of books, jars of herbs, and shelves of arcane paraphernalia.

That day I also met Herman Slater, the owner of the Magickal Childe. Although I didn't know it at the time, there were those who regarded him as disreputable, if not downright evil. Wearing a black turtleneck, his beard in a sharp goatee, and seated high up behind the raised counter, he looked imposing enough. But as I came to know him, I found him both funny and endearing.

Herman invited me to the Pagan Way classes, which met every Sunday. The visit to the store had been enough of an occult experience for Caroline, so the following weekend I made my way back to Chelsea alone.

The first Pagan Way class was a revelation to me. It took place in the temple, which was a private space in back of the store. Flags emblazoned with esoteric symbols representing the four elements hung from each corner of the room. On one wall hung an art nouveau poster of a maiden clothed in a garment of stars, holding her hand up to her mouth as if to stifle a giggle. On the opposite wall hung a banner depicting a beast that looked frighteningly like the stereotypical Christian Devil, complete with horns and tail.

In the coming months, the "evil" Herman would look me in the eye and make quacking sounds until I broke up laughing whenever I seemed depressed or disheartened by some family drama. The impatient woman with the long blond hair turned out to be Valerie, Herman's High Priestess. I came to idolize her for her gorgeous hair almost as much as for her knowledge and stature.

"Witchcraft is a celebration of life," she explained to the class. "There is no heaven or hell. We don't believe in sin, only mistakes." I was fascinated. Here was a model of spirituality that rejected guilt and regarded human life as sacred, beautiful, and worthy of reverence. I felt as though her words were healing my concept of reality. I wanted in.

For the next two years, I faithfully attended classes. Every Sunday morning I would walk to the local bus stop, ride the bus into the city, and take the subway all the way downtown. Looking back, I am astonished at the energy and time I expended. These days I will go to great lengths to avoid public transportation, and tend to choose sleeping late on a Sunday over almost any temptation, spiritual or material.

But I was an eager young teenager, filled with the zeal of the newly converted. Each time I walked down 19th Street toward "the shop," as I came to call it, I was filled with an almost uncontainable energy of anticipation and excitement.

After Pagan Way classes, I would usually stay for whatever lecture was scheduled. I'd go to anything: talks on Tarot, ceremonial magick, herbs, runes, even a lecture given by a group of Satanists. I got to know members of the OTO, or Ordo Templi Orientis. (Members of secret societies love Latin almost as much as they love abbreviations.) These ceremonial magicians followed the work of the infamous but fascinating Aleister Crowley. I even attended a Gnostic Mass, in which celebrants partook of "cakes of light," wafers containing certain bodily fluids of the priest and priestess.

Much like the cakes of light, I swallowed most of this new material with little question. It took years for me to "digest" much of what I was exposed to in those days and to develop the discernment I needed to distinguish between what was nourishing and useful and what was junk food or even poison for me.

I studied the basic ritual and soon was the only woman in class besides Valerie who knew it by heart. I was often called on to lead the Pagan Way circle, sometimes even for public events.

One Sunday, a large public party was being held for one of the Sabbats. When I arrived, Herman grabbed me, handed me his athame, and ordered me to lead the ritual. Looking back at the scene that day, I realize there were several highly respected elders watching the circle, in front of whom I'm sure I would quail today. At the time, I simply took the situation in stride. This kind of fearlessness is a blessing bestowed only on the very young and the very ignorant.

My experiences at the shop were in stark contrast to those of my everyday life, and I fought long weary battles with my parents for the right to keep attending classes.

My weekly trips to the shop were my lifeline to a new world. Each week I encountered a stimulating and baffling array of characters and ideas. Perhaps even more important to a struggling teen: when I was at the shop, I was treated as an adult.

At times my illusion of adulthood would be shattered unceremoniously: My father sometimes picked me up after class. On our way out, he would embarrass me by asking, "Susan, did you remember your glasses?" or "Did you take your allergy medicine?" I would flush with anger and chagrin.

But it was my mother that Herman feared. Though he had never met her, he knew from my stories that she was the family force with which to be reckoned. My first Sabbat made this even more evident.

It was Beltaine, and, as it turned out, it involved more than the usual revelry. The Beltaine sabbats I attended later in life paled in comparison to this one—nothing wilder than a little dancing, a little wine or juice, and a little feasting. Valerie had tried to warn me, saying that I would be meeting a lot of "happy people."

As a rule, the group worked robed. To wind the maypole, the men stood still holding their ribbons, and the women wove in and out around them. Each time a woman passed a man, she would kiss him. The winding process became by degrees slower and slower as the kisses got longer and longer. As the festivities wore on, all of the robes disappeared except mine, and I was confronted with more naked adult bodies than I had seen or imagined in my short time on earth.

Later in the evening, full of wine and food from the feast, I willingly followed a self-styled wizard named Gandalf, who was all of nineteen, downstairs to Herman's basement apartment. There, I finally shed my robe and my virginity, the latter being something I had been wanting to get rid of for some time.

Although society hadn't grown quite as litigious as it is now, I was jailbait just the same. After Beltaine, I was seen as a liability, and Herman made sure that I had my mother sign a statement giving me permission to attend classes and "festivals."

One day, when my father came to pick me up, Herman shuffled over to my dad. "Mr. Taplinger," he said, "Susan is one of the most sincere members of our group, and we'd like to initiate her. But we need your wife's permission."

I sat watching from behind the counter, blushing, giggling like an idiot, and squirming uncontrollably. Here was Herman telling my father that he thought I deserved initiation, something I desperately wanted. I was astonished and delighted, but also dismayed and embarrassed. How could I go home and ask my mother for permission to become a *Witch*?

Asking my mother was something I simply could not find the courage to do, and my father certainly never broached the subject with her. Looking back at this, I wonder whether, with the right words, I could have cajoled her into agreeing. I'll never know. I never worked up the nerve to ask. I continued on as a noninitiate until the group broke up about a year later when Valerie got married and went underground. It was to be years before I could accept an offer of initiation on my own behalf. By then, I was no longer the eager young neophyte, and my original teachers had scattered.

Several years ago, I finally got up the nerve to walk down 19th Street. At first I thought I had turned down the wrong block. The shop was gone. I had to double back a couple of times to be sure I hadn't missed it. By now, for all I know, lattes are being sipped where we once toasted the Gods.

Since that time, I have explored a number of spiritual disciplines, both Wiccan and non. Each one has had something valuable to teach. It is a gentler path now, but the risks I took and the mistakes I made all those years ago serve me well today. I have learned to trust my own judgment and the wisdom of my gut.

Those were wild and precious days, and I am grateful for those who took me in at a time when I craved wisdom and acceptance in equal parts. Many of the wild ones I knew then have left this earth. Others still wander it. I offer my blessings and thanks to them all.

Metropolitan New York

❧ Women's Tales
Dana Kramer-Rolls, Ph.D.

I come from a family of agnostic/atheist liberal Jews, at least on my mother's side. I don't know much about my father. He was a French national who lived in the United States in 1939 as a scholar, and then returned home.

What I was told of my grandmother's grandmother was that she was a very brilliant woman. She was a teacher and a wise woman whom the gentile Russian judges and lawyers would come to for advice. When she came to the United States, she took an interest in theology and was critical of the women in the synagogue who only went to gossip in the gallery (it isn't only in mosques that women are segregated).

My grandmother was a suffragette, as was her maternal uncle, a doctor who was her mentor. More than once she was deposited at her father's shop by the local police after she had chained herself to the gates of city hall to protest for women's rights. She told me wonderful tales of gracious evenings at her uncle's home where she listened to the discourses of his friends, people like the psychologist Alfred Adler and the economist Thorstein Veblen.

My grandmother also had an interest in theosophy, an eclectic spirituality, and I know she attended séances in the 1930s.

She often took me to her favorite tea leaf reader, a devout Catholic Irish immigrant woman, who was really good at it (she also read playing cards). My grandmother taught me to be an intellectual, a grande dame of the old school while at the same time a modern woman and a seeker of knowledge. She was spiritual and in her own way magical.

Even with this individuality of spirit, it was my mother who was the strange one. Caught in the wrong era, my mother was a free spirit. She scoured the fashion magazines and designed her own remarkable clothes, all a little too elegant for an office. Before pantyhose, she dyed her own stockings in colors, something not even thought of. She liked purple a lot.

My mother also did what she had to do to survive. She was an actress and a writer. She started a literary agency and later took a position as an editor. I remember all the wonderful ribald literature on her shelf—*The Decameron*, Rabelais, and that sort, nothing modern. She also had what few books were available on Witchcraft, mostly the evils thereof and titles on the mass hysteria of nuns and that sort of thing.

She also read to me *Winnie the Pooh*, the A. A. Milne poems, *Alice in Wonderland*, and *Through the Looking Glass*. But the most special of all was William Shakespeare. We started with *A Midsummer-Night's Dream* and moved on to *Macbeth*. Looking back, these books were magical texts, and she was introducing me to magic.

My mother taught me a lot of mental techniques, such as full-body relaxation, and kept teasing me about my rationalism (the young scientist that I was at the time). She would ask me if I could hold up a comb or pencil with my mind and would take me to parties to have me predict the roll of dice or the throwing of coins (which I could accurately do about 90 percent of the time. I wish I could still do it). I know this was all prior to my tenth birthday, because when I was nine she left New York to start a life in California. I joined her a year later, but she had a boyfriend and was involved in getting married or whatever they did. I went back to New York to live with my grandparents. My mother and I stayed in touch, but it was awkward. It wasn't until I had experienced the adult world of difficult relationships and failed dreams that I understood.

I saw my mother years later, around 1965, after I had graduated college, completed early grad work, and lived in Europe for a couple of years in the grand bohemian tradition. At that time, she was running a writing camp on a farm she and her husband bought in Oklahoma; it was advertised on the back of *Fate* magazine. She coyly mentioned to me that she had brought me back from Europe with her "yogis," hinting that she had done magic with others.

Following in the footsteps of these independent women, I created my own path. From my earliest childhood, I heard the animals and trees speak. I majored in biology in both college and graduate school. I also rebelled, as is the right of every young adult, and became a Christian, an Episcopalian to be exact, and almost a priest in that church. I learned tons about religion, mysticism, and ritual. But I found my way back to the Goddess, who knew and loved the land and all of the nonhuman people, as the animals and plants are, and who also knew the spirits that lie hidden but that are everywhere.

In time, I was initiated, elevated, and made a Wiccan High Priestess and an elder in not one, but three major branches of modern British Traditional Witchcraft . . . not because I have hunted for more cords, but because I have been around that long. I have even tipped many a horn with the Heathens (those who practice the tradition of pre-Christian Viking Scandinavia) and sat in the high seat as a seidhkona, a seer and witch of the Norse tradition. For me, it isn't the rituals or the names of the local gods and goddesses that matter so much as being one with the magic. I'm not saying that all gods are one god and all goddesses are one goddess, as Dion Fortune said, or that each god and goddess is a different entity. I just don't know. I do know that when we reach for the gods under any name, we become transformed. The Spirit of Witchcraft has infinite names, and no name at all, and Nature is magic incarnate.

For many years, my mother's beliefs remained a mystery to me, but I had strong suspicions of her spiritual practices. The clincher came when an old Irish woman who had lived in my apartment building on the Upper West Side in New York City told me an odd tale:

> *Your mother, she was a clean woman. And kind. Why, I saw her at night in the summer, sweeping, and because it was so hot, she wasn't wearing any clothes, not a stitch, and so as not to wake you, she did it by candle light.*

This testimony had to have come from an observation made some time prior to 1949, long before the 1954 publication of Gerald Gardner's *Witchcraft Today*.

For all I know, my mother, as with so many others, got the sense of being magical and reconstructed her own way from literature, art, and cultural notions. We must not forget that magic was afoot and accessible through the Golden Dawn, the novels of Dion Fortune, and all those other quasi-lodge, quasi-nature religion witches from the Pan and Diana era, as the God and Goddess were often called. There were also writers with Pagan leanings like Kenneth Grahame, who wrote *The Wind in the Willows* (remember when the animals worshiped the spirit of the forest at dawn?). Real Witchcraft was also still in the hands of good Catholic ladies, such as the woman who read playing cards and tea leaves for my grandmother.

My mother died about thirty years ago and my grandmother has long passed through the veil. There is nobody left to ask what she knew and where she learned it. I have no contact with my mother's husband or his family, so I will never know if my mother re-created her rites from what little was published about witch trials and folk traditions, whether she somehow found a family tradition to train her or if she was involved with some pre-Gardnerian U.S. Witches.

But whatever my mother did, or where she got it doesn't matter. What she gave me was wonder, books, and a way to see and trust in my own inner magical abilities. That is far better than a tradition and initiation and all the baggage that goes with it. We have five generations of magical women, counting my daughter; we are a family tradition all by ourselves. From the depths of Russia to the coast of California, we are an unbroken line of Witches, Witches All.

Richmond, California

⮾ Quaker and Pagan
Peter Bishop

I grew up in a bland Protestant church (my family was Methodist on my mother's side, rationalistic agnostic on my father's), but I never felt spiritually satisfied. When I left home for college, I started visiting all the different churches on campus, and I found myself drawn to the Episcopal Church, where the incense, the Gregorian chant, and the Eucharist were so evocative of the presence of the Divine. I spent the summer that I was twenty years old in a Benedictine monastery, with serious thoughts of coming back when I was older to make it a lifelong vocation.

I also joined an organic farming co-op. If God created the natural world, then living in harmony with nature could only bring me closer to God. I grew long hair, gave up eating meat, and began reading books like Theodore Roszack's *The Making of a Counterculture* and some of the mystical ramblings of Wen-dell Berry, especially his collection of poems called *Farming: A Handbook*. This is when I really became Pagan, though years would pass before I found that name for it.

My last summer in college, I visited a left-wing Christian community in Georgia called Jubilee Partners. They seemed to combine the best of the "hippie" values I had found in the farm co-op with a commitment to doing work in the world—both things I'd felt lacking at the monastery. Jubilee presented me with a paradox: though their politics were far to the left, their theology was startlingly conservative. Their founder had been a Southern Baptist, and the community, though ecumenical, still had a strong Baptist flavor. They found their God through a literal reading of the Gospel and had no place in their worship for a personal, contemplative relationship with the Divine. I had always regarded the Bible as poetry and myth—"Deep . . . calling unto deep" (Psalm 42)—but in the Southern Baptist milieu of Jubilee, the same collection of writings became more like a Pledge of Allegiance, recited merely to reinforce a common orthodoxy. In the intense, almost cultish community of Jubilee, I had to face the Bible's literal teachings head-on as I never had before. *Only Christians are saved.* I couldn't escape the implication that Mohandas Gandhi—however much we admired him and emulated his work at Jubilee—burns in Hell, while Jesse Helms, however evil, has his place in heaven assured. It was a contradiction I could not ignore. I was living what ought to have been the ideal Christian life, but by the end of that summer everything I believed in caved in under me.

The loss sent me into a depression. I went back to visiting different churches, but now it was more like flailing around for handholds over the abyss. I went to a Universalist Unitarian (UU) service in Washington, D.C. I liked it a lot. They had a fiery black preacher who talked about his experiences with the Freedom Riders in the 1960s. But when I attended the UU church in my hometown, the local minister was an interim replacement, exhumed from retirement, and his sermon about how Native Americans are really nice people after all was anemic and painfully dull.

I visited the Metropolitan Community Church, a denomination for gay and lesbian Christians where a friend of mine was a minister. I liked their theology and their rather unique perspective as misfit Christians who nonetheless refused to go away, and I thought rather wistfully what a good fit that would be for me if only I were gay.

I took a Buddhist meditation class, but my "monkey mind" was just too busy, and it was there that I learned to crack my knuckles. I went with my landlady to a Kundalini Yoga temple, and found myself allergic to the whole guru-worship thing. I decided to try going back to the Episcopal Church for an Easter service, but changed my mind after waking up that morning from a dream in which the priest who had baptized me was a traveling charlatan revival preacher. He wanted me to be the shill for a fake miracle he was going to perform with a trapdoor on top of the altar.

Three or four times during this period, I wandered into Quaker meetings. I loved the left-leaning, compassionate politics. I admired all of the people I met there. But I just couldn't do the silence. It was that monkey mind again. By the end of an hour of sitting in a room with nobody saying anything, I was practically twitching.

I did read a few books about Paganism and Witchcraft. I identified strongly with descriptions in Margaret Murray's *The God of the Witches* of people in the Middle Ages who practiced a suppressed nature religion and were martyred for their devotion, and Starhawk's *Dreaming the Dark* provided a vision of that kind of spirituality brought forward into the modern world, but I couldn't see any entry points into the religion. Looking in from the outside, it was confusing trying to sort out the relationship among Witchcraft (which looked good), High Magick (which looked kind of bogus), and Satanism (which I'd also seen and which shared a lot of the same trappings and vocabulary as Wicca). It seemed like covens were private and closed, public groups offered seminars for exorbitant fees, and Goddess groups were wimmin-only.

There finally came a day when I just decided enough was enough, and I performed what I later came to see as my first spell. I set up my little Zen meditation cushion, a couple of candles, some sandalwood incense, and a very ripe tomato from my grandmother's garden. I said a prayer along the lines of "Okay, God, I'm tired of this bullshit! I want you back in my life!" and I ate the tomato.

The energy came back to me a day or two later, when a friend of mine invited me to a meeting of a student Pagan group. I went and was blown away by how familiar and right it all felt. That spring I went to my first Pagan celebration. We cast a circle, invoked the four elements and the Lord and Lady, and danced a Maypole. I performed one of the invocations, turning outward from the circle and calling out, "Spirits of Earth! Spirits of soil and wood and leaf! Join us now!" The ritual was held at a place called Temenos, a Quaker-Buddhist retreat center in western Massachusetts run by a couple of retired university professors named Joe and Teresina Havens. They were very curious about our group and what we did and believed. During the after-ritual feast, Teresina peppered us with questions. She asked me how long I'd been Pagan. I told her I wasn't, really, that I was just checking it out, but I realized as I said it that it was no longer true. That day was the first time since leaving Jubilee that I had been able to participate in a religious service and have it feel *right*. It's almost a cliché, how people who find Paganism feel like they've "come home," but that's exactly what it felt like to me.

That was fourteen years ago. I joined a self-trained eclectic coven for a while, and then found a fam-trad Witch* who was willing to train me. I learned to read Tarot, to work with elemental energy, and to draw down the God. I practiced a lot with "shamanic" trance journey, using a tape-recorded drumbeat by Michael Harner to go into a dream state while still awake. My wife and I formed our own coven, and we've passed on our teacher's tradition to a dozen or so students of our own.

One of the tools of a Witch is psychometry—reading the "aura," if you will, of a physical object or place. I had been Wiccan for over a decade when my wife and I walked into a 200-year-old Quaker meetinghouse that had been moved to Old Sturbridge Village, Massachusetts, a historical reenactment museum. The building was empty except for the occasional tourist wandering in and out, but we were amazed at how it still reverberated with the energy of decades of Quaker worship. Hundreds of people had spent thousands of hours sitting in silence there, and the spirit they had welcomed in still rolled off the walls like fragrant incense.

A year later, I attended an active, living Quaker meeting for the memorial service for Joe Havens, founder of Temenos, the retreat center where I'd first realized I was Pagan. Sitting in silent Quaker worship after having been a Witch for ten years was a very different experience from when I'd been in my twenties with a mind full of noise. It was like I'd been deaf to the silence then, and now for the first time I could "hear" it; I could tell what was going on in a room full of people sitting in silence. Quakers talk about a meeting being "covered by the spirit," and as I sat amongst them, I could feel it happening. Like carolers coming into harmony with one another as they sing, I could feel the people around me moving toward unity with each other and with the Divine. The meeting had the

*Fam-trad is slang for a family tradition that is inherited, passed down, or learned from one's parents or grandparents.

same energy as the preserved building at Old Sturbridge, but here it was fresh and green like a new sapling. My wife and I began going back once a year or so just to bask in it.

Then two things happened, one slowly and one abruptly. Our coven was nearing the end of its natural cycle, and with it, our roles as Wiccan leaders and teachers. Our students were moving on or falling away, and we were feeling dissatisfied, as if we'd been running our spiritual lives as a "demo model" for our students. We began finishing off the work of the coven so we could "elder out" of active Pagan leadership, and that left us in something of a void. Wicca has been such a rapidly growing movement that its institutions are almost totally geared to the earnest seeker and the wonder-struck newbie. Once you reach second or third degree, you begin to think there's no one out there who has anything left to teach you. We were sort of drifting, lacking something but not sure where to go next.

Then came 9/11, and in the shock and horror of the aftermath, we found ourselves in acute need of a strong community with a passionate commitment to peace. There was no time for wandering and searching; we went where we already had some connection. A Quaker meeting seemed the obvious place.

We've been attending pretty regularly ever since, and we're now members. The silent worship is sometimes dry, but there are times that it can be pretty juicy. For example, the first time I stood up and spoke in meeting (after about a year as an attender), it had as much of a kick to it as drawing down the God. There was the same sense of being a conduit for Something much larger than myself and of being stretched larger by having it pass through me. As a High Priest in a Wiccan circle, I always felt a powerful sense of responsibility to let the whole message through, but in the Quaker meeting, I could trust that if I missed part of it, if I sat down too soon, others would carry the rest of the message.

The outward forms of a Quaker meeting are very different

from those of a Wiccan circle, but under the surface the two have a tremendous amount in common. In Pagan vocabulary, speaking in meeting marked the moment when I became a priest of the light, or when the divine spark within became my patron deity. In Quaker terms, you could say I'm waiting upon the Gods, or sitting with the magick. Wicca has given me the tools and the discipline to be able to experience Quaker worship in its full depth, and the Society of Friends has given me a venue for continued spiritual growth when the traditional tasks of being a Wiccan High Priest are done. I am both at once, Quaker and Witch, each path giving me what I need to make the other complete.

Northampton, Massachusetts

❧ Wiccans in the Military
David L. Oringderff, Ph.D.

When I was invited to join the U.S. Army in 1968, no one asked me if I worshipped the God of Abraham. They only asked me to protect and defend the U.S. Constitution and to put my butt on the line when called on to do so. And that is exactly what I did, and did proudly, for almost three decades. Having gone from Private to Major in twenty-two years of active and five years of reserve service, I have some concept of discipline, order, and readiness. As a Wiccan for most of that time, I never experienced irreconcilable conflicts between my religious convictions and my military duty.

General George Washington established the Chaplain Corps in 1775 to bring a sense of morality and ethics to the Continental Army and to provide for the spiritual needs of his soldiers. That is exactly what the chaplains have done ever since. Military chaplains have always, it seems, been able to transcend sectarian religion and partisan politics and focus on a far nobler calling: the spiritual welfare of their soldiers, each and every one of them.

Frankly, Pagans have disparaged my military service far more often than military personnel have disparaged my Pagan faith. No military chaplain ever asked me how I addressed my God, or the manner in which I chose to pray. The only questions I was ever asked by a chaplain were: "What is your need and how can I help?" In contrast, I remember one particular Pagan "leader" who told me that it was absolutely impossible to be a Pagan and a soldier. I responded that the ancient Celts, Vikings, and Roman Legions were not Christian soldiers.

In 1994, I helped to establish The Sacred Well Congregation.* We were incorporated as a church in San Antonio, Texas, in 1996. When we started, all we were looking for was the same consideration and privileges that other churches receive. While many of our members were former or currently military, we never dreamed that we would become a sponsor for a widespread network of Pagan groups on military bases.

Our wider role began with a call in 1997 from a group of dedicated Wiccans at Fort Hood, a military base in Texas. They had been trying unsuccessfully to secure accommodation for their practices for a number of years. It's important for faith groups seeking such accommodation to work within the proper regulations and procedures, which are not discriminatory, because they are applied to every group alike. One such requirement is sponsorship from an outside, federally recognized religious organization. They had contacted a number of big-name Pagan organizations that either were not interested, directly hostile to the idea, or who did not satisfactorily meet military

*For more information, see www.sacredwell.org.

guidelines. They were very distraught by the time they stumbled across us.

I was happy to help. Because of my long military experience, I knew how to "work the system." I contacted the chaplains at Fort Hood. Together, we went over the requirements and worked on getting covered. The result was well worth the work. On Midsummer 1997, the Fort Hood Open Circle was certified as a Distinctive Faith Group (a local group functioning on a military base) under the sponsorship of the Sacred Well Congregation. Through the contacts gained in this process, I ultimately became a consultant for the Armed Forces Chaplains Board. The news of our accomplishment at Fort Hood spread quietly by word of mouth, basically through chaplains' channels. Soon, we were contacted by other military groups interested in forming on-base open circles. By May 1999, we were sponsoring seven Distinctive Faith Groups on military bases around the world.

The Fort Hood group existed quietly and peacefully for two years. Then an Austin newspaper ran a wonderful human interest story about them. This story was picked up by the media and soon came to the attention of reactionary elements of the religious and political communities, including Representative Bob Barr, a Republican from Georgia.

So began the controversy of the "Barr Wars." The media blitz that followed over the next six months was horrendous. Representative Barr attacked the existence of Wicca as a religion, correlating it to the rise of violence among youth. On May 19, 1999, Barr issued a press release demanding an "end to taxpayer funded witchcraft on American military bases." To make sure military and congressional leaders didn't miss it, he sent them all copies. Barr's attacks continued to escalate. He issued several strong statements to the media in an attempt to put pressure on the military chaplaincy authorities and on legislators to ban the practice of Wicca on military bases. He went so far as to state, "This move [acknowledging Wicca] sets a dangerous precedent that could easily result in the practice of all sorts of bizarre practices being supported by the military under the rubric of 'religion.'" He then asked whether the military would have to provide animals to the Satanists for sacrifice or marijuana to the Rastafarians.*

But the senior command of the military chaplaincies were not about to back down from their steadfast support for religious pluralism. They had a strategic plan in place long before Representative Barr could even spell "Wicca." By the time the newspaper article was published, the military chaplaincy had already established policy and procedures for the response they would take when (not if, but when) the proverbial shit hit the fan some place.

To illustrate this point, what follows is an excerpt of a letter that Brigadier General Gaylord Gunhus, then Deputy Chief of Chaplains for the Army, wrote to his Ecclesiastical Endorsing Agent in June 1999:

> *During the last several weeks there has been a wave of media hype on the Wicca religion and the coven that meets at Fort Hood, Texas. Most of what has been written or produced has been sensationalized and/or inaccurate. . . .*
>
> *This issue, however, is not a new one. The United States Army Chaplain Corps has been accommodating the diverse religious needs of military people for years. All faiths are seen as equal under the Constitution of the United States with the mandate of "separation of church and state." This idea is further reinforced by the provision of the First Amendment rights of citizens to engage in the free exercise of religion, as defined by the practitioners of respective faiths, not by the government. The mistaken notion, fostered by a newspaper*

---

*For more information on Bob Barr vs. the Wiccans, see "The Burning Times Award," 1999, at www.ReligiousTolerance.org.

*article in Texas, and circulated by other media, that the Army some-
how has "recognized" Wicca, as a legitimate religion is both inaccu-
rate and misleading. The government has no more recognized the
Wiccan faith than it has, for example, the Church of the Lutheran
Brethren, the Roman Catholic Church, Judaism, or for that matter,
atheism. Even now, Congress is working to establish a law entitled
"The Freedom of Religion Protection Act." This is not a freedom of
"some," but of all, religions. We live in a diverse and pluralistic
nation. We are not asked to accept any or all religions, merely to
respect their right to expression and the exercise of their faith. . . .*

*. . . Christian soldiers are extended the freedom to worship Our
Lord Jesus with genuineness and fervor. Jewish chaplains lead Jewish
soldiers in their worship of God openly and freely. Muslim chaplains
lead Muslim soldiers in their prayers to Allah without fear of
reprisal. Soldiers of other faiths and religions, including Wiccan soldiers, have the freedom to follow the spiritual path they have chosen.
I thank God for the Constitution of the United States of America
that allows me to proclaim the message of grace and forgiveness
through Christ our Lord. I will continue to do so as long as I serve
as an Army chaplain. While I do this, I will assure that soldiers are
allowed the opportunity to freely practice their religion. If they lose
their right of religious freedom, I lose mine.*

Representative Barr's very public attack on our freedom of
religion elicited a grassroots outcry and show of support from
the Pagan community. We did, and still do, appreciate the support of our Pagan kin. But the real reason the Fort Hood Open
Circle still lives and thrives is the commitment of the Military
Chaplaincy to provide for the spiritual needs of service members of all faiths, a tradition that actually precedes the U.S.
Constitution. These chaplains, whose beliefs are often quite different from our own, put their careers on the line to stand up
for freedom of religion for all members of the military, and for
all Americans.

As of July 2004, Sacred Well sponsored some twenty-eight military Distinctive Faith Groups worldwide, including the Basic Military Training Wicca Faith Group at Lackland Air Force Base, Texas, two active groups in Iraq, and one group forming aboard a U.S. naval vessel in the Persian Gulf. This group has an annual attendance of some 3,900 personnel. Meanwhile, Bob Barr no longer sits in the Congress!

Military chaplains stand by us and other religious minorities, helping to ensure and secure religious freedom for every citizen of this country. Another quote attributed to General Washington: "When we assumed the soldier, we did not lay aside the citizen."

San Antonio

❧ Rights and Perceptions
Tree Higgins

It is August 16, 2003. Lillith and I are traveling from our home in Asheville, North Carolina, to Richwood, West Virgina. Two of my friends had moved to the dominantly Christian area to open a small publishing office. They told me that land here is cheap, so we have come with the hope of finding property on which to build a home and a place for Pagans to come and gather.

Lillith is both a student and a friend. Her beautiful silver drag pentacle shines in the changing light as we crawl through the winding mountain roads into Richwood. My much smaller pentacle lies underneath my shirt. I am here to do business and will not be thwarted by others' prejudices, although I would never deny who I am if asked.

An old mining and logging company town, Richwood was never really beautiful. The most outstanding thing that strikes me as I drive into the town is the decay. All the buildings on Main Street are in need of facelifts. Sidewalks are broken and uneven. North of Main Street is row after row of houses tightly placed together on the side of a mountain. Every third house emptily glares back at me through broken windows, yawning holes in roofs, and fallen-in porches. The town is ugly, but it is affordable. People stare openly at us on the street. We are strangers in a town where no one is a stranger except winter skiers heading for Snowshoe Resort. I ignore them. Instead, I imagine what good Earth-centered Pagans could do with this place, how we could make it beautiful and harmonious, how we could make this a good environment to raise our children. We could make it a community.

We stop to see Wild and Word Dancer, the friends who first brought me to Richwood. They are in a three-lot trailer park. The park does not have a trailer made after 1970. They all show their age with rusting seams and faded colors. Wild and Word Dancer are pleased to see us. We hug and talk awhile. They have decided to move to Kentucky. Word Dancer tells me she can't stand living here any longer. Men have started following her on her morning riverside walks. She feels threatened by them and is tired of being constantly stared at. They ask me if I am sure I want to move here. I hear their concerns, but my mind is made up.

Lillith and I head to the town's only shopping mall. Lillith goes into a store to buy peppermint schnapps and eye shadow. She returns telling me the people in Richwood are the rudest she has ever met! The clerk gave her a hard time over her ID— a North Carolina driver's license. She is twenty-six and looks it. The female clerk called the manager and they spent fifteen minutes staring at her license. Finally, the clerk relented and rang up her purchases. As she took Lillith's money, the clerk told her she didn't think "Witches used makeup." Lillith was taken back by the sheer spite in the woman's voice.

This is Lillith's first real contact with religious discrimination. People have said things to her about her pentacle, but they were always open questions, not bitter taunts. Even the ones offering to "save" her soul were not malicious.

I told her the clerk has no power over her. The only control the clerk has is what Lillith gives her. I leave her in silence and know she is wandering deeply inside herself. It is ugly to find such people and know there is no way to address it. I think of my Pagan sisters and brothers who endure such places all their lives, loving and worshiping their Old Ones in secret.

We head off to the Monongahela National Forest where we are camping, but I get lost. I find a cemetery to turn around in and find myself staring directly at a tombstone with the name "Gertrude Stull" on it. I am stunned because I am familiar with a sixteenth-century ancestor by that name who was burned as a Witch in Germany, "without the mercy of strangulation." Gertrude must have been a strong woman. She danced with the flames rather than name people who may or may not have been innocent of being Pagan. Giving the inquisitors names would have granted her the mercy of strangulation before being engulfed by the fire. Now, I was staring at her name hundreds of years later in a land she probably never heard of. I wonder if this is an omen. It makes me think about a Pagan woman I recently heard about in Asheville. After giving birth, she was not allowed to take her newborn home from the hospital because a nurse called the state social services and told them the new mother was part of a baby-sacrificing cult. Thankfully, it was resolved in a week and she brought her child home, but it made me question just how far we have come from the elder Gertrude's days. At least, there are no burnings or confiscations of property today. It has only taken us 500 years to get this far.

We get back in the van and find our way back to our campsite by the Cranberry River. The national forest is a place of incredible beauty and Earth power. A week passes. Lillith is quiet at the campsite. I go to the tent to write, leaving her alone with her thoughts. When I come out of the tent, I tell her I am going to the woods where an old retaining wall has made a four-foot pond in a spring fed stream. We call it the "bathtub."

I climb up on a large boulder, cast a circle and pray to Odin and Freya for guidance and thank Them again for a safe journey. Naked, Lillith jumps into the pool, shouting as she submerges herself in the chilling water. I look up and smile. I remember an old line, "By living waters do I call thee, by living waters do I anoint thee, by living waters do I heal thee." It is Celtic, I think.

Lillith is revived now. She dresses and asks me what I am doing. I tell her I am in circle to ask questions without interference of other forces. She nods and heads down the tiny path back to camp, leaving me kneeling here in the great forest alone.

Once upon a time, my ancestresses knelt in great forests alone or with sisters of their kind. They gathered herbs for healing and fertility. They prayed together. They danced in circles. They, too, felt the force of nature course through them and thanked the Old Ones for it all. This forest is why I came to Richwood. Not the people.

Two nights later, two men try to break into our campsite. It is in the middle of the night and we are on our own. There is no cell phone service or police to help us. Lillith has grown up in hard places, as have I, and we fend them off with a show of clubs, knives, and my two dogs. They flee back into the darkness, their truck lights fading into night. Lillith and I debate whether they were from the town intentionally looking for us or if they just thought two women alone would make an easy target. Whatever their intent, they were not expecting us to stand our ground and fight. We finally end up laughing then crying over the incident.

The next morning, I tell a ranger about the incident. He just shrugs it off saying that it was "probably just some bear hunters having some fun." I tell him the men drove back and forth all night, whistling at one point to find out where my dogs were. They also waited until the campfire was out. The ranger tells me there is nothing he can do about it while staring at my pentacle. No report made.

The next morning, I go early to the Cranberry River to listen and pray. I thought if I could survive here and flourish, then other Pagans would be interested in coming and building a Community within this community. Now, I wonder how long I would be here before someone got hurt. Would the law protect us? How would I feel if something had happened to Lillith or anyone else who came to Richwood because of me? (Later, I learned two men from the non-hierarchial, earth-loving Rainbow Tribe were murdered three years earlier in that very forest. All charges were dropped against the accused killers. Our call might have been closer than I originally thought.) I return to camp and tell Lillith we are leaving. She ecstatically begins packing.

As I drive, I review my plans. I am a warrior by nature and always have been, but I weigh the cost of battles carefully. I am not the type to silently endure bigotry and, if I move to Richwood, that could lead me to trouble. I do not feel I would be safe here. Nor do I believe my civil rights would be enforced. On the other hand, I know our silence only strengthens those who would keep us from practicing our religion. But I do not have the money to pursue action every time I am denied a right or faced with harassment. The very existence of coordinated and organized Pagan legal rights and civil rights groups shows me how much we have accomplished, but because there are so few such groups, I can see how much more still needs to be done. I weigh all of this and, somewhere on the long drive home, I let go of my hope for Richwood.

As I drop Lillith off at her house, I tell her I am not Pagan by choice. I am Pagan because I breathe. She looks at me a long time then nods. "Me, too," she whispers as she walks away.

We Pagans are strong. Our faith was strong enough to survive

2,000 years of repression and inquisitions. We will endure. We will one day claim our rights. One day we will stand free and proud in all places in the world, both in large cities and small towns, but only if we do not hide in fear.

Life is good. We have come far. But we still have further to go. Someday, life will be better for all Pagans.

Asheville, North Carolina

◈ A Snapshot in Time
Judy Harrow

In 1986, at a Pagan festival in the New England springtime, hidden from the public eye in a forest clearing, in the hush of twilight, I stood in Circle watching a pregnant woman dance. Her swelling body was painted, covered with flowers, fruits, and vines, emphasizing the growing life within her womb. She was the very picture of abundant fertility. It seemed, in that unforgettable and sacred moment, Mother Earth Herself was dancing before us, clad in the body of Her Priestess.

Eighteen years later, in July 2004, I was at the Fourth Parliament of the World's Religions in Barcelona, Spain. This was a gathering of religious leaders and scholars from around the world to promote interreligious understanding. At the opening plenary session, a young man from the Youth Assembly stood at the podium and introduced himself, "Hello, I'm Donovan Arthen, a Pagan from the United States."

He was the baby, now grown, of the mother who had danced in that Circle in the woods. May the tolerance and acceptance of religious diversity continue to grow throughout the world and may his own children, and all children, dance in freedom and joy on a healing Earth!

Written in Barcelona

∿ The Tulip Bulb of Samhain
Amara

In 2003, I stuck out a hand in friendship to Randy, a man who might have once made me run for cover. He was a Baptist minister. During a period of tension between me and the Christian community, when a local church had gone from witnessing to harassing to stalking, he had come forward to help. Since the incident, we have had coffee a couple of times and spoken at length about our pasts and the very similar roads our lives have taken us on, and the very different places those roads have led. Still, I wondered when "the other shoe would drop" and the salvation pitch to begin in earnest.

The Sunday before Samhain, I was invited to Randy's house for Sunday supper. At first, I wasn't sure about going, but decided that after all he had done in the recent past to clean up after his Christian brethren and stand between me and my harassers, the least I could do is be gracious and accept the invitation.

So off to dinner I went. I took a nice bottle of wine and was welcomed into his family's small home. After dinner, as the plates were cleared, Randy looked me in the eye and asked, "Do you know in your heart where you will go when you die?"

I looked him back in the eye and stated, "Yes, I do."

He nodded and was quiet for a moment. Then he said (paraphrased from memory, of course), "I have to be completely honest with you. You have been on my mind a great deal lately. I've thought about the pain you've been through at the hands of those who have called themselves Christians. I've thought about the happiness and genuine love that seems to be the definition of your character. I've thought about your generous nature, and about your faith. I've prayed about you and how best to witness my faith to you. I've asked God to show me the way to bring you to him."

I waited quietly. He seemed uncomfortable, not quite sure of himself. "Last night," he said, "as I was praying, knowing you were coming here tonight, God spoke to me. He asked me why I thought you needed to be brought to him. I replied that you didn't believe in him, that you followed false gods. He asked me how I knew who you followed. I replied that we had spoken of beliefs and gods. He asked if I had listened to what you had said."

At this point, he folded his hands and sighed. "I knew then that I was in for a bit of a lesson." He grinned. I did too, because I know what those kinds of lessons are like. "He told me that I had already done that which was required of me to demonstrate the fruits of my faith to you. I, however, in my fear for your soul, had not offered you the opportunity to allow the fruits of your faith to be made manifest. For this I owe you an apology."

By then I was hearing a voice myself, prodding me to make the next step in this slowly developing relationship. "I was planning on celebrating Samhain quietly this year, by myself. I am wondering, however, if you would care to join me in Circle to give thanks for the year's harvest and welcome the turning of the Wheel."

It was a bold step. I figured it would be a cold day in the proverbial hot spot before he would even consider such a thing. He looked conflicted for a moment. I thought I had gone too fast, stepped too far in my search for understanding between us. There were tears in his eyes when he looked up at me. "I would be honored to share Circle with you."

It was a bitterly cold Samhain in northern California, as four Pagans and a Baptist minister gathered in a small park to celebrate the turning of the year. One Pagan was overheard cussing out the acting High Priestess for her need to reach out to the world on the coldest of nights in northern California and for forgetting to wear her warm boots. Quietly and quickly, they marked out a circle in the grass.

My minister guest looked very out of place in a suit and tie, and a little nervous. I smiled warmly and introduced the group. "Randy, this is Connor and Maize. This is OakLeaf, Maize's boyfriend. He will not participate with our rite but instead stand outside the boundaries of our Circle and act as our guardian." I took the pastor by the hand and led him into the ritual space. Slowly, we walked the circle, and I explained the Elements to him. We paused in the North and I spoke about the ancestor altar, naming each of the people in the pictures, and explaining each piece of paper. "I invited you to bring pictures of your own loved ones to place here, and welcome you to include them now if you desire."

Almost shyly, the pastor reached into a pocket and retrieved a small snapshot of a man in his fifties who looked entirely unamused to be photographed. "My father," he said quietly as he tucked it in between two frames where it was guarded from the cold breeze.

I nodded and continued around the circle, bringing him back to the center altar where I explained the table and its contents. "I invited you to bring something to represent your faith to lay on the altar, and welcome you to include it now, if you desire."

Another shy dip into a pocket and a small gold necklace emerged along with an odd addition, a tulip bulb. "It represents the resurrection to me," he said, "because it lies in the cold dark ground all winter and returns to beauty and life in the spring."

With a nod, I invited him to place them on the altar. Then, all was in place and the shift in the breeze signaled that it was time to begin. I showed our visitor where to stand, returned to the altar, and nodded to Maize, who stood to the North, behind the ancestor altar, to light the green candle hanging from its iron holder. She spoke of Earth and home, then she walked the edge of the circle to the East where she spoke of Air and movement. Connor addressed the South, and spoke of Fire and passion. He moved to the West, and spoke of Water and emotion.

I picked up the dagger and unsheathed it, pointed it to the North, and drew an invisible line with it from candle to candle,

"From North to East and South to West, we stand apart. As above, so below, as within, so without."

In my mind's eye, the circle shimmered in the various colors, rippling around us as it formed a dome of protection over our heads, extending into the ground. It felt strong and safe. With a deep breath, I gathered myself and addressed the altar. Lighting a match, I lit the green candle, invoking the Antlered God, "Arawn, God of the Dead, Leader of the Great Hunt, on this sacred night we call on you and invite you to join us in this circle." I lit the red candle and invoked the Warrior Goddess, "Morrigan, Goddess of War and Lady of fallen warriors, on this sacred night we call on you and invite you to join us in this circle." Sensing uneasiness in my guest, I hesitated. Modifying my traditional ritual form, I branched out a little. "We call out to the Divine in all its forms, to join us tonight as we honor those who have passed before us and offer our thanks for the blessings of another year. We seek the guidance of our gods for the year to come and the blessing of their company."

There was quiet in the circle as the three Pagans welcomed the presence of their gods. A quick glance at Pastor Randy confirmed that he had felt something and seemed to be quite okay. There was a pause, this one longer than the first. Even the wind had ceased blowing. I spoke then for Randy's benefit, as the others were well aware of the purpose of their work.

"Samhain is a night of somber celebration, for it is a night when the final harvest is complete, and the long, cold winter is ahead of us. It is a night to look back at the year that has transpired and give thanks for those blessings the gods have given us. It is a night also for the honoring of our dead. I invite you to name those who you give honor to tonight."

I nodded to Maize, who tilted her head back as if addressing the skies. "I honor my sister, Margaret, who passed two years ago of breast cancer and my friend, RedTail, who was killed in an auto accident last fall. There are others I honor as well, who I may never have known. They are . . ."

Connor cleared his throat and also tilted his head back. "I honor my unborn son who passed before he could make his way into this world. I honor my brother, Charles, who passed of natural causes last Samhain. There are others I honor as well, who I may never have known. They are . . ."

The air was heavy as I spoke. "I honor my grandmother, Emma, who passed four weeks ago. I honor my companion of ten years, the child of my heart, Brandy, who passed seven years ago this month. There are others I honor as well, who I may never have known. They are . . ."

I nodded at Randy, who stepped forward. Very quietly he offered, "I honor my father, Rev. James, who died when I was ten."

I smiled in comfort and squeezed his arm. "The time has come to offer thanks for those gifts the year has given. I have asked all of you to bring a token in offering, something small that will represent your gratitude. I will ask you now to give it into the offering bowl, and speak your gratitude."

Maize again went first, offering her thanks for her blessings and dropping something small in the cauldron, followed by Connor and myself. Lastly, I turned to Randy to see if he had brought anything. He smiled a silly little smile and pulled a tiny piece of paper from his pocket. "This is a piece of a tract, hate literature that one of the new members of my congregation gave to me. I offer it as thanks, because if not for this, and hundreds of others like it, I might not be here this evening," and he dropped it in the cauldron with the rest.

"Tonight is an ending of one year and the beginning of another. Like the tulip bulb on our altar tonight, seeds are planted on this night for the coming year. I asked each of you to bring your seeds, your needs and desires written on a piece of paper folded twice on itself. We will each light a candle in the cauldron, stating our name and calling on our gods to witness our seeds, and then we will speak our desires for the coming year and lay our seeds in the flame."

Maize picked up a match and lit it from the red candle, touching it to the first black candle. "I am Maize RiverSong, daughter of Morrigan."

Connor likewise lit his candle. "I am Connor, son of Morrigan."

"I am Amara, daughter of Morrigan."

And Randy, "I am Randall, son of God."

Maize lit the corner of her paper, and spoke of the negative things she wished to free herself from in the coming year. Connor and I did likewise. Randy hesitated as he approached the altar.

"I prayed about this all week," he said. "I know there is a lesson I am being asked to learn, and I'm praying that I am strong enough to learn it." His hand hovered over the growing flames of the candles and the burning pieces of paper. "I wish to let go of my preconceptions of others and the arrogance of my faith."

His paper caught and he dropped it into the cauldron. The park was still and quiet as we watched the paper burn. The flames died down and the candles slowly returned to their normal flickering.

In much the same order as it was cast, the circle was closed, Maize and Connor tag teaming their way around the circle. When they were done, I gathered them all once more around the altar to join hands. "Tonight we have gathered and created sacred space, where we have stood together in peace and harmony. Four people from decidedly different places in life stood in unity for this brief hour of time. May it be the precursor of many great things to come. As we leave this place, may we take with us a sense of purpose for the coming year and a path to peace that we may share with others by our example."

When our eyes met, both Randy and I had tears shining in them, for the love was very palpable at that moment. Randy choked on the words, "Take all the love that you need and pass the rest on." The words continued around the circle.

Northern California

2

Air

The Learning Process—Teachers, Mentors,
Students, and Inner Guides

First I must make it clear—I am a humble member of a coven. I am not its head or lead in any way, and I have to do what I am told.

—Gerald B. Gardner, *Witchcraft Today*

ꙮ Walking Between the Stars
Francesca De Grandis

I've fallen in between an electron and a nucleus. And it's lonely. It's lonely being a shaman. Of course, you're not supposed to complain, right? Ever hear of a witch doctor on a psychiatrist's couch saying, "No one understands me?" Does the madman's wife ask, "Have a hard day at work, dear?"

You're not supposed to complain. Bullshit! That's bullshit. Ever hear of the tears of the clown? The fool—who stalks the wildness that only grows during the blinks, between the instant closing and reopening of an eye—is a lonely person. It's a lonely business, being a fool. Nature is lonely, and nature, believe it or not, is the business of the fool.

The fool cries because she is alone at night, cold with her wild soul. When the party is over and she has given her gift of joy and truth to the queen and the court, the fool's beloved humans, given them the gift, she gets tired and wants a backrub. I think you get the picture. Though it's even worse than that, because I'm not just the fool, but also the shaman. The whole cake, big cookie.

I walk the distance between the stars. I once told my spiritual teacher I was lonely. He said all shamans get lonely. He said, "Do you know how far it is between stars?" Well, I'm walking it, going the whole way by foot.

It's not the sort of thing you bring up at parties, either. If Witchcraft or psychic stuff comes up as a topic, everyone else has a cute and amazing story. I'm mute. What would I say, "I walked from star to star today, I felt the wind of the Goddess's breath?" At best, they would think I'm speaking in metaphor. It's not a metaphor.

Sometimes I think I'm having acid flashbacks. I never took acid.

I ask my therapist about all this (yes, I'm in therapy; she helps me adjust to being a wild woman of the primeval forces in a modern city) and she says I'm fine. Not crazy. I just have an expanded consciousness, she says.

My best friends don't know what I'm up to. Imagine if I were to tell them, "Well, you know the Carlos Castaneda and Lynn Andrews books? That's kind of what my day is like. Today, I confronted a demon. I'd made it myself, out of my own fear, but I've started to make friends with her. She really helped me see how I hassle my lover about money. *NO! THIS IS NOT A METAPHOR! SHE'S REAL!*"

I can't tell you why I do this, all the studying, meditation, trances, all the talks with my teacher that might sound to someone else like two high school kids on the phone. (Our sincerity about our lunatic belief ["Oh, so you talked to a fairy today too?"] and uncivilized spiritual longings ["I made love to Gaia. Is that okay?"] are matched only by the zealousness of teenage gossip and the audacity of adolescent rebellion.) There is no *reason* to do all this. Except that it's me. As surely as my arm is. I am alive and happy through these practices of this path. Not because of having done them, mind you; it's the doing of them that is special. This is what grabs me, has grabbed me, God's hand 'round my arm pulling me to Him and saying, "Hey, baby, I got something for you. Check this out." We play, Goddess talks, my teacher talks, I talk, I play, I work.

I love my clients and students. I help them. I enjoy helping them, too. Not only do I like the fact that I help them, but I enjoy the work.

I am a student of the great Mysteries. I am learned, and sound ignorant to so many. What do they know? I can't talk of my life to people; it would be like a physicist trying to casually chat about his latest discovery. Actually, I am a physicist. Like I said, nature is the fool's job.

Someone told me that everyone gets lonesome. Maybe everyone is walking between an electron and a nucleus, and nobody knows the troubles they've seen. Maybe I'm no different.

And for all my complaining about all my loneliness, that dark loneliness is a black horse with wings, who folds a wing about me and presses me to her flank, and I feel that. It's not "like" I feel that. She's there and I feel her, feather and fur, sensual as the frosting off a child's birthday cake. And without that loneliness, I don't think I could stand alone on the plains of my heart and call the moon into my bedroom. Loneliness, that I may be one with the sweet smell of the forest and the night's indigo air.

Between the Worlds, California

Grandmother's Tale
Dana Kramer-Rolls, Ph.D.

When I was asked to write about my experience with spirit and divinity, I found that my own life was too complex, and my reasons too hard to explain. So I was inspired to write this fairy tale, but now as I read it, I see that it says everything about me that I could hope to say. Enjoy this Grandmother's tale.

The old woman sat by the smoky fire, a cat on her lap, telling her tale again to yet a new group of girls. "Tell it, tell it," they would urge. Their eyes would sparkle as the Grandmother told her story, one that needed to be told as long as there were women to hear it. She would rock back and forth, and gently, rhythmically rub her cat's ears and watch the fire as she spoke.

It began long ago. My name then was Hulda, but when the slavers took me away, they called me Silvia, because I came from the forests, and a good Imperial name would fetch a better price. When we arrived in the capital, my master placed me in a house of pleasure. The mistress was hard, but she trained me how to please men, not just in bed, but to play music and sing and dance, and make up poems, and to be witty. Soon, I became a hostess at parties where only the senators and generals came. I became a companion of great men, and they laughed at my carefully contrived gossip, and they told me their heart's secrets, and I grew in beauty and fame. It was a heady time. When my old mistress retired, she gave me two great gifts: my freedom and an introduction to the Temple of the Goddess, the Great Isis.

I was taken to the Temple, and I spent the night sleeping by the altar. The priests interpreted my dream the next morning. I still remember the dream. I saw Her lifted on a cloud of golden light, and She reached down and offered me a rose. I can still smell it, rich and musky, and sweet enough to make you drunk with passion. But it had a thorn that pricked my finger. The pain was terrible, and I could see a spider web of black veins creeping up my arm. I cried out and awoke, shaking. I didn't tell the priests that, only about the rose and Her. Then I was bathed and robed in white and initiated into rites that are secret.

I served in the Temple and rose in rank, until I finally was allowed to assist the High Priestess to bathe and robe the statue of the Goddess. I was then the mistress of a very rich and influential politician. But I was growing older, and my patron was seeking new pleasures. So I prayed and came to believe it was my calling to retire to the Temple to be a resident priestess, as others had before me, and dedicate myself solely to Her. I pleaded my case before the priests, how I had been devout, paid my tithe, observed every fast, and desired to serve Her alone. But I was turned away.

I was cold with shock. Why, I asked the matron who led me from their presence, a tall, aristocratic woman, slender to the point of scrawniness, her neck veins blue. What had I done to fail? She answered coldly, "You are not one of us."

Did I not dress as well as the highborn matrons? Did I not speak the Imperial tongue as well as any? Had I not been welcomed in the finest houses? Was I not free? I was wrong. To them, I was always only the slave girl, a barbarian, trained like a pet dog to please, and now grown middle-aged, graying, and wrinkled. I had thought that devotion to Her was enough, but I was blinded to the truth. The Temple was no different than the Imperial Court, with its politics. There was no Great Goddess there, only rich old matrons who mouthed their prayers and powerful priests who ruled. I would never go back to the Temple again. And I remembered the thorn in the dream of so many years ago.

Shaking and humiliated, my mouth was as dry as my tears were wet. Everything was suddenly foreign and ugly. I took to my bed, saying it was a woman's illness. I sold my house and began to walk north, stopping here or there, but always moving on. I was like a stone inside, cold, empty, and hard.

One day, toward the end of one winter, I sat down to rest on a rock, still damp and dark with a mossy mantle. A small white flower was just forcing itself through the crisp snow. The wonder of it made me smile. I looked out across the broken meadow with its thin stand of trees, the buds now swelling in the delicate pastels of late winter, still no blooms or leaves, but bursting with promise.

A beam of light, golden as the morning, streamed down through the trees, and I saw Her. It was not in her Temple, but Her in her essence, in the buds, the songbirds, the young hares, and the newborn deer. My heart melted. I cried as I had not cried since that terrible day when I left the Temple. Only now I cried with joy.

Every day I seek Her in healing plants, and newborn kittens, and the faces of you, my children, and every day she teaches me something new. Now that the new religion comes to the North, the religion of the Nazarene, his priests call me Witch, but I know who I am. I am Her Priestess, not in ceremony or temple or religion, but in life, in wisdom, in every breath, and I will be Hers when I die. Because She will never die.

•◆•

The girls sat quietly watching the embers. Finally, the cat stirred, stretched, and broke the spell. The smallest girl asked, "Grandmother, will you tell my daughters your tale?"

"No, dear, you must do that for me."

And so it was through all time.

Richmond, California

❧ The Mandala
Laura Wildman-Hanlon

The dark blue metal door of the apartment didn't look any different than the other dozen or so doors in the building but, for me, this door was unique and special. It represented a new threshold in my development as a Priestess, because behind that door waited my new students.

I hesitated a moment before rapping on the metal finish. In my mind, I could see my mentor, my Priestess, as she gave me my assignment.

"You are to start teaching," she told me.

"Well, it's about time!" was my response.

For the last year, I'd been chomping at the teacher/student bit. After all, I had been practicing as a solitary Wiccan since the early 1980s. The last few years I had found joy working with a Priestess whom I highly admired, learning the ways of a structured traditional coven. I was currently working toward my third degree. The opportunity to pass down my vast experience to a couple of new seekers was exciting. I was graduating from student to mentor. I could almost see them sitting around me, trying to absorb my words and thoughts. "How hard could it be?" I thought. "This is going to be a blast!" With confidence, I put knuckles to the surface and waited.

The door was opened by Donna. Smiling, she ushered me down her apartment's long entry hallway, made narrow by the overflowing bookshelves that lined one wall. The hall opened into a surprisingly spacious and well-lit living room. Her husband, John, my other student, sat in a lotus position on the carpeted floor. He uncurled his long legs and stood to greet me with a hug. They were an interesting couple. He was tall and lanky with a dark ponytail that cascaded down his back. Donna was short and full bodied. She kept her blond hair neatly trimmed. John had been practicing a spiritual form of yoga for a number of years but had come to the conclusion that it was too cerebral. Donna came to Paganism by way of herbalism. Interested in exploring Wicca, they met my Priestess at a public Pagan event. Soon after, they began circling with my coven taking Dedication to our Tradition (a commitment to learn) on our last Full Moon. Now, it was my responsibility to prepare them for Initiation to the Craft.

I had brought with me a large ring binder with my lesson plans, notes, and handouts in an oversized tote bag. I dropped it to the floor with a grateful thunk and made myself comfortable on their couch. While Donna puttered in the kitchen, I pulled out the notebook and made a show of flipping through the pages. I wanted to make an impression, let my new students know that I was serious about my role as mentor. No flakey, ill-prepared Witch here! Nope, they were going to learn something from me! I unclipped the first handouts, an overview of their next six months of study, and put it on the coffee table. John began flipping through the pages, waiting for Donna who was brewing a pot of herbal tea. Once she had joined us, I cleared my throat, preparing to begin the first lecture.

"Excuse me," interrupted John even before the first words left my lips. "Before we start, I would like to give you something."

"A gift . . . for me?" I said, confused and pleased all at the same time. "I would love to see it."

John reached over and retrieved a large white piece of cardboard that had been tucked next to the couch. With a look of pride in his eyes, he turned it over revealing a design etched on the other side. "This," he explained while handing it to me, "is what I hope we will learn from you over the next few years."

There in my hands was a beautiful black-and-white, hand-drawn mandala in the shape of a lotus blossom. The center of the flower consisted of nine petals, each containing one word: Mind, Body, Synergy, Craft Lore, Language, Mythology, World, Divinity, and Objectivity. The petals that radiated from the center created columns five layers deep. Each petal held objectives directly related to the word on its corresponding inner core. Each layer indicated an increase in difficulty and a step toward mastery. For example, "Mind" blossomed from basic meditation practices to astral projection. The numbers zero, one, two, and three (indicating degrees) were inserted at differing layers, creating a spiral effect within the flower. Obviously, a lot of thought had gone into the creation of this mandala. I sat there staring at the work in awe and fear.

"This is beautiful," I finally managed to say, meaning every word.

"You can take that one home with you," John replied. "I have copies for each of us to study." Donna nodded in agreement. "I was hoping we could use the mandala to talk about the process and our expectations," he continued. They sat back with satisfied and expectant smiles.

The rest of the class was a blur. Thank goodness for my notes or I might have spent the entire time sitting with my mouth open and nothing coming out. All I could think of was the learning flower. At just one glance, I knew a number of petals represented gaps in my knowledge.

Later, when I was safely at home, I spent more time reading over their goals. While all the topics were familiar to me, I had mastered very few. Coming to terms with the realization that I knew less than I thought about magic, the Craft, and its various aspects was sobering. Self-doubts surfaced. How could I take on the responsibility of guiding students through the learning process when I didn't know the way myself? How could I call myself a Witch and a Priestess? In tears and feeling defeated before I even began, I visited my mentor and her working partner to show them the learning mandala and to admit to them that I was not worthy of the task assigned to me.

My teacher looked at the drawing with admiration then said, with a twinkle in her eyes, "You've got live students, don't you. Guess you're going to have fun with these two. By the way," she added, "I don't know if I could adequately teach half of these either."

My mouth dropped open. My teacher, mentor, friend, Priestess, the woman who I thought knew everything couldn't teach all of the petals?

My Priestess handed the drawing to her partner, a competent Witch who had degrees in three different Pagan Traditions. She also studied it for a moment. "Well," she said while pointing out a little more than a dozen petals, "I would feel comfortable teaching these but I'm not too sure about the rest.

But," she added looking straight at me, "this shouldn't be a surprise to you. I've told you many times that you're better at divination than I am."

A soft pop and hiss came from the bubble of perfection I had fashioned around my teachers. I looked at my Priestess and her partner and the realization hit. The expanse of knowledge is unlimited. There is always another petal, another area to explore. The learning does not end with leaving formal studenthood. It is a never-ending circle of exploration. With each pupil, the teacher again becomes a student. Both learn from each other, pushing personal boundaries and expanding individual consciousness. The relationship between student and teacher is therefore reciprocal. The outcome of this process is a group of equals.

As my understanding grew, I began to laugh. My teachers and peers laughed with me. Together, we looked over the flower and came to the conclusion that, between the three of us, we could competently teach a little more than two-thirds of the mandala. For the remainder, we would either have to research the topic, find someone else to teach it, or ask John and Donna to do independent study.

John, Donna, and I worked together for a year before our lives and responsibilities caused us to go in other directions. I don't know whether I ever imparted any wisdom to them, but they taught me an invaluable lesson. The mandala hangs in my study. Before agreeing to teach a new student, I gaze upon its petals and the kernels of knowledge it holds. It helps to open me to the lessons that are being offered to me. It keeps me humble.

Upper West Side, New York City

❧ The Darker Side of Teaching
Brook Willowbark

I never intended to teach. That was something that other people did, not me. Teachers were the ones who had the inner call to share their knowledge with others. They were the ones with the talent to create lesson plans and who were organized. That definitely wasn't me.

But then one day my calling came. It took the form of a ringing phone. It was my Priestess. She was a formidable woman in her late sixties who didn't take kindly to hearing the word no. She reminded me that she hadn't spent years training me as a Witch only to have me sit around doing solitary work. Just to emphasize the point, she told me to expect a visitor. A friend of hers was looking for a teacher and I was it. So Meg, my first student, showed up on my doorstep. My Priestess must have sent out some sort of psychic call as well because, with the number of students who spontaneously approached me looking for training, it felt like a flashing arrow reading "Priestess here, just ring bell" had been installed over my house.

During the next year, four students, Dragonwing, Allyison, Hawthorn, and Stephon, joined Meg. We worked and trained together for two years, becoming a solid working coven. To my amazement, I found that I loved to teach. I enjoyed watching my students learn, grow, and come into their own as a Priest or Priestess in the Craft. Over the years I also took on other new students. Most of these were happy experiences. But one thing my Priestess neglected to tell me about was the darker side of teaching.

When a student enters training, it is normal for her to develop a deep and personal relationship with the teacher. But if a student enters with unresolved personal emotional issues, such as childhood abuse, she may subconsciously see the Priestess and Priest as surrogate parents and the coven as a stage on which dysfunctional behaviors can be replayed.

I first met Darla at our local occult supply store. Standing among the oils and candles, I was immediately taken by her appearance. She was a tall woman, large boned with a mane of salt and pepper hair. Her flashing gray eyes showed her Welsh heritage. After being introduced by the shop owner, Darla cornered me by the book shelves and dazzled me with her knowledge of Celtic mythology. She was warm, friendly, and charismatic. Before I knew it, I was inviting her over to my Lammas holiday potluck party.

The day of the party, Darla arrived early wearing a typical Pagan outfit, a loose fitting peasant blouse that showed off a little bit of cleavage and a flowing Indian skirt. She brought a gift bouquet of wildflowers she had picked from her garden. Seeing I was behind in my party prep, she went to work, unstacked the plastic chairs, arranged the furniture on the deck and helped to set up the food table. As the guests arrived, Darla flitted around greeting and talking with anyone who stood still long enough to listen.

At the end of the party, she approached me asking for coven training. I was taken aback by her request. We hardly knew each other. My psychic alarm bells started ringing—something didn't feel right. I sidestepped answering her. Within a week, my phone rang, with Darla again asking if I would train her. I put her off and told her I'd think about it. A few days later I found Darla knocking at my door, asking if I had come to any conclusion. With the third request I was obligated by the rules of my Tradition to bring her appeal before the other members of my group.

After our next Full Moon circle, my coven sat around my living room talking about Darla. While a few nagging doubts seemed to surface, no one was able to articulate a solid reason why she should not be allowed to circle with us. And so Darla, along with three other students, began training.

Coven circles and classes with her were wonderful. Darla could always be counted on to ask deep questions, the kind that motivate others to reevaluate themselves and their ideas. When I became ill with the flu, Darla immediately volunteered to take care of food shopping and light housekeeping until I was able to handle it again. Over cups of warm tea, we spent hours talking about life, the Craft, and other topics of interest. I thought we had a wonderful student-teacher relationship and any doubts that might have been tugging at my mind completely melted away. She and the other members of the class completed their initial training and formally dedicated themselves to the coven, making a promise to the Gods and the group to study with us for a year and a day. They all began their training for Initiation.

Five months later Darla surprised me with a visit. "I want to be Initiated to First Degree at the next Full Moon," she said as soon as we sat down. "Also, because my health could take a turn for the worse at any minute, I don't want to wait. I want you to elevate me to Third Degree within the year." She then sat there looking at me with an expression of complete expectation. I was flabbergasted!

In my Tradition, a form of British Traditional Witchcraft, we have three levels of study after Dedication. We also have a strict policy of at least one year between each degree received. Darla knew this. In essence, she was asking me to bestow a title that many within our Tradition, including me, spend well over the required three years working to obtain. She had just begun to experience our Tradition, never mind understand the depth and breadth of our beliefs and practice. Understanding can only come through time, maturity, practice, and study. Concerning her health, before joining the coven we had discussed her disease, a liver ailment. While it could shorten her life, it didn't appear it would happen anytime soon. Besides, we're not in the Make-a-Wish-Foundation, granting last requests to the terminally ill. Many people die to face their Gods and Goddesses without a Third Degree. I'm sure the title, which simply indicates a level of training, means little to Them.

Darla pursed her lips together and scowled at me when I told her no. I watched her nostrils flare with anger as I gave her my reasons why. But she said she understood and gave me a hug as she left. I thought that was the end of it.

A few nights later, my phone rang. It was Darla. "You've got to talk to Maureen," she said, referring to one of her fellow students. "She is all upset about our last class but is afraid to tell you. I just spent the last two hours talking to her and calming her down." As soon as I was off the phone with Darla, I was dialing Maureen's number filled with dread. But Maureen was fine. True, she had one small question about a reading but nothing as earth-shattering as Darla had implied. I put it down to lack of communication between the two students.

But the phone rang often after that. The calls consisted of Darla wanting to "tell me something that I really should know about another incident." Each time I would check, only to be told that nothing was amiss. I became tired of the false alarms and I finally sat Darla down and told her that I did not want to receive another call. I explained that if a student had a problem with me then I expected that individual would contact me directly. The calls stopped.

A month later I began noticing a sharp change within my other three students. They were becoming more distant. Talks with the members of the class revealed nothing. All said that they were happy with the class, the coven, and with me as their teacher. I was beginning to think I was imagining things.

Then coven circles became challenging. Where she was once warm and friendly, Darla was now rude and cold. She was often sarcastic, increasingly argumentative and condescending. I discovered that she was manufacturing cruel gossip, twisting innocent words and intents, and whispering the poison to the coven members in what could only be seen as an attempt to breed mistrust among us. She told one covener that I hated her children and didn't want them attending any of our circles. The mother, who often brought her children to open events, was terribly hurt. It took a few conversations before trust was reaffirmed between us. When I confronted Darla about the issue, on one hand she adamantly and angrily denied her behavior, while on the other she ardently promised to change.

After many tears, I and the other members of the coven concluded Darla's presence was damaging the group. We decided to ask her to leave.

Darla surprised me by arriving at the scheduled meeting with the other students in tow. They all sat in a line across my living room couch with Darla in the center. The conversation that I had planned to have alone with her was unexpectedly thrust into a group discussion. But instead of her behavior being questioned, I was put on trial. The entire confrontation was focused on a list of my alleged misdemeanors. I was heavily chastised for asking that they conform to our Tradition's practices. Aspects discussed and agreed upon at the beginning of their training were suddenly turned into atrocities. I listened and watched as Darla played upon the other students' insecurities as if she were a violinist and they the strings. She would take an issue, such as our ritual structure, and somehow correlate it to fears on sexual deviation. The words coming out of their mouths didn't make any sense. My voice was drowned out, my questions left unanswered or unheard. I felt overwhelmed, vulnerable, and betrayed. When they had finished, they got up and abruptly left as a group. Darla's last words to me were a veiled threat indicating that if I were ever to speak of the incident, she would use both magic and manipulation to destroy my reputation within the Pagan community.

I have not heard from Darla since that day. Immediately after they left our group, Darla and the other students attempted to form their own coven, but it didn't survive for very long. I think it had something to do with Darla's attempt at breaking up the marriage of someone within the group. She has since moved away from Pagan practice and now focuses her attention elsewhere.

In a perfect world, a teacher would immediately pick up on the emotion and psychic disruptions and guide the student through the healing process. I'm not perfect. I missed the subtle signs and became caught up in the student's drama. In other words, for all the students whose lives we touch for the better, there are others for whom we fail. This is the difficult and often painful side to teaching.

It took two years before I, and the coven, healed enough to accept new students. The experience taught me a great deal. We are more careful and cautious when talking to potential students. I now expect the candidate to prove him- or herself before opening my heart and embracing him or her as a member. The coven carries a scar from the experience. The memory will always be there, haunting us each time a potential student asks "the question" three times.

The wildwoods of New Hampshire

✒ Lessons from the Dark Gods
T. Thorn Coyle

I had it made: a solid magical practice, engaging students, a book deal in the works, a long-term love partnership, and good posture.

It was probably time to learn a new lesson. I teach magic as spiritual practice, with students around the country. I love my work. During the time of this story, my students sometimes said they found me to be intimidating. I had never received a good explanation for what they meant by this and usually chalked it up to their own process. But in the back of my mind, I was starting to suspect that my own practice was too distant from theirs.

Then my issues began to surface. My relationship was breaking up. This solid, wonderful partnership that I'd come to count on and was depending on to carry me through the vagaries of my new successes had to be radically changed. Not yet realizing the outcome, I began the processes that would end my marriage.

I continued to practice. I cried and aligned my soul. I sat quietly, breathing, in the midst of my obsession with a new lover. I grew angry. I lost weight because of stress. While taking my classes on trance journeys, I wrestled with my demons. They were messy, sloppy, and transformed my magic and the way I moved in the world. I was grief stricken. I was integrating emotions I'd barely touched for years. Inhale. My magic grew stronger. Exhale. I was letting go. I was expanding.

Here's a little preamble: months before this, the Dark Gods—the Gods of midnight's passing and our shadow spaces, the Gods who cull what needs to die so new growth can occur—had spoken to me in a vision. "You may no longer take responsibility for anyone's life but your own," they said. Damn. I knew this already, of course. One key tenet of Feri tradition, which is what I teach and practice, is to not coddle weakness. Another is do not submit your life force to anyone or anything. Meaning, don't give over responsibility for your life's choices to another and don't expect this from others, either.

Oh yes, I knew these things. But the charge from the Gods still felt like a knife in my gut. I was afraid. The child of an alcoholic, I had struggled with codependency my entire life. I'd grown strong and fierce and could take care of myself, thank you. But it was a slap in the face to realize that I was still taking care of others. And worse, I was taking care of their emotions without their permission. This realization began the collapse of my marriage.

I had coddled my partner, sheltering him from the things I wanted and needed to be whole. I made decisions based on what I perceived to be his limitations: "He won't be able to handle this, and it's not so important anyway." Unwittingly, I had boxed myself into a life that no longer included my own burning desires. I scrambled to change, to save the marriage, but the patterns had been set so deeply that a gentle shift was no longer an option.

Let me be clear on what I mean by coddling weakness.

I'm not talking about lending a shoulder to a friend in crisis or making soup for the terminally ill. I'm talking about making decisions about my own life with an eye toward what I thought another person wanted. As a survival technique in my childhood home, this made sense. But for an adult woman, a powerful Witch and Magician? No. The Dark Gods were right. I began to listen. And that is when things started to shake down, bust open, and fall apart.

All of a sudden I didn't feel graceful. I didn't feel pretty. There were times that I felt very weak, small, and vulnerable. I exposed myself to friends, lovers, and students. And do you know what? Friends and lovers stuck around. And my students thanked me for my honesty. All of a sudden, they could see into my process—a pattern that had been obscured to them before. They saw me using the tools we worked on together to bring myself back into balance in the midst of this whirlwind my life had become. They heard me apologize for not getting back to a question sooner because of my own personal upheaval and heard, too, that I was continuing to sit in silence every morning as an anchor. My *practice* was real to them for the first time, because they could see that my *life* was real, not some perfect spiritual haven.

I teach that we can expand our capacity to be human. I

believe that spiritual practice—that our magic—has evolutionary capabilities. In the midst of my crisis, one student wrote,
"When you share your personal life, we see you with your own
emotions and vulnerabilities, living in your full humanity. We
see that this work can lead to major life changes and that we
can use this work to grow. We see that your life is not perfect,
either, but see you use the tools for your own healing and transformation. You are also teaching us to cope."

These tools included standing tall, breathing, and running
energy as consciously as possible while in the midst of emotional upheaval. In order to keep my life force running strong,
I frequently called upon the points of the Iron Pentacle—sex,
pride, self, power and passion. I continued to use the tools of
unbinding, cleansing and aligning. All of these helped me to
move forward out of anger, grief, guilt and sorrow. They kept
me teaching, writing and dancing—and got me out of bed in
the morning.

I was learning. I was scared. I also began to feel more liber-
ated and more powerful. *This* was teaching, this messy soup held
in the strong cauldron of my practice. I was recasting the spell
of my life and rewriting a childhood story that told me perfection was inviolate and unchanging. The Dark Gods were moving in my life, reshaping my work, love, and body. They were
putting me in danger. As soon as I embraced that danger, freedom began to enter.

And the playing field was leveled. We were all in the work
together. Yes, I was teaching, but my learning process was finally
apparent to everyone in the circle. We were all students. We
were all needed for the work to open, and for the magic—the
cauldron of transformation and healing—to be formed. This
was something I'd always known in my head, but I was coming
to know it in my gut, my heart, and my bones. No longer inviolate and unapproachable, after more than twenty years of
magical work, I was becoming whole.

My life now? I still have it made: a solid magical practice, engaging students, my writing, and a lot of love. My posture is still good, too, but I'm a lot more relaxed these days.

San Francisco

℘ Midwife to a Spiritual Birth
Autumn Amber Fox

Ten years ago my son and I stood with friends and strangers in a moonlit glade. As a circle was formed, the sounds of the city faded until only a woodsy song could be heard; the rustling of leaves, birds in their twilight chorus, and the evening dance of squirrels getting ready for slumber. A woman spoke of her spiritual path and explained to us the ritual to come. It would include, she said, "calling the elemental spirits and acknowledging both God and Goddess." I glanced at my sixteen-year-old son and wondered why I had come here this night. What had Dominic talked me into doing?

Taking a deep breath, I calmed myself. It was a lovely evening and Dominic seemed interested in and happy with the ritual's beginning. I had agreed to come so I could learn more about my son's thoughts and beliefs. In the previous year, I had realized that Dominic was no longer a little boy. I began searching for ways to connect with my teenaged son. During a heart-to-heart talk a few months earlier, Dominic told me he had found a spiritual connection with a faith called Wicca. After asking several questions about his beliefs, I realized the Protestant church I attended would not accept my son as a member. Dominic was becoming a gentle and caring young man, but he did not believe their God was the only true God. Yes, he believed in God, but he also believed in a Goddess.

So we left that house of worship and joined the local Unitarian Universalist (UU) church whose theology was more accepting of diversity. The UU congregation embraced both of my sons, Dominic and his younger brother, Patrick. I also felt welcome, but there was still an elusive spiritual element missing from my life. Listed in the church's weekly newsletter was an announcement for a newly formed Full Moon group. Dominic decided to attend. He had learned about Wicca through reading several books and was interested in meeting others who shared similar beliefs. He pointed out that it would help me understand his new spiritual path and encouraged me to come with him. This brought us to standing in the glow of the moon.

We began our ritual, a celebration of the sacredness, wonder, and beauty of Earth. As the moon rose, we sang and laughed, drummed and danced. The moonlight glowed on the tree branches and among the shadowed underbrush. It felt like waves over my face and body. I was caressed with a sense of peace that had not touched me for years.

Twenty years had passed since my home had been a big red school bus settled in among trees. It was a life of contentment and joy, awakening with sunrise and resting in gentle moonlight. At night the tree frogs sang, the trees whispered in the cooling breeze, and the mission bells outside the door chimed a soothing lullaby.

How did I wind up living in a city, working Monday through Friday, worshipping only on Sundays, sitting inside a building, in a row, listening to someone else speaking about life and religion? When had I stopped celebrating the sacred beauty of each and every day?

More memories rose from their slumber. I found myself recalling the girl-child who found peace wandering in the woods on her grandparents' farm . . . the girl who was calmed by the softness of early summer dusk . . . the child who marveled at the beauty of star-blazed night skies.

I remembered in joy, and as we stood in that moonlit glade,

I looked at my son, Dominic, with new eyes. At that moment, under the embrace of the night Goddess, a new bond was forged between us. Since he first emerged from my womb, I have been his mother, guide, and teacher. Now, it was he who was becoming my mentor, helping me find my way back to a spiritual path I had walked unconsciously in previous years. Across the circle, we exchanged a knowing smile.

For two more years my son and I gathered with friends to recognize our connection with the Divine through celebration of the Full Moon's beauty and energy. With Dominic's guidance, I explored the Wiccan ways and reopened my heart to the sprites of nature. Dominic graduated from high school and moved to another state. I continued to participate in the Full Moon circle, becoming more involved with the creation and facilitating of Earth and Sky's rituals. Our informal circle became Earth and Sky CUUPs Circle (Covenant of Unitarian-Universalist Pagans) and our celebrations of the Full Moon expanded to include rituals to honor the eight Sabbats in the Wheel of the Year.

Ten years ago, I came to a circle on an early autumn evening as a mother hoping to understand her teenaged son. What I found were my own unrealized beliefs. Nowadays, I often wander among uniquely beautiful trees. I listen to Spirit's lessons in the whispering of the wind; I feel cleansed by the gentle rain and renewed by invigorating sunlight. And so it was that my first-born child, Dominic, became midwife to my rebirth as a Witch and my first teacher on my true spiritual path.

Rockford, Illinois

❧ My First Teacher
Wren Walker

My first "teacher" literally walked into my life when I was about four years old. A feral cat gave birth to a litter of kittens in the old log pile under the apple tree behind the barn. This apple tree was my favorite because it was the old-fashioned kind with spreading branches low down on the trunk. Even a young child could reach those first limbs and then have a good climb on such a tree. That was exactly what I was doing when I first heard the strange little crying sounds coming from under the log pile. So I climbed down and, as any self-respecting curious toddler would, took a wary peek.

Within the dimly lit hollow were three very small kittens skittering around chasing leaves and tails and whatever else dared to move inside there. One black-and-white kitten spotted me. I have no idea what he was thinking, but he seemed to take two big blue eyes suddenly appearing at his bedroom door as a not totally unexpected occurrence. I made that pursed lips sucking sound that cat lovers are probably born knowing how to do. (Cats seem to find the noise rather pathetic coming from most people, but will grudgingly admit that it's a somewhat adorable ability in their own humans.) He came out, I picked him up, and that was that. My very first cat had found me.

Looking back on it now, I think that this particular cat decided—probably somewhere during that prenatal auction that cats attend to choose their Witches—that he was going to volunteer to be my "training cat." There is no other explanation that I can think of for why he would let me dress him up in baby clothes, run him around in a doll carriage, and tie bells on his tail. I named him "Blacky-Wacky" and he let me get away with it.

Blacky-Wacky taught me one of the first tenets of magic. For the nonmagical layperson, these are: to know, to will, to dare, and to be silent. Being the advanced soul that he was, Blacky-Wacky went straight to the last one first.

I grew up in a pre-1800 farmhouse. In the kitchen, we had a huge cast iron, four-legged, wood-burning stove. In the winter, Blacky-Wacky would crawl under the stove and nap the long cold New England nights away.

Somewhere along the line I noticed another kitten. I don't remember how long she had been living with us prior to this incident. In fact, it seemed she didn't really live with us as much as she alternated between being in the house and not being anywhere at all. I didn't question her appearance but figured that she must be Blacky-Wacky's sister. I named her Fluffy. My only excuse for reaching such an obvious name was that she was gray and fluffy and I was four and my vocabulary was still pretty limited.

Anyway, Blacky-Wacky and Fluffy were snoozing away under the stove one night when I needed my "cat fix" which meant rubbing my face in my beloved kitty's fur. So there I was, feet kicking out from under the stove, trying to grab two squirmy kittens that undoubtedly would much rather continue sleeping. Finally, Blacky-Wacky, resigning himself to the fact that sleep was now totally impossible, came out from under the stove on his own. That left just Fluffy . . . a little closer. . . . I almost could reach her.

"*What* are you doing under there?"

Startled, I bumped my head on the underside of the stove as I shimmied out and into the middle of the kitchen floor. Looking up, I knew that there was going to be trouble.

My parents and I lived in the family homestead where my dad and his family had grown up, where three generations of our family had lived, where everyone always gathered on the weekends. The good part of two of those generations were seated around the big harvest table playing cards, drinking the coffee that came from the pot that was always perking, and all of the eyes of all my relations were suddenly on me.

When you are four, you generally feel pretty small anyway. I felt even smaller than usual right then.

"I'm trying to get Fluffy out from under the stove, " I said in a smaller than usual voice.

Then came the words that if I had only been a wee bit older, a wee bit wiser, and a wee bit less small, would have warned me that something was a wee bit askew.

"*Who* the hell is Fluffy?"

My mother had that look on her face. The look that mothers and fathers get when their children are embarrassing them in front of people. I knew the look. I saw it a lot. I should have known better, but I didn't. And besides, by now I was also more than a wee bit confused.

"Fluffy. You know, Blacky-Wacky's sister. I stammered and looked frantically around for an understanding face. "Fluffy is the little gray fuzzy kitty. She's Blacky-Wacky's sister, I think, and she's under the stove and she won't come out."

"There is no fuzzy gray kitten in this house," my mother said rather curtly. "There never has been any gray kitten in this house. We have one cat and that's Blacky-Wacky and he's sitting right there."

I looked back at the stove. Blacky-Wacky was sitting right in front of it, paws neatly pressed together, silent and still as a statue. Right next to him sat Fluffy. Paws neatly pressed together and still as a statue. I looked from one perfectly solid cat to the other in utter confusion, which is probably the reason I remember the entire thing so clearly. It was one of those emotionally charged moments that continued to rummage around in my mental attic for years.

In fact, I didn't get it until Blacky-Wacky curled up his paw and proceeded to casually examine his kitty-cat manicure. Time seemed to stop. No one moved for what seemed to be a very long time. Blacky-Wacky lifted his seriously green eyes and looked straight at me. Then he glared at the table filled with very silent people, at Fluffy, and back at me. He put his paw down and neatly pressed his dainty feet together again.

And in that strange nontime between one second and the next, I got it. The grownup people saw one small black-and-white kitten and one small blue-eyed child sitting on the kitchen floor in front of the big wood-burning stove. They did not see the small fluffy gray kitten. They never had seen a small fluffy gray spirit kitten anywhere in or out of the kitchen, and they never would. The world started to move again. But it was a different world and, for me after that, it always would be.

I had no idea that a cat face could hold an expression so wise and profound, but Blacky-Wacky looked all of that and a whole lot more. He yawned and stretched as if to signal that his work here was pretty much done. Yep, he almost smirked, went according to plan.

So now I know: Some things are meant for me and me alone and there are things, like Fluffy, that others will never see or understand. Perhaps they just didn't want to. It is better to not try to explain such things to those who would just rather not see them. They find it more than a wee bit disturbing.

Fluffy slowly began to fade after that night. She just seemed to become dimmer and dimmer until one day she was simply gone. I don't really know who or what she actually was or how she came to be hanging around with Blacky-Wacky under the big wood-burning stove in my parents' kitchen.

To this day, if I see certain things—and I do all of the time—it has become second nature to scan the faces of the people around me. If they didn't see it, then I don't bring it up. I have learned to "be silent" about such things thanks to one small black-and-white cat. He was my first teacher and my friend.

Clearwater, Florida

✺ Memories of Gerald Gardner
Frederic Lamond

On an afternoon in June 1956, I stood among the stacks of books in Hatchard's on Piccadilly in London. The bookstore was only a short walk from my office at the Economist Intelligence Unit in London where I worked as a market researcher. I smiled as I thought of what my fellow workers might think if they saw the books I was browsing. Here I was, a professional, well-dressed gent examining titles like *Sex in History* by the English anthropologist Gordon Rattray Taylor and texts on comparative religion.

On the other hand, they probably wouldn't approve of the company I kept after work either. My friends were members in the Progressive League, which promoted world government, European federalism, pacifism, socialism, Jungian psychology, nudism, and free love.

I came to the bookstore on a quest. Two years earlier, I'd had a mystical experience in the arms of my first fiancée. There, I encountered the Goddess, the Great Mother, the Lady of Life. That meeting changed me forever. So, after my relationship with my fiancée ended, I felt a great need to find others who shared similar visions. I wondered if they could tell me what it might have meant. And, most important, could they help me find my way to Her sweet presence again. An abiding desire to touch again the divine bliss remained deep within me.

I was familiar with Margaret Murray's theory that Witchcraft was a survival from Pagan antiquity and that Witches worshipped a goddess. I was seeking more knowledge of their ways when I came across Gerald B. Gardner's book *Witchcraft Today*. *Perhaps*, I thought, while turning over the volume in my hands, *I'll find the answers in here.*

I took *Witchcraft Today* home and settled down to read it. The more I read, the more Gardner's book rang my inner bells. He spoke of people in our own time who continued to worship the Mother Goddess of life and love. Their worship took place at the full moon, when I had always felt closest to the mystical Spirit. They practiced ritual nudity.

In the foreword to *Witchcraft Today*, Gardner expressed interest in hearing from other covens and "anyone who has any further information on the subject of witchcraft."* While I didn't have any more information on the topic, the statement made him seem approachable. Using the address of the publisher printed in the back of the book, I posted a letter to Gardner. He responded within days, inviting me to visit him in his Holland Park flat. With excitement and some trepidation, I boarded the subway to West London.

With Gerald's letter in hand, I walked the few blocks from the station down the rows of Holland Park apartments until I found his address. From the outside, it was a normal London apartment house, looking just like every other building in the neighborhood. I took a deep breath and knocked on the door.

I don't know what I expected, but what I found seemed a disappointment. The man who answered was a very lovable, unassuming old gentleman. He was dressed in the informal dress of the time: tweed jacket over colored shirt and trousers. He had a narrow goatee and white hair. I later learned he liked to style the sides of his hair upward in an attempt to make them look like horns, an effect I found more humorous than demonic. I felt no spark of recognition from a past life, no charismatic pull, and no mysterious occult flare. Gerald B. Gardner was just an average, elderly man. For a brief moment, I wondered if I had gotten the wrong address.

Gardner invited me into his home, which turned out to be just as ordinary inside as out. He led me into his living room and invited me to sit. We made small talk while his wife, Donna,

*Gerald B. Gardner, *Witchcraft Today* (London: Rider, 1954; reprinted, New York: Citadel, 2004)

who had no interest in the occult, served refreshments and withdrew. We continued to talk a bit, sounding out our common interests. I found Gerald to be an excellent raconteur with a fine feeling for the absurdities of human life and a great sense of humor. While not charismatic, he did elicit an instant affection. It almost made up for my disappointment that he was so normal and ordinary.

The conversation soon turned to my reason for contacting him. I explained that I was interested in Witchcraft and then gave him my reasons why. How do you explain a vision? An epiphany? My heart raced from the fear that he might laugh at me even as I told him my story.

He must have liked what I said. At the end of the visit, he invited me back to meet the rest of the coven.

I returned to the Holland Park flat in September 1956. There I met another invited candidate and the members of Gerald's coven. They were a strange mixture of people. In addition to Gerald, there was a financier from London, a retired British Indian Army major, Dayonis, and Jack Bracelin. They all seemed pleasant enough, but not particularly magical.

After the informal meeting, the coven members held their rites, but neither I nor the other guest was allowed to attend. The first time I participated with the coven was at my initiation in February 1957.

Doreen Valiente, perhaps the most well known of Gardner's High Priestesses, had recently left the coven over a disagreement concerning coven privacy. Dayonis became the new High Priestess. She, and Gardner as the High Priest, officiated over my initiation rite. While I did not feel the same mystical connection that I found in my lover's arms, it did give me a sense of a permanent spiritual contact with the eternal Goddess. I felt "welcomed home."

I continued in the Craft, receiving my second degree in February 1958. I did not feel any stronger connection to the

Mother Goddess and Horn God at the time, but two days later I had an intense experience of cosmic consciousness.

Gerald was not what could be called a mentor or teacher in the traditional sense. He did not hold formal classes. The circle was the classroom, the coven a warm extended family. His stories, often told during the cake and wine section of our rite, were certainly not factual, but nonetheless conveyed mythical truths.

For example, Gardner would speak about witchcraft traditions in "preBurning Times," implying that we had an ancient unbroken tradition dating at least from before the Witch hunts. We all knew that this was improbable.

Recently, I realized that he was using, consciously or unconsciously, a historical mirror-image technique. When he said, "This is what happened before the Burning times," he really meant, "This is what you should do when times have become sufficiently tolerant for you to emerge from the broom closet, go public, and acquire a lay following."

As I recall my fifty years as a Witch, I can't help but be amazed at how far Wicca has come since the day I found Gardner's first nonfiction book about it in Hatchard's. Wicca has become a great religious movement since then; one that I'm sure goes well beyond Gardner's visions. But as its numbers have grown, I fear it has also become, on average, more superficial. I wonder sometimes where the Craft is headed.

London

✌ The Crystal Ball
Lady Rhea

When thinking of teachers in the Craft, most people have a vision of a wise, gray-haired crone or maybe the figure of an earth mother. The Goddess blessed me with four wonderful guides, all of whom were men.

My journey in the Craft began in 1971 with the desire to purchase a crystal ball. What followed turned my life around, putting me onto a new spiral path, one that has been fulfilling and nonending from that first day.

One of my friends gave me a book for my birthday called *The Gypsy Fortune Teller*. It contained an assortment of different methods of divination, the most fascinating of which was the crystal ball. Visions could be seen in its shining depths, or so the book said. I was hooked—I had to have one. I remembered seeing an advertisement in *The Village Voice* for an occult store called the Warlock Shop. So on a Sunday in September 1971, I made my way to Brooklyn and to the shop that would forever change my life.

To say that the Warlock Shop was otherworldly is an understatement. It totally existed on another plane. It was small, crowded, and jam-packed with stuff. The place smelt of herbs, oils, and incense. If one could have captured the fragrance of the store and put it in a bottle, he or she would have made a fortune. It was totally intoxicating, and I was enthralled with it. When I arrived, Herman, the owner, popped his head out from behind a string of talismans that were suspended over the counter like a metal veil. When I told him I wanted to purchase a crystal ball, he lit up, a charm I was to see for many years to come. Herman was as much a great Witch as he was a businessman. He was excited because he knew the person standing before him was not only a potential customer, but a future Witch.

Herman produced a crystal ball. I then asked if he had a black cloth I could buy to use while scrying with my ball. He hobbled to the back of the store. I heard a mumbling and sultry male voice ask, "Who is that?" Little did I know that the voice belonged to Eddie, the man who would soon become my mentor. I heard a ripping sound of fabric being torn and snickers coming from the back of the shop. Herman came out with a flourish carrying a piece of black cotton cloth. He said, "At my store, it comes free with the ball." Later, I found out that he tore off a piece of an old robe hanging in the back. Then I asked, "Do you have a stand?" He started to do this peculiar dance with a perplexed look on his face. I learned this was Herman thinking. He said, "Just a minute." In a flash, he was again in the back of the shop. I heard Eddie saying, "Herman, what are you doing?" When Herman returned, he handed me a stand that he said belonged to my crystal ball. It was a hard rubber circle, the kind that you use to keep your couch from moving around on a wooden floor. He had taken it from under a chair in his upstairs apartment. Of course, at the time I had no idea, so I was happy and pleased.

With the sale complete, I was ready to leave. "Would you like to become a Witch?" he suddenly asked. "We have Pagan Way classes every Sunday." He explained that there would be other Witches, and, of course, beginners just like me. I was hooked again.

Pagan Way was held in Brooklyn Heights. The apartment had an exceptionally spacious living room that held about twenty-five people comfortably. Once I arrived and was seated, my eyes were riveted to the statue on the central altar. About two and a half feet tall, it was a beautiful art deco rendition of a woman with long hair. I was enchanted. I had brought a beautiful white blossom to give to the Goddess. The High Priest bade me to place it on the altar. It was my first true act of devotion.

We formed a circle around the altar and the High Priest,

Lord Tammuz, introduced himself and his High Priestess, Lady Vivienne. They instructed us in the ways of the Craft, saying that if we worked hard, developed self-discipline, and proved the ability to work in a group, we would be considered for training in an outer court leading to initiation of the first degree.

Lord Tammuz was Arthur Jamison, affectionately known today as Ol' Grandpa Witch. He took a liking to me right away, and I to him. He became my first teacher, initiating me into the Welsh Tradition, which is based on Celtic and Druidic practices of tree, plant, and nature worship of the Goddess and her consort. The Welsh tradition is derived from the teachings of the *Mabinogian,* the four lost books of Welsh, Celtic, and Druidic magic. It was brought here by Gwen Thompson.

Herman's lover was Eddie Buczynski, also known as Lord Gwydion. Herman was the businessman, Eddie the artist. They lived together above the Warlock Shop, sharing a magical bedroom where the vines and large white flowers of a moonflower, a night-blooming plant, entwined their bed frame. When I first laid eyes on Eddie, I said to myself, "Ah, here is the epitome of the androgynous God." Having a tall lithe body, long red hair, and liquid green eyes, the sensuality of this man was total. I just stood there and melted, totally entranced by his beauty. Emotionally, we fell in love. He became my High Priest.

With the enthusiasm of a new convert, I longed to be around my mentor as much as possible. Eddie was trained in the Gardnerian Tradition. He oozed magic as he walked. All manner of magical beings emerged from his mouth as he spoke. This meant when Eddie spoke, you could see magic happen. When he spoke about the Gods or Elementals, you were so transfixed it was as if they appeared out of thin air. His gaze could make me see the secrets of the universe. He opened my world, affirming that the beliefs I had held were true and valid. My heart and soul belonged to him and the old Gods.

He set me free. On that broom, I flew to my freedom. Goddess, I was alive!

Eventually, Herman relocated the Warlock Shop to New York City and renamed it Magickal Childe. Eddie remained at the shop, but their relationship had died and only the business partnership remained. I was hired to come and read Tarot, manage the floor with stock, oversee sales, and help people with spell work. Each day at the Warlock Shop or the Magickal Childe was filled with wonder and surprise. It was like living in Hogwarts. You never knew what you were going to find: Witch bottles, which are glass jars stuffed with pins, needles, and other nasty stuff, including vinegar and such, crammed on the shelves, hidden jars full of graveyard dirt, bones, skulls, bats, scorpions—it was a magic emporium of everything you could imagine. It was here I was to meet my next great mentor: Clinton Stephen.

Clinton was my "Louisiana swamp Witch." With a choir boy face of innocence, soft pouty lips, and the most delicate expressions I have ever seen, he could spin magic and voodoo out of nothing. Spells, blending oils, and making mojo were his domain. Clinton was a dear friend to my Eddie, and we instantly became paramours. Clinton would flutter up and down the aisles of the Magickal Childe, while Eddie gracefully glided. Together, in less than two minutes, they would have spells flying galore. Herman would yell and scream as books flew off the shelves because one of them left the watchtower of the North or East open, releasing playful gnomes or fairies, leading to hell and pandemonium.

The three of them, Herman, Eddie, and Clinton, were masters of magic, herbs, and oils. Although I had been in the Craft for over eight years and had learned much on my own blending oils with Eddie in the Warlock Shop, I still jumped at the opportunity to expand my knowledge. Clinton introduced me to the world of Voudon. Having been involved in Santeria in my earlier years, I found it familiar and fascinating. He taught me many stories about the Goddess and gave me the veve, which are magical seals of the Gods in Voudon that were later included in my book *The Enchanted Candle*.

Sadly, this wonderful time in my life came to an end, but the legacy of these special teachers continues. Eddie, who was the acting High Priest in all three of my degree elevation rituals, my then-wife, Carol Bulzone, and I started the Minoan Tradition. The Minoan Tradition was one of the first all-gay working groups in the New York area. It consists of both an all-male group practicing the men's mysteries and an all-female group practicing the women's mysteries. The two come together to celebrate the greater sabbats.

In 1982, I followed in the footsteps of my mentors and, with Carol as my partner, opened Enchantments, an occult store. Later, when I chose to leave the store, Carol kept it open. Enchantments continues to serve the Pagan community, offering occult supplies and public circles. In 1995, I went on to open Magickal Realms, Home of the Enchanted Candle, with my wife, Lady Zoradia.

Lord Tammuz (Ol' Grandpa Witch) and I have an active circle with many students and teachers of the Craft working together in a Pagan Way offered at Magickal Realms. Many of my initiates have become prominent speakers and Pagan authors including Phyllis Curott, author of *Book of Shadows*, and Lexa Roséan, author of the *Supermarket Sorceress* series.

All of us have gone through many transitions. I am proud of our accomplishments in the Craft. With the help of these magnificent men, and all of my friends, teachers, and mentors, I learned to make my dreams become manifest. My crystal ball still remains. It has been with me since the beginning, helping to guide my way, serving as a watchful eye through my journey in the craft, and ever projecting my future onward.

Bronx, New York

ॐ Lord Theodore Parker Mills, Pagan Elder
Ellen Evert Hopman

Another word for "priest" is "father." My biological father died when I was thirty-six years old. He had been fairly typical for his time, somewhat distant and preoccupied with work. In my forties, I was fortunate to meet my next "father" in the person of Lord Theodore Mills, Priest of Isis and Witch. He was the first and only person in my life who cheered my projects and ambitions without reservation. No matter how far-fetched my dreams and visions, he always encouraged me and gave me unconditional support.

Lord Theo, called "Ted," was housebound with emphysema by the time I met him, the outcome of a lifetime of smoking. He trailed good-naturedly through his apartment, dragging a small container of oxygen, plastic tubes twining around his nose and ears. I would visit him once or twice a month, bringing a small gift of food or fresh flowers; the flowers inevitably found their place on Ted's altar, dedicated to Isis, Stella Maris, Star of the Sea.

Ted and I would converse, always at the kitchen table over a steaming cup of tea. Ted was very proud of his Salem, Massachusetts, ancestry. He was a direct descendant of Rebecca Church Nurse, who was executed during the infamous Witchcraft trials. He was equally proud of his military service during World War II. We had much in common: as children, we both had to covertly worship our Goddesses to avoid upsetting our parents; as adults, we both had spent time with Native Americans and admired their magic and ways. We did not always see eye to eye, of course! Ted was a fan of George Wallace; I was and still am an ardent liberal. Ted felt that religion and politics should not mix; I am a Pagan activist for peace and for the environment. He was a Witch; I am a Druid. But such discrepancies never got in the way of our friendship. He always spoke to me as a peer, telling me not to mind the criticism of others, that one day I would be an international Pagan leader. "Brush them off as if they were gnats," he would advise.

Ted set a profound example for what it meant to be dedicated to a Goddess. He constructed an elaborate altar in Isis's honor in his bedroom, with a boxed niche for his Goddess's statue. Every evening he would pray to Her and then close the doors of the niche for the night, so that She could safely travel away to Her realms. In the morning, he would reopen the doors and pray to Her again. He had a small bottle of lavender water that he would spray for Her pleasure and a sistrum that he used to make music for Her. He always made sure that his bedroom was immaculately tidy so that the Goddess would not be offended. He commissioned elaborate robes and beautiful headdresses to wear in ceremony, in Her honor, as a mark of respect.

One day, I found a museum replica of a ring worn by the followers of Isis during the time of the Roman Empire, and Ted suggested that we each buy one as a symbol of our friendship. The rings consisted of two intertwined snakes, with one head pointing to the left and one to the right. "They mean that we are protected by Isis, coming and going," Ted explained. For six years, Ted told me his stories, such as his vision of the Goddess, who appeared to him one night as a woman with long dark hair and green eyes and told him, "Take care of my children." From that day on, he assumed that anyone who came into his sphere was one of Her children, deserving of respect, care, and support.

There were many who felt the touch of Ted's love. In his later years, some came to his home on a weekly basis to wash his hair, cook food, or clean the apartment. Others took him on outings so he could escape the monotony of his elder-housing unit. A friend who happened to be a countess gifted him with a beautiful set of bedroom furniture. Respected Craft elders such as Elizabeth Pepper and Laurie Cabot called on the phone.

Ted is gone now. He is buried in his family plot in Ludlow, Massachusetts. A small Egyptian ankh decorates the headstone where he lies with his relatives. Ted was a shining example of a true Priest of the Goddess. He set the highest standard for how a Priest should behave, toward people and toward the Gods.

Sometimes, when I am praying to the Goddess statue on my altar (She happens to be Brighid), I know that he is watching from the Other side. Once, for example, I was particularly worried because I didn't know how I was going to come up with money for the rent. I heard Ted laughing behind me, like he thought the whole situation was hilarious. A few days later a check arrived in the mail for $450, paid by a student of mine who had owed me tuition for an herb class for eleven years! She said she "just happened" to walk by a store window and saw one of my books, after which she tracked down my address.

Ted embodied the best attributes possible that one would wish for in a father, and that was how everyone who came into his sphere experienced his presence. His was the gift of unconditional positive regard, respect, and love, qualities all too rare in the earthly fathers we have been born to and equally rare in the priests of most religions.

Toward the end of his life, many of us who knew him threw a big party in his honor. Each person who had been touched by Ted's affection designed a page of tribute, and all the pages were bound into a large book. The bookbinders were astounded by the love that poured from the pages and said they wished they could have met such a great man.

My page said simply, "In this world there is no other whom I call father."

An oak forest in western Massachusetts

ॐ Leon's Template

John Yohalem

Orianna was a lovely tall Texan who had studied with some Dianics back home—some weird Dianic group that accepted men, I gather, because Orianna's then husband had joined them, too. She used to say that he'd become a witch for love of her and she'd become Jewish for love of him. Anyway, the point of the story is that these were not orthodox Dianics (who tend to be all-female) or by-the-book anything. But if you ask me (I'm aware you didn't) there are too many people in this supposedly Earth-centered religion who get what they know about magic and the Gods out of books. (I'm a prime offender, of course.)

I once asked Rolla Nordic, a ninety-eight-year-old Witch, if she thought Gerald Gardner had made his stuff up. She said, "Well, somebody made it up. Does that answer the question?" In other words: If somebody made it up and it works, then you, too, can make something up, and it will work just as well. Our ritual books weren't handed down from the Gods. That's some other religion (and they're lying).

I'd attended a couple of Orianna's rituals when she led them at Tom and Star's home. Tom and Star used to host monthly full moon rituals for the entire local Pagan community in their town. They used their backyard, weather willing, or their capacious family room downstairs otherwise. A different coven would lead the actual ritual each time, and up to eighty people would show up, expecting to be entertained. The thing that amazed me was that Star, who was a social woman, managed to keep this up for nearly two years before she had had it.

Orianna's rituals at Tom and Star's were different from the rituals led by everyone else because she hadn't read those books or studied those templates. Her rituals were spontaneous. One time, after celebrating some seasonal change or other, she produced the proper chalice and her husband produced the proper knife and they looked at each other and dropped the props, and she jumped laughing into his arms and (though clothed) they mimicked the proper sacraments that way, to enthusiastic response all around. Another time she sprayed us from a water pistol to invoke that element.

Now, I had been a Pagan since I was eleven years old. I got my Paganism out of books of Greek mythology to begin with. When I stumbled into Wicca twenty-six years later, I had no idea how to lead a ritual or what was required to create one. I'd been to Christian rituals a few times (when the music was Haydn or Mozart, or if someone I knew was singing) and the Mass, of course, has roots in Pagan rituals, but what parts of the Mass were specifically Christian and what parts were useful for the sort of powers I wished to raise, and praise, and adore, and invoke were not clear to me at all. When I wanted a Pagan ritual, I went to the opera. I still do. Try it. Superb for raising energy, and the Pagan rites in *Aida*, *Idomeneo*, and *The Magic Flute*—to name just three—though bogus, are impressive and thrilling.

So when I found myself among Witches—I had never connected Witches with Paganism before—I went to a man named Leon, who taught the most widely praised class in ritual design and other aspects of witchery in the region—perhaps in the country. Leon would take anybody as a student (of course, he or she had to be eighteen) who showed up on his doorstep between sunset and sunset on Candlemas. For years only two or three people ever did show up, but in my year, eleven aspirants came. Later the numbers got higher. Eventually, he had to change the rules and limit the number of students. Now he has given up teaching entirely, but back when I was his student, Leon devoted a lot of time to teaching a two- to four-hour class

every Thursday for a year and a day (Thanksgiving off). He
liked to feel close to each individual's energy. He said he used
to visit each of us on the astral, while we slept, to see how our
studies were affecting our spiritual natures. You're responsible
for the students you teach. Leon didn't charge money to teach
magic (Tarot, yes); his conditions were that should we eventually decide to take on students ourselves, we would not charge
for teaching. Each of us, however, might teach in his or her
own way—I did it through starting my magazine.

Leon brought in visitors from all the groups around the area
(he knew and was respected by everybody, perhaps because he
never engaged in feuds). They came not only to assist in the
teaching, but also to scope us out—on that initial Candlemas
he promised to place us in groups if we wanted to be. My pantheon had been so very Hellenic for twenty-six years and most
people in the region were so very Celtic or Native American
(Leon was both, with Hindu thrown in) that he didn't think
he could place me, and indeed he couldn't.

Regardless, I got a lot from that class. I learned more there
than from almost any college course I ever took. There was history, anthropology, and magical theory and discussions on traditions, seasons, methods of prognostication, spellcasting, and
every magical lore imaginable except herb lore and Tarot,
because Leon taught other classes on those subjects. But,
remember, for the Tarot, he charged.

And there was ritual design.

I feel very sorry for anyone who did not study with Leon, and
for those who studied with Leon in the years after I did. Because
up till then, Leon taught in the front room of his little dark
house on the side of the bay. That house was the spookiest, jol-
liest, most magical place I've ever done magic in (aside from
the occasional grotto or long barrow). It had St. John's wort
drying from every spare rafter, and there were yards and yards
of strange books here and there, some very creepy plumbing

and a whole temple room dedicated to nothing but ritual, festooned with amazing art—glorious and tacky, handmade and crafty, folkloric and pornographic. Ritual in the near darkness in that space had a tang that ritual has never had for me in any other urban space. (Out in the country it is obviously a different matter. That whole year was a year of discovering the country, and going to it not just to enjoy it, but to bring in something tangible, to gather inspiration for ritual. I went to the woods to encounter the Gods, and found They had always dwelt within me and that the woods were a coming home. Like the opera house with less glitzy decor.)

Leon taught required steps, and when we got his pattern down, we were allowed—no, commanded—to replace his concoctions with methods of our own. They would all achieve the same thing: a song here, a chant there, how to raise power, and how very easily misbehavior could dissipate whatever energy we had raised. It was very real to us there in the dark. "But you'll get so you can do it anywhere," Leon said. It was a course in how to make yourself superstitious again (after going to school to get rid of it) for the purpose of healing your spirit and turning yourself into a tool to heal the spirits of others.

So I got the template down. I found a song to cast directions that I still often use—Purple Mark, a local solitary, wrote it, based on Sumerian deities—and developed a style of when to do this and when to do that. All of these things were fixed within my soul by those classes. I can see echoes of the lessons I learned in other rituals I've attended, and recognize how other ritualists go about achieving the same thing by similar/ dissimilar means. (This includes Giuseppe Verdi in the temple scene in *Aida* and Richard Wagner in the final scene of *Parsifal*.) Now, when I attend full moon rituals with unfamiliar covens, I know what they are doing, and why, and how, and I can admire them and appreciate (and steal) ideas.

Still, the idea of performing publicly made me nervous, as

I was only used to orchestrating ritual for Leon and my fellow students. But when I had done my year and a day with Leon and was making ready to leave town, I knew it was time. I threw a ritual, my own parody sabbat, for the whole community at Tom and Star's. Star said it was the only time she ever forgot she was a hostess and just enjoyed herself. I invoked the directions with limericks composed for the occasion, and consecrated the Elements with Tom Lehrer's "Elements" song (102 of them, to the tune of "Modern Major-General"). I had the attendees charge the first issue of my new magazine, *Enchanté*, and I invoked the Moon Goddess with a hymn sung to her by the natives of the island where I was born, Manhattan: Cole Porter's "You Do Something to Me." (I didn't have to change a word.) At the height of it all, I had myself stripped naked, blindfolded, and bound and responded to ritual questions from a Witch who then consecrated me to the community of the Witches. From the moment I was blindfolded, I never again feared being naked in the company of strangers. (I was kind of sorry when the blindfold came off.)

Two or three years later I was passing through town and I learned there was going to be an open full moon—not at Tom and Star's: they'd closed up shop, and someone else was now hosting the monthly circles—but no one had volunteered to lead it. So I was happy to do it—having had plenty of experience by now. About twenty folks showed up, among them Orianna, who had never seen a rote Leon-template ritual before. I did it by the book—Leon's book—this time. Orianna was very impressed. She never ever did the same thing twice and the way things just fell into place won her admiration. She said to me, "Perhaps I should go study with Leon."

I told her, "No you shouldn't. A template is fine, but it's a crutch for people like me who haven't got what you've got: a natural gift for it."

The very first rituals must have been spontaneous ones, and

the first Witches were like Orianna, inspired from within. The rest of society saw that energy and made what use they could of it and developed a pattern, a template. That template is very useful—it's a path to the center. But keep an eye out for the ones who can get there untaught. The power is for all of us. There are the Leons who show us the path, but there are the trailblazers, the Oriannas, who discover it.

Watch them. And follow their lead.

Formerly of the Pacific Northwest,
currently in New York City

3

FIRE

Magical Transformation—from Wow!
to Oops!

The tiniest movement of one of the threads will set a web a-quivering, and so it is with the workings of magic, as they send tremors through the Web of Fate.

—Diana Ferguson, *The Magickal Year*

ᗡ Magic Is Not Easy
Oriethyia

Magic is not easy
not Presto Chango
Hocus Pocus
snap your fingers
all is changed

Magic is not easy
ABRACADABRA
will not do it
spin around twice
and all is changed

Nothing changes
nothing
Magic is not easy
nothing moves
unless the heart is in it
unless the will is in it

Cutesy-pie
rainbow light magic
think good thoughts and all
    will be well
budges nothing
flits along
like a half-turned smirk
unable to grow
into a laugh
Magic is not easy

If you would do magic,
listen,
everything is connected
everything
like it or not
never mind that it does not
    compute
everything is connected

If you would do magic, listen
start here
everything is connected
nothing moves
unless the heart is in it
unless the will is in it
Magic is not easy

Simple words won't do
chanting the same song
day in day out every full
    or new moon
is not enough
if the mouth is singing
"Hail unto Thee Spirits of the
    South"
while the mind is humming
budgets and schedules and
    where did I leave those keys
this is not ritual

only rote
and we have more than
   enough of that
thank you
Magic is not easy

If you would do magic
listen
Magic is fed by the heart
made manifest by the will
the minister who leads his
   flock
to pray for the death of a
   Supreme Court justice*
is doing magic
BAD magic, murky stuff
but the heart is there
a heart full of pain
and no one can doubt the will

The adolescent boy who
   dismembered my cat
or the one who stuck knives
   through the lungs
through the heart of his
   former friend
singing some crap
all the while about
Satan or the devil†
was doing magic

Bad, bad medicine
but the heart was there
a heart full of fear and pain
and the will was clear
made manifest through a
convenient channel
It is always easier to invoke
what you have learned to
   name external
when the demons inside
the ones whose true names are
self-doubt and self-hate
have grown sufficiently strong
when our children search for
outlaw status
seeking to flee the mirrors in
   our,
in their own eyes
sometimes purple hair
or a pin through the cheek
some punk version of Jesse
   James
won't do it

When we will not
cannot
touch our own demons
we invent others
or worse

---

*In 1986, "Rev. R. L. Hymers, Jr., pastor of a large fundamentalist Baptist congregation in Los Angeles, urged his congregation to pray for the death of Justice William Brennan. He later prayed for the 'repentance, death or retirement' of five justices who voted that a couple could withhold medical treatment in the 'Baby Doe' case." *Freethought Today* 20, no. 6 (August 2003).

†The alleged murderers were Ricky Kasso, seventeen, and Jimmy Troiano, eighteen, of their friend, Gary Lauwers, seventeen. According to reports, Gary was forced to his knees and made to repeat "I love Satan" as the knife was plunged into his body. See *Rolling Stone*, 22 November 1984, 30.

sing the names of demons
invented for us

Magic is not easy

If you would live magic
Listen
you must move beyond your
    pain
listen
you must turn and face your
    fear
listen
you must touch the demons
hold them
ignore your scorching flesh
(it is illusion)
cradle the flailing thing
cradle it
cradle it

Madonna with child
Madonna Madonna
Mother-gift
cradle your demon self
until you can love it into
    healing
Magic is not easy.

If you would be magic
then listen
dance your demons with love
dance your demons until
they become love
fill your heart
with the mother's love

and dance your
shattered pieces into her love

Listen
there are two rules
just two:
"An you harm none, do as
    you will"
listen
"everything you do comes
    back to you,
a thousandfold"

Magic is not easy
nothing changes unless the
    heart is in it
unless the will is in it
Listen
true magic demands two
    things
only two
Integrity and
Clear intent
Intent
because you must see truly
    what
you desire
before you can call it out
Integrity
because only fools foul the
    well
where they daily
must drink

Magic is not easy.

Albany, New York

✍ Ancient Texts and Venerable Tales
K. A. Laity, Ph.D.

I became a medievalist for the stories. Reading *Beowulf* and *Njal's Saga* for the first time in my thirties, I knew at last what I wanted to do with my life. These tales of epic struggles and matter-of-fact magic piqued my imagination. I had thought of the Middle Ages in terms of Arthurian romance (bleh!) and the church's oppression of women. While most think the Christian church maintained a kind of stranglehold on the lives of people during the Middle Ages, this is not really the case. I quickly found out just how different the reality of medieval literature was from my prejudiced notions. But I didn't know that my academic studies would be a source of enchantment that would turn my life around, inspire new creativity, and open my heart to the mysteries of these long lost worlds.

As I struggled to learn Old English, Old Irish, and Old Norse, sometimes I lost track of the words while puzzling through the grammar. I was startled to realize that some of the works I was translating were charms—magical charms. This was different from Gerald Gardner's "discovery" of a secret coven or Margaret Murray's fanciful imaginings of an "ancient witch cult." This was real magic, practiced by real people. Even more surprising, most were probably written down by devout monks of the church.

Most of the charms that have come down to us were recorded in books of healing like the *Leechbook* or in monastic collections of poetry and knowledge as were the metrical charms. In large part, I came to understand that the charms' existence was due to the definitions of magic at the time. *Maleficium*, evil magic, was forbidden by various laws. But magic that had no intent to harm was often considered *cunning*, especially if it dealt with healing. While the modern meaning of this word implies a shifty sort of shrewdness, the Old English root has to do with knowledge. Divination, too, has a mixed history; for a long time in England, it was tolerated in the early laws, then discouraged by the first penitentials, and finally outlawed as an effrontery during the tenth-century Benedictine reforms—how dare one seek to know the mind of God? Of course, it never really went away, which is why folk charms for prognostication (Whom will I marry? Will I be rich?) continue right up to the present.

Yet, healing and other benign forms of magic also endured for quite some time in the Christian era. I read with great excitement charms that told how to fight off creatures like a "wen" or a water-elf. I also learned how the Anglo-Saxons asked saints to possess stolen cattle to bring them home. The spell also cursed the thief, declaring he would be left "limp as a thistle." The monks recording these charms may have Christianized them, substituting saints and Christ for the original gods, yet even those changes were not complete. After all, the Nine Herbs charm calls on the healing powers of both Christ and Woden (Odin) within its list of the most effective herbs against poison. Genealogies of kings, too, feature the old Pagan god, who is usually sandwiched between Adam and Eve and the early biblical patriarchs. These blendings of the Pagan old and Christian new show an unwillingness to let go the past, even as innovations are embraced.

For me, the best thing about these texts is the reality of this distant life. Here were people who lived in a world full of magic—yet, it was completely normal to them. If they felt a pain in their leg, they could be sure they had been elf-shot. Those little arrows of poison could leave quite an ache! We may find it easy to dismiss this "primitive" view of disease and medicine, but when we consider viruses and bacteria, are they really so different? Tiny beings attack your body and you must drive them out to regain health. The elves and wens and their arrows and darts that afflict people, horses, and cattle are simply a metaphorical understanding of how illness works. We can see how much more real the "battle" is when we read their charms, many of which threaten or cajole the intruders. Consider, too, how alternative physicians use creative visualization. They recommend that patients imagine the radiation or drugs doing "battle" with the disease. Sounds very similar, doesn't it?

Understanding the medieval past helps me to realize more vividly what it means to live a life of magic. Intent, the most important aspect of magic work today, was the guiding force even then. When stepping out on a journey, Anglo-Saxon travelers focused attention on their walking staff. They begged it to take on a mantle of protection and use the power of the gods to ward off everything from stomach aches to "grim horror" and loss of life. Charms of the Middle Ages often tell the supplicant to declare or sing the words aloud, to announce his or her intent to the world. The charm to restore fruitfulness to a field, known as Æcerbot, requires that the farmer stand in the field, face East, and bow nine times and call on the Lord and Lady and Earth herself to hear the entreaty to return the bountiful crops and also to protect the field from counter-charms of crafty men and word-skilled women.

The more I understand the long history of magic and healing, the more I feel that the same intent of these charms can be captured now. I know, because I have used them by slightly adapting them for modern problems, such as using the charm to make a "wen" disappear in order to get a negative person out of my life:

> May you shrink like coal on a hearth;
> May you shrivel away like dung;
> And evaporate like water in a pot.
> You shall become as little as a linseed,
> And much smaller than a hand-worm's hipbone,
> And you shall become so small, that you shall become
> nothing.

Nine days, nine repetitions, and the person's influence did indeed disappear from my life. A thousand years later, the poem still has power. While we once thought an unbroken tradition had been rescued by people like Gerald Gardner, we now find that a genuine history—fragmentary and for a long time lost with the manuscripts and the knowledge of medieval languages—can be recovered, understood, and utilized. While my colleagues appreciate the work I do as a recovery and contextualizing of history and literature, I hope for more from modern Witches and Pagans. We can see ourselves being part of a long tradition that continues today in our languages, fighting against our own monsters (illness, hatred, poverty, or materialism). I have learned a rhetoric of magic that worked for people a thousand years ago and have found that it works just as well now. While not an unbroken ancient tradition as Margaret Murray had hoped, the medieval charms preserve a practice that survived the conversion to Christianity. Remember also that the church recognized that here was good magic worth being copied by monks. While the practices did not live on unchanged after the Middle Ages, the manuscripts preserved them for later discovery, unlocking a treasure trove of "new" old knowledge.

Willimantic, Connecticut

☙ Oh, Lady Moon: A Vignette
M. Macha NightMare

Through the fog of years past, memories arise to the surface—memories of twilight beginning to fall on a sun-baked canyon; hills burnished with late-summer grasses and the dark presence of oaks, clumps of rock; the scent of the nearby sea on the breeze coming down the canyon.

Four hundred Witches assemble in a dry open clearing, forming a large circle. A priestess steps forward and begins to tone. Others join in a spontaneous attunement of everyone present. Voices join into a single precious tone, reverberating like a bell, now stronger, now fainter, now stronger again. The ethereal sound rises over the assembly in a dome of sound and suffuses the people and the meadow with its magical sweetness.

A circle is cast. A priestess and priest from four quarters of America call the Guardians at each Quarter.

The dulcet sound of a bell fills the circle. From a small altar in the center an elder priestess enkindles a glowing sphere of light and offers it up. Out of nowhere dances the White Goddess Herself. Garbed in a flowing white tunic, long pale yellow hair spilling over her shoulders, she accepts the sphere in her hands. Her creamy skin and long graceful limbs glow in the gathering dusk as she dances, holding the sphere aloft. The celebrants clap rhythmically, encouraging this Maiden priestess as she honors Lady Moon.

Just as the ball of light begins to fade, the Maiden hands it back to the Crone priestess, and it disappears.

A Mother priestess steps to the center of the circle, faces East, and begins with the words, "Oh, Lady of the Glowing Moon, Oh, Lady of the Night," . . . in a clear, strong voice. Her song intensifies with the words, "Diana moves with Strength and Will, to bend the arrow's bow." As the Mother priestess addresses Our Lady, She slowly rises over the hills. Her silver light illuminates the grasses and silhouettes the gnarled contours of the ancient oaks. The glow spills into the clearing and fills 400 hearts. All 800 hands remain clasped round the circle; all 800 eyes brim.

The priestess concludes with the words, "We must remember who we are. We must take back the Night," sealing a spell.

Malibu, California

Note to "Oh, Lady Moon": This remembrance is filtered through the fog of many years and the emotions it evoked within the author, so it may not be precisely accurate. Memory and emotion, magical and mutable as they are, can alter objective reportage. This event, which occurred in Malibu, California, in August of 1995, is one of the highlights of my long and varied magical career.

ஒ The Lights Were Extinguished
Carl McColman

My journey into the practice of Paganism began in 1990 at a beautiful meadow on top of the Cumberland Plateau in southeastern Tennessee.

Surrounded by forest and stretching out to a bluff that overlooked a lush valley, this acre or so of land was filled with grass and wildflowers such as thistle, Queen Anne's Lace, and coneflower (Echinacea). In the distance stood a huge old southern home where my married friends Thorn and Casey lived. Thorn was an herbalist and an organic gardener; to her, Paganism was not about initiations or rituals, but about simply living in tune with the earth and the turning seasons. Casey's spirituality ran more toward an odd mixture of Buddhism and Amerindian Shamanism. They were my two compatriots in our first intentional foray into the world between the worlds.

We had met several months earlier at the local food co-op, although our friendship really took off only after I overheard them talking about the esoteric work of Rudolph Steiner. Thinking they might be kindred souls, I tentatively asked Thorn if she were interested in magic. She studied my face carefully before counterasking, "Are you?" It turned out that she, like I, had read a number of books by Starhawk, Z. Buda-pest, Scott Cunningham, and Raymond Buckland; but also like me, she had never felt much of a tug to find a Priestess to study under.

Even so, my question and the many conversations that followed stirred within us a shared desire to enact our devotion to the Goddess—to make it more real than mere words or ideas. I cannot now remember which one of us first said to the other, "Would you like to do a ritual?" But I do recall that, whichever one of us was on the receiving end of the question did not hesitate to say yes, enthusiastically. Soon, we had identified a purpose for the ritual (to send love and healing energy to the cove beneath the bluff on which we lived), a format (generic Wicca, basically our own amalgamation of Starhawk and Cunningham), and a date (the fall equinox). We told no one of our plans, beside Casey, who was perfectly willing to lend his energies to a Wiccan ceremony.

It seemed like forever, but finally the weekend of the equinox arrived. We planned the ceremony for Friday, September 21; it felt as if my workday would never end. When it finally came time to drive out to the bluff, I studied with dismay the ominous presence of storm clouds covering the entire sky. Sure enough, I had barely made it inside Thorn and Casey's house before the heavens opened, with rain pummeling the ground, cheered on by frequent and exuberant thunderclaps.

We sat patiently on the porch, enjoying the invigorating ionized air and the rich darkness of the stormy night. Our forbearance was eventually rewarded, as the rain turned to drizzle and the drizzle finally stopped. Hurriedly, we took flashlights out into the inky darkness and gathered items for our altar: autumn leaves, pine cones, and a few brightly colored rocks. Thorn had a small figurine to symbolize the Goddess and a set of deer antlers to represent the God. Casey brought out his drum, and I set up tiki torches at each of the four directions, with incense, a candle, a bowl of water, and a stone marking the directional correspondences. Our altar, torches, and quarter symbols were set in a ring of stones that Thorn and Casey had set up earlier that day.

Once everything had been set in place, we returned to the house one last time, to change into our magical clothes and remove our shoes, so that we might begin with a procession into the circle, accompanied only by a solemn drumbeat. Just as we left the house for the last time, all the lights in it suddenly went out. Indeed, the streetlights up and down the country road that snaked off through the woods also disappeared. Clearly, the storm's final gift to us that evening was a power outage.

With only the flickering flames of the tiki lamps at our circle to guide us, we made our way slowly through the darkness that covered the bluff like the interior of a womb. When we arrived in our ritual space, Casey continued to drum as he walked sunwise along the perimeter of the circle. Behind him Thorn cleared the space with her besom, and I followed her, with clouds of incense billowing forth from a thurible attached to a chain I held. Thrice around the circle we drummed, cleansed, and censed. Then we called the quarters and invoked the Lord and the Lady. When Thorn said, in a hushed tone, "The circle is cast, we now stand between the worlds," it was less an affirmation than a mere statement of fact. Beyond the pale glow of the torches and the few candles we had lit, a dark universe separated us from all that was normal and mundane in our lives.

For ninety minutes we danced, sang, prayed, meditated, and played within our sacred space. We drummed until we could feel the presence of those whose habitat was not our own. We listened for the loving whispers of the God and Goddess, and we laughed whenever someone did something "wrong." The tone of our ritual was reverent yet joyful, playful yet heartfelt.

Finally, it was time to end. Holding hands, the three of us spoke in unison, thanking the Lord, the Lady, and each of the Watchers in turn. And right when the last syllables of "Merry meet again" left our lips to fade slowly into the darkness, the lights in the house and on the street blazed forth again.

Sewanee, Tennessee

➥ The Blasted Heath

Oberon Zell-Ravenheart

In 1977, Morning Glory and I left "civilization as they know it," and moved onto Coeden Brith—a 200-acre parcel of a huge 5,600-acre ranch called Greenfield Ranch, located off the grid in the mountain wilderness of Mendocino County, NorCalifia. The land had been purchased in 1972 by a bunch of hippies, who had created a wonderful back-to-the land community of about 100 families. At that time, much of it was deeply forested with Douglas fir, oak, madrone, and even some redwoods. However, the loggers had gone through about fifty years before and had clearcut some areas. These areas were a mess—old tree stumps, gouged-up "cat-skinning" roads, and "slash" (trimmed-off branches) everywhere. One wide flat place above our main spring looked like Isengard after Saruman tore up all the trees! (A reference to *Lord of the Rings*, for those who have been living on the far side of the moon . . .) We called it "the Blasted Heath." Over the next few years, we started doing annual New Year's tree plantings all over the land, with seedlings we got free from the Department of Forestry. These were cedar, Coulter pine, and redwoods, which were intended for commercial timber. And we planted thousands of them, starting with the Blasted Heath.

We moved off the land in 1985 and just go back for rituals that are still held there. At Beltaine a couple of years ago, the present caretakers, Jack and Tamar, said they wanted to show us something. They took us on a hike up the hill to where the Blasted Heath had been. Only now it was a deep, lush forest of fifty-foot Coulter pines. Nesting birds sang in the branches, and rabbits scampered off through the undergrowth. There was a stillness and peace that radiated through the place—it felt like the Elven forest of Lothlorien in *The Fellowship of the Ring*. We just stood there in awe with tears streaming down our faces. And all this was a magick we had created simply by planting for the future.

Mendocino County, northern California

ᕙ Youthful Hubris Meets Elementals
Penny Novack

In 1969, not long after my initiation into the Craft, my husband and I were employed for the summer at a camp. The staff cabin we were given was small but pleasant and our children were sort of "fudged in" with the camp's children even though the youngest was a bit too young.

Some time well into the summer program, our staff scheduled a bit of on-site R&R. Once the campers were safely bedded down for the night, the staff would have a gala costume party.

That evening we were all in a good mood. The weather had been warm and clear, so most of the preparations had gone ahead without any trouble. As it held the only stove, all those preparing cooked goodies for our contribution to the evening were in the staff meeting cabin. Rather than being with the regular campers, our children were with us.

In the midst of our babbling enjoyment of food preparation, the screen door slammed. Someone announced that storm clouds were moving in. Wails of dismay erupted. We contemplated carrying our newly cooked treats across the common in a deluge.

Since my hands were full, I turned to my eldest son, "Steve, would you run out and ask the clouds to hold off the rain for a few minutes so I can get the food out of the oven and over to the rec hall?"

"Sure." My son, who had just turned nine a week before, felt very important to be performing this at my request.

I was just getting my food out of the oven and preparing to carry it across the campus common when my son slammed back into the room exactly as a huge crack of lightning and thunder introduced a massive wall of rain. It was ferocious.

"What did you do?" I cried in dismay.

My son's face was massively satisfied as he described how he had gone out there and commanded the winds and clouds to do as he said. He told me he cussed them out and told them who was boss. Blissfully unconscious of how unsuccessful his demands had been, he looked truly proud as he described his masterful diatribe.

All I could say, in the face of the debacle was, "Honey, Storm Elementals are a *lot* bigger than you and when you're asking for a favor of somebody bigger, it is always a good idea to be *very* polite."

We waited for a little break in the deluge and covered our food as best we could to finally join in the party at the recreation hall.

My son was perhaps too young to understand the relationship between a hedgewitch and Elementals. I've noticed a lot of newer magicians are so impressed with the power that Elementals appear to give them that they presume upon the relationship. I highly recommend one remember one's manners when dealing with beings who move vast forces.

Bucks County, Pennsylvania

❧ The Wicker Man, or How I Learned That Magic Works

Susan G. Curewitz Arthen

We wanted to burn a Wicker Man, a giant human-shaped effigy that is traditionally filled with offerings for the Gods. The idea was to ask attendees at the Rites of Spring, a springtime Pagan festival held in western Massachusetts, to bring a piece of trash from the neighborhood where they lived, to be burned with the effigy and released in a magical act of transformation and healing for our Mother Earth.

The debate: Would the Pagan community that formed Rites of Spring be able to do a magical working that called on fire in a transformative, as opposed to a destructive, way? Would burning a humanlike figure be too provocative? We pondered, discussed, argued, and put it to a vote. In what was to become a tradition of pushing the boundaries at Rites of Spring, the vote was to go forward with the idea. Having left his hand in the air too long after the vote, my husband found himself in charge of building and transporting the "Man."

The Wicker Man slowly took shape in our garage. We sacrificed our wicker laundry hamper as the basis for his chest and as a receptacle for the trash offerings. His body was woven from reeds and straw gathered from various small wooded areas, havens of nature in our concrete town. He grew to over seven feet tall, and it started to feel a little creepy having him living in the garage. He somehow looked real, or felt real, and when we wrapped him in blankets and lashed him to the roof of the car for transport, it felt like we were moving a body. As we finished tying the last knot securing him for the trip to Rites, we suddenly realized that between building the effigy, packing, and organizing for ourselves and our two small children, we had not given a lot of thought to what we wanted to bring to burn.

We lived in Lawrence, Massachusetts, an old depressed mill town on the Merrimack River enveloped in a miasma of defeat. The river coursing through the middle of the city was so polluted that, although we often strolled the footpath that edged it, we feared dipping so much as a toe in the water lest some serious bacteria come home with us. Our favorite path traveled through the sparse woods along the Merrimack. It was a good half-mile stretch that ended in a small promontory. The way was heavily littered: cans, bottles, diapers, and trash were strewn among the brush. After we finished packing, we went for a quick walk to the river and gingerly grabbed a few burnable pieces.

Arriving at the Rites site, we suspended the Wicker Man from the farmhouse porch. Throughout the weekend people came and thoughtfully placed their trash inside him. Then it was time for the ritual. The effigy was moved to a triangle-shaped pyre in the ritual field. Four lines of people processed, chanting and weaving themselves into one large circle. The chant ended, and a robed priestess came forward. She charged us to recall how we, as part of the human race and as individuals, had contributed to (literally) trashing the Mother. The Priestess recognized the Wicker Man as the embodiment of the neglect of our responsibility to the planet and led us to invoke the fire as a vehicle for change. We chanted. The fire was lit. Small flames caught at the base of the Wicker Man and soon he was ablaze against the night sky, sparks shooting up toward the stars. As he burned, we called out our wishes for change and healing, and soon he was ash. I had rarely felt so alive, so ecstatic, and so profoundly capable of enabling change with magic.

The weekend came to an end, and with no small amount of sadness, we parted from our Rites of Spring community and drove home. My husband went back to work, I went back to Mom, Tot swim class, and laundry, and we all felt a little low.

The first Saturday after Rites was a warm, sunny day and we

decided to walk the path along the river. When we came to the promontory at the end, our conversation was stilled abruptly. It was clean and clear of trash, with raised flower beds, newly planted shrubs, picnic benches, lighting, and docks. Bewildered, we looked around us, mouths hanging open. We later learned that, over the Memorial Day weekend, the City of Lawrence had designated this place as part of a municipal boating program—a project that must have been in the works long before our ritual. But no amount of fact diminished the wonder we experienced coming across the new park. And the memory of the ritual ecstasy, of the message of the Wicker Man, of the promise to work toward healing the earth around us, carried and the wonder of that transformation is strong within me still. Magic works.

Lawrence, Massachusetts

A Maiden's Passage from Crone to Mother
Angela Huston

Some things in life are simply universal. They reach beyond the bounds of time and place because they speak to the human spirit instead of speaking to only one particular culture or era. A smile is a fine example of this. A graceful, upward curve of the lips transcends language barriers, cultural differences, and even oceans of time. Rainbows are another universal symbol; their arched columns inspire hope. They remind us that no matter where life leads and no matter how bad things seem at the time, it *will* get better. The Witch is also a universal symbol. I formed my own deep images of the Witch as a small child, just as we all do.

I was a very young woman when I came into the Craft. I started reading books as a teen and my avid interest quickly turned into active practice. I joined my first coven when I was twenty-one years old. I can still remember in vivid detail my first meeting with my High Priestess. As I drove home, a rainbow graced the sky. It didn't take long before I settled into coven work and began to focus on getting to know the nature of "Deity." Wiccan practice requires participation equally from all members. Each Witch develops her own personal connection with the Gods. There's no go-between offered. We choose our Gods purposefully; we know full well that the energy we invoke most frequently into our circles and hearts also touches our inner selves, influencing and shaping our future. Research, meditation, and sincere invocation are paramount to Witchly practice. Since I was so young, one might think that I'd have been captivated by the Maiden aspect of the triple Goddess, but when I gazed into the looking glass, it was the Crone who peered back at me.

Coven work focuses on developing raw talent into true skill. Each individual brings his or her own interests, affinities, and abilities to the circle. The diversity adds depth and dimension. Everyone learns and grows as the joy of discovery and development is shared. One member may have an affinity for scrying, another may enjoy the dance, and yet another may be particularly fond of reading omens. The idea of reading omens may seem difficult or even supernatural to some, but the trick of it is really quite simple. Imagine life with a *knowing* inside of you, and this *knowing* tells you that all life is delicately interwoven. Like a fine tapestry, each thread is intricately connected to become the whole. By virtue of this "bond of becoming," all of life not only touches, but also interacts. While operating from this base of experience and viewing everything through the lens of this unique perspective, it's easy to see how the wind might whisper back to those who listen. It's also easy to see how

the appearance of a rainbow might bode well for a new enter-
prise or some new way of life.

As the seasons turned, my beginning years in the Craft
stretched into more than a decade of practice. I started shifting
into the life stage of motherhood and my inner drives and
desires changed. I found myself yearning for a child. Concep-
tion proved elusive and infrequent. Carrying a pregnancy to
fruition proved difficult. With this type of health history, I
decided to approach the situation rather aggressively. My strategy encompassed mundane and magickal approaches. By day, I
found a skilled and reputable doctor. I kept temperature charts
to guide our efforts as we started down the arduous road of
blood tests, clinical procedures, and exams. By night, I turned
my expectant face to the Goddess to ask for Her blessing. All
witches know that deep desire churns the ethers, stirring the
cauldron of possibility. It excites the force behind all form and,
with a lot of skill and little luck, pure potential becomes the
undeniable. My desire for a child enticed the Mother Aspect
of the Goddess, luring Her to me, but the Barren Crone still
held sway in the secret recesses of my soul. When I called to
the Goddess, it was the Crone who answered.

Some of the most profound insights can emanate from a
fresh perspective that's on the outside looking in. Adepts can
learn a lot from novices if they only listen. In a strong coven,
each member offers his and her own particular experience, per-
ception, and prowess. An apprentice of mine looked at me very
intently one day and said, "You're trying to have a baby. Perhaps you should start beseeching a fertile Mother Goddess
instead of a Crone." I had several years of experience beyond
his, but his words pierced the veil with clarity and brilliant truth.
His fresh perspective changed the course of my moonlit strategy
and, in time, it eventually changed the course of my life.

Night after night I'd step out onto my porch and sit beside a
cast iron cauldron to bask in the pale moonlight. The cauldron

was filled with half-barren soil that was long depleted of nutrients, and so it lay fallow. I'd sit quietly for a while and meditate, and after I felt centered I'd let loose the rivers of my desire. When I felt the presence of the Mother Goddess, I'd whisper an invocation to Her.

> Beguiling Lady of the moon, and of old night's eternal
>   bliss
> Bestow upon my waiting brow your lasting, loving,
>   tender kiss.
> Bless me as I come before you, make my body your
>   fertile ground,
> Fill me with your ancient power! Make me strong, my
>   judgment sound.

The night air can be very inviting and I found myself on the porch a lot. I wasn't the only one either. As spring faded and the fireflies of summer started lighting up the nights, I noticed a grayish, odd-looking toad keeping company with me. It had burrowed beneath my cauldron and it emerged to join me almost every time I went out onto the porch. It was surprisingly bold. It didn't seem to fear me and it liked being touched. I was so interested in the toad that, for a time, I failed to notice something else that was strangely peculiar. A plump, succulent-looking vine was reaching up out of the cauldron and I hadn't planted anything there! It didn't take long for the vine to mature and bear fruit, and I eventually recognized it as a pumpkin. Shortly thereafter I discovered that I was pregnant. Only then did the full weight of the omens hit me.

The warm nights of summer eventually gave way to autumn, and each new turn takes its start from the influences that are passing away. The lessons of my maidenhood were successfully met, and these hard-won personal victories inevitably empowered me. I transitioned into the life stage of motherhood. I wasn't able to carry that pregnancy to term, but I've come to know the Mother Goddess intimately. The mother within me has not only taken root, She has blossomed deep within my soul.

Not long after my loss I found a sense of peace and self-acceptance with my physical infertility—in essence, an inner rainbow's end. I am no longer afraid of whether or not I'll have a child. I *know* that I'll find rewarding outlets. There are so many children in our world who need a stable, loving home. Perhaps someday I can be a rainbow of hope for a child who desperately needs a loving mother. Now that I'm filled to overflowing with the Mother Goddess, I'm utterly compelled to parent. An acquaintance of mine, Dana Morgan, once wrote "REAL witchcraft is the art of making exquisite lemonade with whatEVER the universe sends your way." I concur wholeheartedly!

> In the Appalachian Mountains
> of western North Carolina

๛ Because I Am a Shaman
   G-

It wasn't necessary for him to be at the planning meeting, but he came anyway. We did ask him to be there . . . sort of. We wanted him for festival security. We needed his muscle, not his mouth. He was a pain in the ass. He believed it was his mission in life to teach others what their reality should be. He *loved* to push buttons and leave his victims quaking in a corner.

That evening, we were meeting at a local restaurant to discuss an upcoming festival. There must have been a dozen people there representing different traditions including Reclaiming, Faery, Pagan, Eclectic . . . and there he was, the Shaman. During the course of the evening's planning, the Shaman kept interjecting his point of view, which would have been perfectly reasonable if he hadn't prefaced each statement with, "Well, speaking as a Shaman. . . . You know, as a Shaman. . . . Being a Shaman. . . . Shaman . . . Shaman . . . ShamanShamanShaman Shaman."

We were sort of taking his claim of actually *being* a Shaman at face value. In a community where "Solitary Eclectic" is considered a tradition and coven secrets abound, actually asking someone to prove his religious practices are valid seemed to be bad form. The truth is, this guy came across as all talk and no walk. We never saw any outward signs of any training or faith. He had never tried to put forth any sort of credentials. He would occasionally mention that he had been to some ceremony far away, with people that we didn't know, doing stuff that he couldn't talk about. But there was very little to call him on, as there was no one else in the group qualified to dispute his claim.

Part of the reason that we were there was to get different points of view so that we could make this festival as accommodating to everyone as possible. But this was a bit much. Okay, it was way too much. We caught on early that he was a . . . Shaman (yeah, that's the word I want to use), so there was no need for him to keep pointing this out. Truthfully, I believe he was trying to remind us just how spiritually superior and important he was . . . you know, being a Shaman.

This little insinuation that he was better than we were was starting to grate on several of the participants, myself included. If he wanted to organize a festival for Shamans, then he could bloody well give it a shot, and I for one would support him. But as is the case with most open, public, Pagan festivals, this one took on a decidedly Wiccan flavor. He objected and blocked the discussion repeatedly with comments about how, speaking as a Shaman, he would do this part of the meditation differently or would change that part of the invocation to something else.

At one point during the evening, when we had had just about enough of him, thank you very much, a half-dozen of us got up and went to the ladies room (a fairly innocuous gesture, considering that women go to the loo in packs anyway), to blow off the steam that had been boiling most of the evening. We left the other half of the group, which included another half-dozen women and at least two guys, including Shaman-man, bantering about the best time to schedule the potluck feast.

I am not sure who started it, but someone balled up her right hand into a fist and started smacking it into her left palm—a nice, quiet way to release frustration. It beat screaming all to hell—that would have attracted attention. So we all started doing it, packing one hand into the other while muttering the mantra "I'm a *Shaman*! I'm a *Shaman*! I'm a *Shaman*!"

Now, if you have ever been in a restaurant bathroom, you know that the acoustics are fabulous. You just want to go in there and sing your heart out, because the sound of your voice bouncing off the walls makes you dizzy. We found out that energy bounces the same way. The more we chanted and packed our hands, the more the room reverberated. It was great for everyone—except the poor lady who just wanted to come in and use the potty. I think we scared her. After getting it out of our systems and finding some sort of peace in the symbolic act of cramming the word "Shaman" back down his throat, we returned to the table, ready to face the subject of our ire once more. The meeting came to a successful close and we went home and thought no more about it.

Several weeks later, I was out with a bunch of friends, including our Shaman buddy, when he excused himself suddenly. Once he had left the room, his girlfriend confided that she hoped this meant he was getting some relief from the wicked constipation he had been suffering for the past few weeks!

Pioneer Valley, Massachusetts

৵ Love Lost

As told by Kate

She arrived at my door one cold, wet night looking like William Shakespeare's Ophelia. Rain dripped from her unkempt, bleached blond hair. The exposed dark roots of her bleached blond hair mirrored the black rings beneath her eyes, which showed stark against her pale, white face. Her clothes, blue jeans and a nondescript t-shirt, were covered by a well-worn denim jacket. It hung heavy with moisture, making it look a size too big. She held onto the door frame, bracing her slight body with her hands as if the earth would claim her if she let go. The eyes that met mine contained sadness, fear, and a touch of madness.

"I'm Heather's friend," she said. Heather was a member of my coven. She told me that she had a friend in trouble and asked if I would meet with her. "My name's Amy." Her voice was barely audible over the storm. Please forgive my appearance," she added with a tired laugh, "I haven't been sleeping very well."

Unsure of what I was getting myself into, I invited Amy into the kitchen and got a dry towel. As a Priestess and active member of the Pagan community, I have always tried to make myself available to those in need. So this left me standing in my kitchen, toweling off a strange young woman like she was one of my children.

With a warm cup of herbal tea in hand, I led her through my house to my office, my personal sanctuary, and made her comfortable on the couch.

Amy took a deep breath and began her story, her words dribbling off her lips in splashes of emotion.

"I met Ryan eight years ago in our senior year of high school," she said, almost in a whisper, "and I immediately fell for him. In my mind, I can still see him standing in the hallway.

He was talking with a couple of other guys from school. You couldn't help but notice him. He was tall, handsome, and funny. His light brown hair had this way of falling over his eyes. They were green, a shade that could catch your gaze and pull you in until you couldn't see anything else."

With the memory, Amy let out a dreamy sigh. She wrapped her hands around her warm mug of tea and pulled her legs up under her body. She looked so young. I could easily see her as a teenager in the throes of a crush.

"Ryan was everything I had ever dreamed of in a guy . . . everything I had ever wanted. Every girl in school wanted him as her boyfriend. They would flock around him like seagulls, all screeching for a bit of attention. With all that noise, it was hard to get close to him. I tried everything to get him to notice me. I flirted with him. I laughed at his jokes. I even worked my course schedule so that we would be in a few of the same classes. No matter what I did, he just walked by me as if I didn't exist. The more he ignored me, the more I wanted him. I couldn't focus on anything but Ryan. I couldn't eat. I couldn't sleep. All I could think about was Ryan . . . wanting him . . . wanting him to want me. It was eating me up. I was desperate."

She took a sip of tea and closed her eyes for a moment. I couldn't tell if she was trying to remember or to forget. After a moment of silence, she continued.

"One day, a friend of mine suggested I talk to this Witch she knew, a Strega. She told me that the Witch might be able to work a spell that would get Ryan to see me and make him want to be with me."

A chill went through me. I don't believe in working love magic or, for that matter, any magic that manipulates another person's will. But not everyone in the Pagan world holds this opinion. Some believe that, as magic workers, we should use our talents to create change in whatever ways are requested or needed. I suddenly became worried where her story might lead.

"I take it you went to see this person?" I asked, while dreading the answer.

"Yes," she replied. "I couldn't wait. I called her the same day my friend gave me the number and arranged to meet with her that night. I figured, what the heck, I'd tried everything else. I'd never actually met a Witch before, and the idea scared me, but I was obsessed with Ryan and it was killing me. So I went to meet the Witch."

Amy stretched, took another sip of her tea. Her hair was drying in the warmth of the room. Using her fingers as a comb, she took a moment to try to brush a few untamed strands into place. The action also seemed to reflect an attempt at smoothing her tangled emotions. Finally, she continued.

"The Witch handed me a charm and then asked me a bunch of questions about Ryan. They were strange questions like: What is the tone of his voice? The texture of his skin? What are my feelings whenever I see him? I told her everything, from the way he walked, to the ringing in my ears every time I saw him. I remember she cautioned me. 'Be careful what you wish for,' she said. But I was in love. My need for him burned inside me like a sun. It blinded me to everything except my desire.

"After I had poured out all my longing, she took the charm and wrapped it up in a piece of cloth. She handed it back to me and gave me specific instructions of what I needed to do to cast the spell. She said that if I followed them exactly as written, Ryan would fall madly in love with me. He would be mine forever. I left feeling happier than I had in months."

"It took me a while to get together what I needed for the ritual. Then I waited until the full moon. I crept out of my house after my parents were in bed and went to the woods. I did the ritual exactly as I was told. When it was finished, I was disappointed. I had thought that something would happen . . . the wind would blow, an owl would hoot, something . . . but nothing. I thought that it hadn't worked and I went home upset and disappointed."

A shiver passed through Amy's body.

"I was wrong."

Her hands clutched at her mug, as if pulling warmth from the remaining liquid. She gazed into the bottom of the cup for a moment in contemplation before she went on with her tale.

"The next day, I saw Ryan looking at me. I was thrilled. Wow! He was actually looking at me! A few days later, he said hello to me. I thought I'd faint with joy. Two weeks later, he asked me out on a date. I never thought I could feel so happy! We soon began seeing each other regularly. It was a dream come true. He told me that it was fate, but I knew differently. I knew that fate had been tweaked a bit, but I didn't care.

"We dated all through our senior year. As soon as we graduated, we moved into an apartment together. My parents were furious. They didn't like Ryan. They said he had no direction in life. True, he didn't know what he wanted to do after high school, but I figured how many kids do? Plus, we were happy and in love. We married a year later.

"It was then the troubles began. He couldn't seem to keep a job . . . any job. I was working as a waitress and I wanted to go to night school to become a nurse but all my money kept going to pay the rent and food. His paychecks, when he was employed, just kept disappearing."

Amy put her empty cup down. I watched with concern as she brought her legs up to her chest, wrapping her arms around her knees and pulling herself into a fetal position.

"It wasn't until I came home and found him snorting cocaine in the living room that I finally figured out what was going on. God, I felt so dumb. He, of course, denied that he had a problem. He told me that he was bored and just experimenting. He said he wouldn't do it again. I was stupid enough to believe him. But he didn't stop. It only got worse. Next came the lying, then disappearing for days. He always came back begging for forgiveness, promising to change.

"Finally, I couldn't take it anymore. I asked him to leave, but he refused to go. At one point I even threw his belongings out on the street. He just banged on the door for hours crying. He followed me everywhere I went. He called me at work so often I lost my job. He said he needed me, he couldn't live without me. He said we were one person sharing a soul. It was then that I realized what I had done when I cast the love spell. I had bound him to me and now I couldn't get rid of him!

"Be careful what you ask for," Amy said with a crazed laugh. "Boy, she got that one right.

"Over the years I tried everything from restraining orders to pleading. Nothing worked. I tried to find the Strega to undo the spell but she had moved. I went to the site where I had performed the ritual, to dig up the charm bundle and destroy it. But years had passed and I couldn't remember the exact location.

"In the meantime, Ryan was getting worse. He had become addicted to heroin. With every year, the drugs took a greater toll on his body. His looks were gone. He had dropped weight, making him look like a walking skeleton. His beautiful eyes were dull. He stole from me and from others to support his habit. I kept trying to make him leave so I could create a life without him but he wouldn't, he couldn't. The bond between us was too strong. It kept pulling us back together in this crazy dance. He was right; I had somehow cemented our souls together, never to be apart."

Amy began to rock back and forth, softly crying like a young child who was trying to console herself. The mother in me wanted to go and comfort her but I knew that she had to finish her story.

"Last month they found him at a friend's house," she said between sobs. "He would go there when he was on a good bender. He had overdosed. It took his friend, another junkie, a full day before he realized Ryan was dead. He died alone, without me." She sat crying, her body trembling with anguish.

I let out a sigh of relief. This was a simple case of loss and grief!

"I know a few good books on death and grieving," I began, using my best consoling Priestess voice. "We could write a lovely memorial service—"

"You don't understand!" she screamed. Her body shook as she cried out on the edge of madness. "It isn't over. He isn't gone! Every night, as soon as I close my eyes, he is there. I hear his voice crying, echoing around me. He comes to me, begging, pleading for me to join him . . . to come be with him forever on the other side!"

Hartford, Connecticut

ꙮ Birthing Magic
Victoria Slind-Flor

The breeze shivered the branches, and the cherry tree released a blizzard of pink petals onto the four of us. We were standing in a circle, holding hands, on a mild late April afternoon in the University of Washington Arboretum.

The tree was so heavy with blossoms that the branches seemed to bow under their weight. And my niece was so heavy with child that I could see her rocking back and forth and looking around longingly for a stone or a bench on which to rest.

But we couldn't let her leave the circle yet because the deep magic we were doing was for her benefit.

We represented three generations of my family: my elderly favorite aunt, my sister, her pregnant daughter, and myself. My niece, Nicole, was three weeks away from giving birth to the first of our next generation.

I'm the eldest of my own generation, and am the oldest

daughter of the oldest daughter of the oldest daughter, as far back as anyone can remember. But life events had skewered what had been the natural order of things. My own mother died at an early age, so she could not be here. And my first-born turned out, to everyone's surprise, to be a son.

Still, a deep and powerful connection had grown among the four of us, even though we weren't in the usual straight line from generation to generation. My aunt had stepped up to take my mother's place as matriarch. And my younger sister's daughter was the first to come forward and ensure the continuance of our line by bearing the first grandchild.

We worried about this pregnant young woman. She would be the first of us ever to give birth away from home and family. We all knew that in the best of all possible worlds, we'd be the three attendants at the birthing, encouraging and supporting Nicole through her work of bringing the new baby to us all. But, at the end of this ritual, she would be leaving for Oregon, her mother and I for California, and we'd drop my aunt off at her home in Seattle. Like many other American families, we had scattered, and many of us lived far from those sisters, cousins, and aunts who are the sustainers of the web of life. (In fact, the only reason we all happened to be in Seattle that day was for a rare family gathering to celebrate my father's eightieth birthday.)

We had further concerns for Nicole. She had inherited a dreaded bleeding problem that had killed so many women in our family, and we knew that childbirth was often the riskiest time in the life of a woman with this genetic disorder.

So we gathered to make magic. We held hands and hummed. Then each one of us, in turn, faced a direction and summoned the spirits, powers, and guardians associated with that quarter. I placed my hands on my niece's head and called in the grandmothers, great grandmothers, and all the women in our family from times beyond time, asking them to bless and protect this daughter of all of ours and the child she carried.

Then I took a spool of red Japanese silk thread from my pocket. I wrapped it thirteen times around Nicole's wrist, then thirteen times around my sister's. Without cutting the thread, I circled my aunt's wrist thirteen times, and then, somewhat awkwardly, made the same number of circuits around my own left wrist.

I went back to Nicole, and wrapped her wrist another additional thirteen times. And all of us started to talk about how this thread represented not only our shared bloodline, but the strong cord of love and affection that tied us to each other.

Each of us talked about babies, mothers, grandmothers, birthing, bleeding, loving, and connecting. And each of us promised we would keep this red thread on our wrists until Nicole had safely delivered the baby as a sign that we would be with her as she labored. I made a cut between the wrists, and we each tied our section of the string that had circled our wrists thirteen times into a corded bracelet. Thirteen times around each wrist for the thirteen moons in the year, with moons a symbol of the moon-blood that had flowed from each of us women.

I handed Nicole the birthing charm I had made. It was a small folkart appliqué of a primitive Viking ship taken from petroglyphs I'd seen in Norway. In the ship, I placed a simple image of the Norse mother goddess Nerthus, who looked very much like the primitive figure I'd seen in the original petroglyphs. I set two primitive figure matrons in front of the Nerthus figure. They attended a figure of a laboring woman, who was seated on a chair shape. They were accompanying her on those last perilous hours of the woman's journey to motherhood. Nerthus was holding aloft a serpent representing rebirth and healing.

The figures were all made from a deep blood-colored fabric dyed and sent to me by a Witch friend in Latvia. I had dyed the background fabric in the blue of a summer sky over a Norwegian fjord. This charm was for Nicole to hang on the wall of the labor room, to help her remember she was never alone.

Finally, we sang "We All Come from the Goddess" and blew kisses to the ancestors and the spirits of each direction. We passed a kiss around the circle, then opened the circle, secure in our knowledge that we had blessed Nicole with all the mother power we had within us.

I kept my thread bracelet on my wrist, even though it got wet in the shower and grungy from the ink that always rubs off in the newspaper office where I work. And, honestly, I felt silly, because I had a couple of power-suit interviews to do, and my raggedy red wrist cord was not an elegant accessory.

One night in mid-May, I could not fall asleep. At first, I thought it was the general insomnia that hits women at menopause, but I wasn't too hot and I didn't have any of the other usual symptoms.

My main complaint was that no matter which position I took, I couldn't get comfortable. I thrashed around in my bed all night, pulling up and tossing off my covers, grabbing and rejecting my pillows, alternately sprawling out, and contracting into a fetal position.

Finally, the dawn washed through my window, and, when the light level was high enough, I noticed something surprising. The red silk thread was gone from my wrist, even though I hadn't remembered pulling it off.

About five minutes later, the phone rang. My niece's husband, who was calling from the birthing suite at a Portland hospital, told me the news I'd been waiting to hear, "Aunt Victoria, it's a girl, and Nicole is just fine."

I've been watching that baby girl for six years now. Poppy's her name, which goes well with her ginger hair and her love of dancing with all the flowers in the garden. She's long and lean and inexhaustively curious about everything.

And her favorite song? She's introduced her class to the song "Who Were the Witches? Where Did They Come From?" by Bonnie Lockhart:

> Who were the witches?
> Where did they come from?
> Maybe your great, great grandmother was one.
> Witches were wise, wise women they say,
> And there's a little witch in every woman today!
> There's a little witch in every woman today.*

I know she's one of us. Our line continues, the future is secure. A very real cord connects us with those mothers from our past, and off into the future, to generations far beyond even Poppy's imaginings.

Oakland, California

ঔ The Talisman
Judy Harrow

Landlords in New York hate long-term residents. Rent stabilization laws keep rent increases within sane limits for people who stay put. Whenever an apartment is vacated, the owner jumps the rent up to slightly above market rate. These days, it's not unusual for folks to spend more than half their pay on rent.

We'd been living in the same apartment for some twenty-five years, so our rent was comfortably within our means. We also

---

*"Who Were the Witches? Where Did They Come From?" by Bonnie Lockhart, as recorded on the CD *Dreams, Drums & Green Thumbs*. For more information, go to www.bonnielockhart.com

worked with the tenants' organization. So, naturally, our land-lord hated us.

We received several spurious eviction threats and harassing lawsuits that forced us to spend a small fortune on lawyer's fees. One night, the landlord's pit-bull of a son came shouting at the door. We heard stories from other buildings about even more serious violence and vandalism directed against "hold-outs." In truth, it got pretty frightening.

But this apartment was also a covenstead, a place where Witches regularly gathered to study, work magic, and worship the Ancient Gods. And a coven can offer much more than empathy to a Priestess whose home is threatened.

Alice made a charm for us. It looked like a decorative object—a bunch of pretty seashells in an ornamental jar, with some glittery purple ribbon tied around it. The other ingredi-ents in the container—minerals, oils, and herbs symbolic of safety, stability, and a secure home—were not quite so apparent. Within our long-term worship space (our living room), and in a sacred circle, our coven blessed and empowered the talisman. Very soon after that, coincidentally of course, the harassment ceased.

A few more years went by. The building deteriorated from lack of proper maintenance. We needed more space for our books. The tree outside my study window snapped off near the roots when a careless truck driver backed into it, and that seemed to snap my emotional link to the place. After twenty-eight years in that apartment, and nearly forty in the neigh-borhood, it was time to move on.

We found and bought a house. Our closing date was April Fool's Day, probably a mistake. Delay after delay kept us from moving into our new home. First, the seller's new house was not ready. Then, once we finally had access, the contractor we'd hired for remodeling stalled and fell far behind schedule. Frus-trating months dragged by with us still in our old apartment.

Finally, somebody in the coven remembered the jar of sacred seashells. Duh! We circled in the old covenstead to ritually sever the invisible tendrils connecting the talisman and us into the fabric of the building. In the next circle, in the empty new house, we reinstalled our anchor, attaching the group and my family to our new home. It was very much like repotting a plant. Not long after that, just two weeks short of the next April Fool's Day, we finally moved in.

Is there a lesson to be learned here? I think so, one about magical housekeeping. Obsolete magic, ignored or neglected, can keep you enmeshed with obsolete needs or desires. Remember to turn off your spells when you want them to stop working. And remember to update your magic to serve your current goals.

Metropolitan New York

4

WATER

The Seasons and the Cycles of Life

 inter, Spring, Summer, Autumn—birth, growth, fading, death—the Wheel turns, on and on. . . . We fall in love; we suffer loss; we consummate relationships; we give birth; we grow old; we decay . . . we are renewed, we are reborn. . . . As the season changes, we arouse the power from within, the power to heal, the power to change our society, the power to renew the earth.

—Starhawk, *The Spiral Dance*

THE CYCLES OF LIFE

﹋ Vision of the Goddess
Kathi Somers

When I was growing up, in my very religious, Southern Baptist family, I desperately wanted to have a vision, see an angel, or have some other kind of truly mystical experience. I memorized Bible verses, I prayed, I meditated . . . but I never saw anything.

Whenever I thought "godly" thoughts, I generally had good feelings and positive sensations, but I never felt a sense of empowerment—only powerlessness and smallness and, often, fear. That was my reaction to the God I grew up with. And, of course, I always thought I needed to transcend the physical in order to be spiritual. As a physical creature, I had no idea how I was supposed to accomplish that.

In April 1992, my pregnant daughter asked me to be with her during her labor and delivery. I was honored and pleased that she wanted me there, but there was no way I could have known what was in store for me.

That whole night, between contractions, I watched my daughter handling this momentous event in such a lovely, human, normal way. But often, during the contractions, I saw something else: I saw Woman—even more than that—I saw Goddess. The face of this laboring woman relected the faces of all women in all labors from the beginning of time. I'm sure my relationship with my daughter heightened this vision, but I felt such female kinship with her—and at the same time a genuine spiritual awe, a reverence, and worship. It was the first time in my life I ever sensed the Divine in such a profound, gut-level way—and It was totally Feminine and totally Powerful!

There was such a contrast between the earthy, physical event occurring, with its blood and pain and the holy, shining, all-encompassing transcendence I saw in Her face. When she was pushing so hard, completely consumed by giving birth to her child, I couldn't take my eyes off her face. I saw my daughter, but so completely suffused with intensity and light that I would-n't have recognized her on the street. At that place and at that time, I worshipped Her. She had become Woman in the most physical, most holy, most female sense possible. She was all women, all femaleness—so terribly awesome.

For the first time in my life, I knew that God is our Mother. She labored to bring us forth and gave every ounce of Her effort to bring us into Being. When we finally arrived, She looked at our misshapen heads, our mashed faces, our bloody mass of hair and as Her face softened into radiance She pro-claimed, "Beautiful!"

Rancho Santa Margarita, California

ཉ Unto Us a Child Is Born
Oberon Zell-Ravenheart

I'd like to share some of my own feelings on the subject of birth. Yeah, I know, I'm a guy. Surely giving birth is a woman's prerogative and doesn't have much of anything to do with men, right? At least that was the attitude back in 1963, when my son, Bryan, was born.

Excerpted from "Personal from Otter G'Zell—Unto Us a Child Is Born," *Green Egg*, 24, No. 95, 1991.

I had spent most of the summer building a Skinner Aircrib—the famous "baby box" proposed in *Walden Two*. This was a complete infant environment at waist level, like a mini-habitat designed specifically for human babies, addressing all their needs for climate control, temperature, humidity, hygiene, and protection from germs. When Martha started going into labor one evening, I dropped my tools and bundled her off to the hospital. I stayed right with her for the next thirty-six hours of agonizing labor, holding her hand, mopping her brow, and doing whatever I could to reassure and comfort her with my love.

And then came the fateful moment. Her contractions reached that critical frequency and the doctor and nurses came to take her into the delivery room. I tried to accompany her, but they wouldn't let me. This was something I had not anticipated nor been warned about, and must seem incomprehensible to my current readers. Despite my strongest protests, I was torn from her side as she was wheeled away, screaming, on the gurney. She gave birth to our only child in a sterile white room, under blazing lights, and I wasn't there for her. I fumed in impotent fury in the waiting room. I remember one other man in there with me. When the nurse came to tell him his child was born dead, he fainted. Given that example as a possibility, I raged at the nurses, but to no avail. It was hospital policy to not allow the husbands into the delivery room, and my protests had no effect.

Although in subsequent marriages I have become stepfather to two other great kids, Rainbow and Zack, Bryan was the only child of my loins, as it were. With my vasectomy, I joined an ever-growing Pagan sterility cult and so the miracle of childbirth, from which I had been excluded, seemed forever lost to me.

Twenty-eight years later, still feeling a hole in my heart over that loss, I met a very pregnant woman named Bethany. She was glowing—golden-red hair, freckles, and all. She had been brought to our Lughnasadh festival by two midwives in our circle, Macha and Willowoak, and she was glad to hang out in the zero-gravity of our wonderful swimming hole at the Old Same Place on the Rushing River. We played the traditional Games of Lugh, circled up, danced, did magic, feasted, sang songs, and caroused far into the evening, most folks sleeping that night on the lawn.

The next morning, Bethany went into labor. Everybody else went into action, boiling water, bringing her pillows and blankets, walking her around, massaging her back, singing songs, weaving magic. She was the center of the cyclone. Kids and kitties danced around her, unicorns nuzzled her, Archimedes, our owl, watched over her sternly, and an osprey soared above. We were all there for her every step of the way, as her water broke and the baby lowered. Finally, a little head crowned and he emerged through the crimson Portals of Life to be placed on the sun-warmed naked breast of his beaming Mother. There wasn't a dry eye in the yard. It all happened right here on the green grass of "the world between the houses" and I was there!

I've never felt such an intensely overwhelming sense of magic—of miracle, even. I felt a great healing within my soul; the lifting of a veil.

What is this evil thing that Western medicine has done, removing the father from his partner and baby at the moment of birth? How much of the alienation between men and women in Western society comes from this? I think on some deep level Martha never forgave me for not being there with her in that moment. Certainly, she suffered major postpartum depression, and our relationship was somehow never the same.

Having finally experienced the miraculous sharing of childbirth brings into sharp focus the obverse: the not-sharing, and all the ills conveyed thereby. I think that the recovery of this kind of sharing is an important part of our mission as Pagans, re-creating our once and future partnership society.

Mendocino County, northern California

❧ Growing Pains
Laura Wildman-Hanlon

Birth, graduation, marriage, initiation into a religious institution, and death are traditionally the rites of passage that our culture publicly acknowledges with a formal ritual. These rites help to transition both the individual who is experiencing the transformation and those whose lives are affected by the change.

There are, however, thousands of other points in life that are equally pivotal and emotionally challenging. Yet, these important moments are often ritually ignored. For many, this void is grudgingly accepted as a normal part of our society. But for others, a lack of acknowledgment or community support during a crucial life passage would leave a spiritual wound.

As our Pagan and ritual community has developed, so has our ability to identify and create rituals for these moments. This story is about one such ritual. It was created for a mother and her child, to help both of them through a rite of passage that many in our culture consider a normal part of growing up.

Since the first cells divided in her womb, they had not been separated. She could remember stroking her belly with wonderment and joy at the changes happening within it. To her, the morning sickness was an act of purging her past life. The marks that formed with the expanding of her flesh were scars of pride. When she first felt her baby's spirit fluttering inside her, she sang with joy. When the child moved, giving her a sharp and unexpected kick to her ribcage, she laughed.

When she gave birth to her daughter, the midwife was the only spectator. She held the mother's hand and helped guide the child out through the living tunnel to take her first breath. The man with whom she had once shared a moment of passion had long since left. She did not regret the meeting. He was a tender god who would not have survived the radiance of his daughter's face. The memory of the creation night, his mouth upon hers, his powerful muscles melding with her softness, would bring a nostalgic smile to the mother's lips, but she did not long to seek him out. All she needed, all she wanted, she found within the tiny life that nuzzled at her breasts.

Time passed, as it always does. The baby grew. The mother watched with pride as her child pulled herself up to stand on two feet, supported by her mother's fingers. As her legs became stronger, the daughter no longer needed her mother's hand to hold her steady. The mother felt a pang, a tug of loss at her heart, but smiled at her daughter's accomplishment.

The days continued to move on. The snow fell and covered the ground, to melt in a burst of renewal with the spring sun. The mother taught her child the patterns of the earth around her, the calls of the birds, the footsteps of the beasts. She instructed her in the ways of planting and of the wonder found in the harvest. Each morning brought new joy and discovery for them both.

Then the day came when the daughter turned to her mother and said, "Mama, when will I go to school?"

The mother felt a wave of coldness pass over her. The thought of watching her daughter step into the yellow bus filled her eyes with tears. The bus would take her daughter away. She would no longer be a part of her child's every waking moment. At school, her daughter would meet and play with new friends. A stranger would teach and guide her. She would not be there to see the look of accomplishment flash across her daughter's face when she answered a question successfully, nor witness the look of disappointment when her response proved to be wrong. That first step onto the school bus would begin the process of growing up, becoming a separate being no longer dependent on her mother.

For this mother and child, the traditional ritual of buying school clothes and supplies would not satisfactorily mark their rite of passage. In the late summer, as her garden grew heavy with fruit, the mother gathered her friends and their children to her home. She watched as the parents mingled in the yard beneath the shade of the trees, drinking lemonade. Their children, of varying ages, wrestled and played in the grass.

She asked her daughter to stay by her side. She watched her child look longingly at the others playing. She could sense how much her daughter wanted to join in their games. Still, she listened to her mother and stood holding her hand.

The mother took a deep breath to steady herself for the rite ahead and nodded to her friends. Leaving their children to their play, the parents formed a circle of love and friendship around the mother and child. Then a long yellow ribbon was produced. One end was tied around the daughter's wrist. The mother tightly grasped the other end. The laughter of the children running through the field in the back of the house filled the air. The daughter, shaking like a young racehorse waiting for the starting bell, absently fidgeted with her ribbon while straining to see the other children running in the backyard.

The parents made an opening in the circle. The mother looked down lovingly at her child and spoke the word her daughter had been waiting to hear, "Go!" Mother and daughter were off. Side by side, the yellow ribbon rustling between them, they ran after the children. The children took the cue and the chase began. Round and round the two ran chasing the others. Through the fields, around the trees, under the swing set the couple flew.

The mother began to tire. She clutched the end of the ribbon.

"I can't let go! I won't let go!" her heart cried.

Still they ran, the children always before them, edging them to go faster, further. The daughter laughed with glee at the game. She failed to see her mother begin to fall behind, the ribbon start to lengthen.

The mother's lungs began to burn. She no longer had the endless energy of youth. She felt the ribbon begin to slide between her fingers.

"No!" she silently cried as she realized that she could no longer keep up with her child. "No, don't leave me!"

Then her daughter turned to look back at her. The child's face shone with excitement and joy. The mother smiled back at her daughter and, with love, released the cord that joined them. It fluttered in the breeze as the child skipped off to join the other children. They welcomed her with cheers.

The mother stood alone watching, her hands empty, holding only a sense of loss. The children scampered off to play another game. Suddenly, from out of the fray, her daughter came running back across the yard. She jumped into her mother's arms, hugging her tightly and kissing her cheeks.

"Later, can we play together again, Mommy?" she asked.

The mother nodded her head yes, "I would like that."

The daughter screeched, "Yeah!" then squirmed out of her mother's arms, dropping back down to the ground. She ran to rejoin the other children, wrapping the ribbon around her wrist. Later, when she went to school, a snip of the ribbon would go with her.

"So this must be how Demeter* feels each fall," the mother thought, as she wiped away tears of loss and cried anew for the joy of self-discovery that she knew awaited her daughter.

Western Massachusetts

*The story of Demeter and her daughter Persephone is a part of the Eleusinian mysteries. Persephone is stolen by Hades, Lord of the Underworld, and brought to his realm. When her mother, Demeter, Goddess of agriculture and growth, finds out what happened to her, she goes into mourning and stops producing the crops. Demeter manages to regain her daughter but, because while in that world Persephone ate six seeds from a pomegranate, she is required to return to Hades for six months out of every year. From this we get the seasons and cycles of life. In spring, the world explodes with Demeter's joy as her daughter returns to her. In summer she is content and all is green. In fall, her daughter leaves and the world cries. And in winter, Demeter mourns again.

❧ Marriage in the Cathedral
Judy Harrow

One of those moments when Witches often feel the need to compromise is when we marry. Most of us want to marry by the ceremonies of our own religion. Most of us want our close relatives, and perhaps some of our workmates, to be with us at this moment of great joy. So, how far out are we going to come? Do they know? Would they approve? A hurtful family fight would spoil the day for sure, and, in all honesty, the last thing we want to do is hurt, frighten, or offend our non-Pagan loved ones.

So we sometimes marry in their churches, and often see what we can sneak in. If we interpret Mary as a form of the Great Mother, we can use "Ave Maria" as a Goddess hymn. Meanwhile, the minister will think it's a gesture to the bridegroom's Catholic parents. Or we might hold our weddings in "secular" spaces, outdoors, or in some rented party room and make the ritual look secular as well. We can't call the Lady and Lord by name, but if we refer to Earth and Sky, they'll think we're environmentalists or maybe throwback hippies. In most of the handfastings I've done, the game seems to be making our religious commitments recognizable to our own and transparent to the others present. Nobody's completely happy, but everybody's sort of content. And besides, it's the marriage that matters, not the wedding, right?

In that spirit, Spellweaver and Shadow arranged their church wedding. They expected disapproval, and perhaps downright discrimination, as they explained to the Christian clergyman that they were also involved in a spiritual practice that centered on the female aspect of Deity and that they wanted a female

First published in the *Covenant of the Goddess Newsletter* (Midsummer 1993).

cocelebrant (me) to call on and represent the Divine Feminine in the marriage rite.

In an attempt to "pass," they wrote a script for the ceremony that was dignified and poetic, but also pretty bland and generic. We wondered together about how much this minister was going to let us get away with. And then the four of us—the bride, the groom, the minister, and me—met in the church office to read through the script together.

We had a live one! He seemed to have radar for every vague phrase in the script. He also surprised and humbled us with his open-minded and welcoming attitude. In our expectation of prejudice, we were the prejudiced ones. Again and again, he asked, "What exactly do you mean by this?" And, still carefully avoiding the words "Wicca" or "Witchcraft," which I feared would offend him, I found myself explaining, "Well, you see, this is one of the places where our two traditions conceptualize things somewhat differently. As I understand it, your model is like this (for example, monotheistic), and ours, in contrast, is like that (polytheistic)." Every single time, he encouraged us to be clear and specific. The second draft was much more explicit.

Two days before the wedding, we gathered in the church to rehearse. Not everybody in the wedding party was watching their language, and all of us were beginning to relax. What's more, somebody's loud organ practice forced us to yell our lines. The rehearsal got silly, rowdy, and Pagan. The minister seemed unperturbed.

The morning of the wedding, I sat down with my copy of the script and changed many of my speeches to the actual language of our Book of Shadows. Now, I'm notorious for not usually going "by the Book." I much more often speak spontaneously, guided by the inspirations of the moment. But this time, I felt that blending classic Wiccan phrases with equally classic Christian ones would be magical and healing for all.

Let me give you just one example. Here's how we blessed the rings:

> Rev. Joel: This wedding ring is an unbroken circle that symbolizes unending and everlasting love, and is a visible symbol that represents your inner commitment to each other.

> Judy: Remember your experiences and memories of loving. Remember your hopes, wishes, and dreams for Shadow and Spellweaver. As the rings are walked around, would each of you please empower these rings with your prayers and hopes for their future.

The maid of honor and the best man then carried the rings around the Circle (yes, we had cast a circle and invoked the Quarters within the church building!). Each of the people who had called a Quarter offered the rings to that quarter and called that Element's blessings on the marriage.

> Rev. Joel: [Drawing the Sign of the Cross above the rings] Dear Lord, bless these rings and those who will wear them. May their marriage be filled with understanding, vitality, goodwill, and prosperity in all things.

> Judy: [Drawing a Pentacle above the rings] Bountiful Goddess, Great Mother, bless these rings and those who will wear them. May their marriage be filled with health, wealth, joy, strength, peace, and that fulfillment of love that is perpetual happiness.

That's typical of the script. What we did not anticipate was that the "audience," more than two-thirds Pagan, got the surprising message that they were in a safe space and began responding noisily and enthusiastically, as though they were in Circle. Well, they were. So we didn't after all merely take some of our phrases and symbols out of context and use them with an alien, churchly kind of solemnity. We also never dreamed that the minister, by the end of the ritual, would be enthusiastically joining in our chants. When the newlyweds finally jumped the broom, the big, old sanctuary rang with our shouts and cheers!

Afterward, many of us thanked him. One guest questioned him a little further. His response was interesting. He said that he believes that, in a joint celebration, instead of some bland compromise, both Traditions should be fully present. And now, I believe it can be done.

From that beginning, let it grow!

Metropolitan New York

❧ Stepping Aside for Death
Bob Barraco

I grew up among Witches. My grandmother was a Witch. She was a card reader and the local practitioner whom people went to for advice. We have a deep appreciation of the spirit world. You know how some families get together to drink and play cards—well my family got together for séances. We keep in touch with our ancestors that way. So my childhood led me down the path of magic and working with spirits.

At the age of sixteen, I was diagnosed with a very rare form of cancer that required extensive surgery. During the operation, I had an out of body experience. It was very typical as far as descriptions go, with the tunnel, the light, the sense of leaving my body, and all that. Then suddenly I found myself back in body and I woke up. The doctor confirmed that I had indeed died during the procedure.

Since then, I have had prophetic dreams and experiences. I became a nurse. In my job, I use the foresights and inner voices, guides, and guardians quite effectively, primarily in working with the dying. I have had a lot of experiences where I have come face to face with the reapers or harvester spirits. I actually see them out of the corner of my eyes, feel them, and sense them.

There was a day when I stood in the doorway of a hospital room filled with people frantically trying to save the life of a woman who had just had a cardiac arrest. During the commotion of attempts to resuscitate her, someone tried to leave the room. I stepped aside to let him pass.

I said, "Excuse me, let me let you out."

He replied, "That's okay."

There was so much action going on in the room that I didn't pay close attention to him until it struck me . . . he had been wearing black. How many people in a hospital wear black? I turned to another nurse standing near me and asked him who had just left the room. I got a puzzled look. "No one left," he said. Suddenly, the woman's pulse went back to normal, as did her other functions. It was at that second I realized just who it was I let out of the room! The specter, Lord of Death!

This is my life, working with the human spirit. This is why I am a Witch. I work with people, but I also work with spirits. To me, a lot of these entities are my Gods and Goddess, even though they may not always have names.

Salem, Massachusetts

∾ What to Do with a Dead Husband
Victoria Slind-Flor

He was one of those cradle Catholics who'd gradually drifted away from calling the church "Holy Mother." There was no big dramatic break, but over the years he connected less and less with the liturgy, the Catholic community, and with the church's increasingly dogmatic stance on issues like birth control and homosexuality.

So, when he lay dying at Davies Medical Center's AIDS unit in San Francisco, my own Catholic-trained reflex action to call in the priest felt silly, but prodded me nonetheless. Finally, when my husband was in one of his few lucid moments, I asked him if he wanted to talk to a priest. "Sure, fine, send him right in," was his expansive response, reminding me of the warmth with which he greeted his lawyer buddies over an Irish coffee at Brennan's bar on Friday nights.

I was at work when the priest dropped by the hospital, and the only way I knew there had been a visit was that he had left his business card on the tray table.

"So what did you think of the priest?" I asked.

"Who?"

"The guy who came to see you. The guy who left this business card."

"Oh him. He wasn't a priest. He was a plumber. Came to look at the pipes."

My husband's AIDS-related dementia was so advanced, anything could, and did, pop out of his mouth. This was the end of any attempt to help my husband reconnect with his Catholic roots in his last days.

Gradually, the fungus in his mouth and throat spread through his body. The brain plaque that clouded his judgment and memories covered more and more of his brain. And the bright, funny, elegant lawyer I had known and loved faded away to someone who rarely recognized me as familiar, who seldom spoke, and, if not watched carefully, was liable to unplug his IV or fingerpaint the wall with his feces.

Finally, the day came when I sat at the side of his bed holding his hand, breathing every rasping breath with him, and, finally, feeling the last flutter of his pulse under my fingertips.

The "arrangements" had already been made. The nurses had helped me find the budget crematorium, and I'd bought a $19.95 ceramic urn from the discount coffin shop. The paperwork for death certificates had all been done.

But then what? How does one commemorate the death and honor the life of a loved one who had let go of the old traditions, but never had a chance to know, much less embrace the new ones?

Tilden Park in the Berkeley Hills was our sacred space. We had celebrated our marriage there, and every Saturday and Sunday, as long as he was well enough, we'd hike its trails. Over the years, I grew to know every turn of every trail, and when to look for familiar wildflowers as their season arrived.

So I knew we had to go to Tilden Park. But beyond that, I was at sea.

Now, years later, when I look back on all we did, I realize that my turn into a Pagan, Witchen life is not so much a matter of learning the new as it is remembering from some deep place the practices and rituals of my pre-Christian ancestors.

Ask me how I knew how to priestess my husband's memorial, and I really cannot answer. Something from the ancestors spoke to me and helped me connect with the roots.

I knew we had to have an Irish bagpiper, and that IRA songs had to be played. My husband was one of those Irishmen who wore a "Return the Six Counties" button on his lapel. He was also a frequent donor to those "widows and orphans" funds that are collected in the Bay Area's Irish bars.

So we—all the friends and relations—processed into one of the park's large meadows, led by the bagpiper whose pipes were wailing "The Rising of the Moon." We made a large circle because something told me this was the symbol of the cycle of life.

We had a reading of William Butler Yeats's *Lake Isle of Innisfree*, which talks about a wonderful place of peace and repose, a "bee-loud glade," not the heaven of the patriarchal religion in which my husband and I had both been raised.

I brought my husband's blackthorn cane, and we passed it around the circle, with each person saying something about my husband's life as the stick passed. This was years before I learned about use of "talking sticks" in the Dianic circle to which I now belong.

The meadow faced West. For some reason, I knew we had to have a site that faced West, toward the Pacific Ocean, the source of all our watery beginnings. I had asked each person who came to the memorial to bring a fist-sized stone and wildflowers from their gardens.

In the center of the meadow, we laid out the outlines of a Viking ship; prow pointed to the West, and filled the outline with wildflowers, herbs, and loose buds of garlic. (My husband was a great cook whose favorite ingredient was garlic.)

Then we took his ashes from the urn, and each of his or my blood relatives took a turn pouring out some of them within the outlines of the ship. I watched the ashes—really cinders and bone chunks—pour out and realized that this was all that was left and that it really wasn't terribly different from the bonemeal I use whenever I plant tulip bulbs. It was then that I knew that whatever he was would indeed be recycled into the raw stuff of the cosmos, that what was left of my husband would be part of the compost from which new life would arise.

I poured out a whole bottle of Jameson's Irish whiskey into the boat shape, remembering all the times we'd drunk wine on picnics and my husband would only half-jokingly pour out what he called "a libation for the gods." And I started to giggle because I could hear my husband's voice always telling the bartender to make his Irish coffee with Jameson's, and "none of that Protestant piss," as he used to call Bushmill's whiskey.

The traditional New Orleans band struck up two somber tunes that are played at New Orleans jazz funerals. We passed around a pitcher of water and a large bowl to catch the water, so each person could wash hands and feel purified from the grief of death. And then we returned the water to the earth.

Then the band started to play "Saints" and we all second-lined—danced—around the circle, back to our starting places, and then somebody yelled "let's eat." So we all bellied up to the picnic tables and had the roasted potatoes and poached salmon that are the sacred foods with which my family blesses every significant life event.

No, we did not call the quarters or cast a circle. If I'd seen an athame or smelled a sage smudge that day, I would have flinched and been fearful of something I was not yet ready to re-member—as writer Mary Daly would say—and incorporate into my life.

But I know this was a Pagan way to deal with death and that somehow the Goddess and my ancestors gave me the tools I needed to mark in an honorable and dignified way the passage of someone I had loved. I thank them and I hope that others who are on their way to Paganism will find a way to listen carefully to what is within and find their own paths to the Goddess.

Oakland, California

❧ Owls

Holly Heart Free

I live along a river on a small farm in southeastern Wisconsin. It is lovely here, with the river, the wetlands, a small wood lot, pastures, and a hill. This farm is home to all kinds of wild creatures, our fold of Highland cattle, and a small flock of rare Jacob and Cotswold sheep.

It was a cold and wet evening in early April. It was lambing season, and I visited the barn both night and day to check on the progress of the expectant sheep. I had just returned to the house when I felt a strong and strange "urge" to go back. I was quite sure there were no problems in such a short period, but this feeling was pushing me out the door. Grumbling a bit, I put on a warm coat and hat, found my gloves, and slipped into my boots.

It was during that very small window of time between sundown and actual dark, when the sky is sapphire and the stars are already bright. With my hands sunk deep in my pockets, I headed blindly down the walk.

An owl lives in an old dead tree that stands behind the house. I know this because I sometimes hear her who-who-whoing. A couple of times I saw her as she flew from her tree, startled by car lights that flashed over her home in the dark. I have also seen her hunting at night, under a moon that illuminates but leaves shadows and shapes to the mind's imagination.

But on this night and in this time that was neither dark nor light, an amazing thing occurred. I was just a few feet from the house when I heard an owl call off to my right. Another answered from a row of pine trees on my left.

I stopped and looked around in the near dark. They were so close to me and I was thrilled to hear them. Then I realized this wasn't what I was used to. One owl I heard infrequently, but several owls, early in the evening?

From the owl tree came another call. It was then that I realized what was occurring: the owls were "courting." It was beautiful, it was raw nature, and it sent shivers down my spine. This was indeed a gift, to see and feel a seasonal event between these very reclusive birds. A fourth owl answered from down in the willows along the creek bed. Four owls, were singing in a native song that is far removed from most of our lives. How magical!

I stood and watched as the dark descended around me, listening to the calls of the owls echoing back and forth. In a softer voice than their usual song, they flew from tree to tree, never repeating their cry from the same location. I seemed to be encircled by them, by the soft whirring of their wings, and by the sense of them flying past me in the night.

Twisting, turning in midflight, soaring and diving, all the while softly singing to the partner they desired, these beautiful large birds swooped and called, dancing a ritual in the air as old as time, as new as this night. And while I knew that owls have the same mate for many years or a lifetime, still the process of actively selecting that same mate again, of courting and winning her was an event that would take place every spring for as long as there would be owls. To the female, it reaffirmed that in his ardor of wooing her, in the song and the dance that only she understood, the male would stay near her and their nest, bringing food to her as she first layed and then brooded the eggs, and providing tasty morsels and safety for their chicks once hatched. He would herald danger from his watching perch, teach his young to fly and hunt, and spend the quiet of the dark winter months near her until the circle would renew itself next spring.

I had never been sure what kind of owls lived in the tree

"next door" until that night. One landed atop an electric pole and I shined my flashlight up at him. The great horned owl was so caught up in the night and the mating dance that he was impervious to the mere mortal who watched with awe.

I have no idea how long I watched and listened, ears finely tuned and eyes wide with wonder. Then the moment ended. Just as dark came fully down, one pair flew to the top of the silo. I could see them silhouetted there, back lit by the sliver of the waxing moon that hung just above them. Mates chosen again and life would go on for the owls in this tiny part of Wisconsin. With tears in my eyes and a lump in my throat, I sent a prayer and a blessing to them, and to Her who brought me outside at just the right moment.

These words do not convey the sense of absolute awe that I felt. It is with me still. I've witnessed so many things since moving to this place, but nothing will ever quite compare with the beautiful night I was shown the majesty of the great horned owls, courting, singing, soaring, and mating.

Bullthistle Farm, Wisconsin

๑ The Fecund Cold Dark: Walking the Alum Cliffs
Douglas Ezzy, Ph.D.

It is usually approaching dusk when I begin my walk. The cliff track is muddy black, sometimes slippery, and I am almost always alone for my journey. Few like to walk in the fading light when the shadows lengthen and day turns into night.

She draws me into her fecund cold dark valleys, caves, and wombat tunnels with an often overcast sky moistened by soft rain and the rhythm of breaking waves. Sweet rotting leaves scent the wavy curled branches of the short eucalypts and shrubs that forest her valleys with damp soft stream banks in their depths. She is a lover to me.

Today, I am walking the track with my friend Ani. Ani walked the track while she was growing up. I have walked it intensively in recent years. Her memories of the track are longer than mine and I have invited her to share them. It is late afternoon as we arrive, parking the car at the end of the street close to her childhood home that I purchased recently.

The first thing I feel is water and the green. It has been raining regularly over the past weeks and the bottom of the first gully is muddy for the first time in nearly two years. All last summer was dry, and the winter before, and the summer before that. The slippery track and mud under my feet feels so good. In Tasmania, winter rain is life, and the hot dry summer is death.

As we climb out of the first gully, Ani says, "It's so different now, all the richness of the forest is gone. The layers of bark and decaying leaves that made the forest alive and smelt so rich are all gone." Ani recalls the day of the fires, five years ago, when her brother stayed with the house, putting out the spot fires. The road was closed and she was unable to help. The houses were saved, but not the forest. We exchange stories of lovers, boyfriends and girlfriends, and their place in our exploration of the track. There was Richard and Paul, Kristy and Anna, from whom we learned how to kiss, how to caress, how to love. I point to the leafless skeletons of small shrubs and mourn their death in the great dry of the last eighteen months. Walking the track in the great dry hurt. Plants died, trees lost limbs, the animals dispersed, or retreated to the watered grass around the houses. But the dead leaves, bark, and twigs are re-creating anew a bed of rich fecund rotting fertility. Life and death lie entangled in our stories.

At the second gully we pause. "I've never seen it that open," says Ani. "It used to be so dense that you couldn't see more than a few meters." Now, we can see twenty or thirty meters up and down the valley. A small stream is flowing for the first time since winter two years ago. Following its course down, we jump from one side to the other with that fleetness of foot that only comes naturally to someone who has grown up in the Tasmanian bush. You have to be able to read the mud, the moss, the half-broken branch, and know that it is safe and will hold your weight. At the end, Ani hangs on a tree and leans out over the thirty-meter cliff that the stream cascades down into the ocean. It is perhaps two or three kilometers to the other shore of the river mouth. There is not a boat in sight, nor a plane in the sky. At this angle, most of the city is hidden further up the river, and we look out to the ocean and across to the fields and light woodlands on rolling hills. The river is dark. We wonder what lies in its hidden depths.

Just slightly back from the cliff is an abandoned wombat hole. There are several along the cliff track. It was deserted when I first saw it and Ani can't recall ever seeing a wombat. There are plenty of eastern barred bandicoots, evidenced by their distinctive triangular digging. Possums, both brushtails and ringtails, are commonly observed on the roof of the house at night, or in the vegetable patch. Rabbits have become more common. I suspect there's a platypus in a nearby valley, or at least there was before the big dry. We wonder if her father recalls seeing any evidence of wombats, such as their improbable and biologically inexplicable cubic scats. Ani promises to ask him for me.

It doesn't take long before we are at the halfway point, walking along Kingston beach. We stand on the beach, where a small river meets the sea. Ani recalls the day she saw the dolphins from here. After walking back to the other end of the beach, we watch the waves from a prominent rock. As I admire the tidal zone, Ani sees the wave coming and decides not to move. Unaware, I jump with surprise when it hits. We are both drenched and laughing.

As it often does in Tasmania, the weather comes in short phases. A rain shower arriving from the southwest darkens the sky. To the northeast the sun is still shining on the opposite shore. A rainbow bends across the sky. The visual echo of the rainbow is also there, like an admiring outer ring. I have never seen a sky quite like it. To the south of the rainbow it is dark, to the north it is light. There is something magical about the moment. Not only are the colors in the sky brilliant, right down to the purple on the inner rim, but the brilliance of the rainbow is also reflected in the water. The reflection stretches out to meet us as we stand in awe and silence.

Back up the cliff, and down the valley, we begin our return journey. Standing once more on the edge of a high cliff, I wonder aloud if Ani has ever contemplated going over the edge. "As a teenager," she says. More recently, when my marriage failed, I contemplated it, I reply. "I knew of one person who did jump," says Ani. "A friend of a friend." Our conversationless descent into a particularly dark and quiet valley absorbs our mood.

On the return journey, we notice the houses that used to not be there, the new fences, the bulldozer tracks, and the boundary posts marking the edges of new subdivisions that will soon be backyards. I was shocked when they first bulldozed that path, I say. "It feels like a wound to my body," says Ani. "As if all that matters is building houses and the wants and pleasures of the people who will live in those houses. There's no recognition of other reasons, other purposes for this bit of bush that used to be so remote."

It's easy to romanticize the good old days, before development, before the fire, before the big dry of the last two years, before the wombats left. But that is not the heart of our story. In many ways, the track just "is." Life and death that keep coming and going. The bush is remade ever anew. Our story is of walking with, not just on, the Alum Cliffs. It is a story of her voice, the joy and pleasure we shared with her, and the pain of her passing. Make no mistake, the Alum Cliffs are dying. The wombats are gone, the old trees are burned, the undergrowth is changing under the pressure of global warming, the invading European plant species are more common, and the subdivisions more intrusive. But it is not her passing that upsets me the most. It is that so few people stop to listen.

The Alum Cliffs spoke to us, and we were both nurtured in her embrace: the rhythm of the waves echoing to the cliff tops; the depth of the ocean along her borders; the temperamentality of the weather's moods; the harsh cruelty of death by fire and drought; the dark quietness of her valley; the warm embrace of her folds; and the sweet fecund scent of rotting plant matter. She is an intimate friend to me, comforting me with her caress when I cry, refusing to compromise when I do not agree, and challenging me to be true to myself. As she moves on to new things and perhaps passes away, I will miss her.

Tasmania, Australia

The Evolution of a City Pagan
Jennifer Hunter

Throughout my childhood, I was forced into a nonconsensual relationship with nature. My mother, a single mom and pseudo-hippie, dragged me on numerous hiking, camping, and canoeing excursions. This was either an attempt to raise me with a healthy appreciation for the outdoors, or the inevitable result of a lack of overnight babysitters. I do not remember developing a healthy appreciation for the outdoors. What I remember is having to climb out of a tent in the middle of a chilly evening to walk a quarter-mile to bug-infested communal bathrooms and trudging along on hikes where the scenery was secondary to the goal of just getting there already. I sat bundled up in a life jacket and blankets in the middle of a canoe traveling down the Delaware on a frigid and gray October afternoon; all I wanted was a television and some civilization.

Each year I tried out a new summer camp. I packed my suitcase with optimism about the new friends I would meet and the swell activities I would participate in. Each year, after arrival, I realized it was yet another filthy prison where I would be attacked by mosquitoes, forced into competitive sports, forced to eat slop, and be tortured by cliques. The only brightness in my day was the chance to buy candy bars from the cantina.

Then at age sixteen, I discovered Wicca. Blinded by the giddiness of new love, I forgot all about the past. I saw no connection between sun-drenched Beltane meadows and sunburns, moonlit magical forests and mosquitoes, sleeping on soft moss, and peeing on one's shoes while trying to squat properly with no glasses on.

When I started going to Pagan festivals, the honeymoon was over as I discovered I was back in summer camp. True, the emotional torture was absent and the food was better, but I was back in those buggy bathrooms. It's not that I don't like nature. What I don't like is being cold, dirty, itchy, and sleeping on a cot. Don't you think the Pagans of old, who lived "close to the land," would have been thrilled if presented with a luxury hotel room and a hot tub? Let's face it: they lived close to the land because they *had to*.

As if my own preferences weren't indication enough, the course was set for me to wind up a city Pagan* when I joined my

---

*The term "city Pagan" is an oxymoron, since the Latin term *paganus* originally meant "country-dweller." But being a Jewish Pagan as well, obviously I have no problem with that.

first coven at age nineteen. It was in the Bronx. Skyclad in candlelit rooms, we cast circles, called the Elements, and worked magic as salsa music thrummed in through the open windows.

As an adult, deciding where to live, I again figured the issue was creature comforts. As long as I had my real bed and indoor plumbing, of course I would (should?) want to live in a cottage in the woods. The most rural home for me was in Southborough, Massachusetts, where the business district is about a block long and the only sound you hear at night is crickets. It was pretty and peaceful, but I felt lost. I realized that the happiest time in my life was when I lived in a college dorm. I moved to Somerville, Massachusetts, the most densely populated community in New England (77,000 people in four square miles), and breathed a sigh of relief.

Cities are not dead spaces, you know. I love watching the squirrels dash along phone lines and fences, their voluminous tails twitching with excitement. I like chasing them around trees, in a game that's peek-a-boo to me, mortal terror to them. I may be the only person who likes to look at pigeons, seeing orange eyes and dinosaur feet, watching the males puff up as they follow the females around. Neighborhood dogs play; neighborhood cats lie in the sun. Bees, sparrows, butterflies, worms, slugs—it's *Wild Kingdom* if you know where to look.

I wake up in the morning with birds chirping in the peach tree outside my window. My own yard has raspberry bushes, mint plants, and wildflowers. I show my three-year-old daughter how the trees have pushed up the sidewalk, scoffing at our attempts to civilize the place. We smell all the flowers. We blow kisses to the moon when we see it. She reminds me of these things, if I forget.

In some ways, living in a city allows me to be gentler to the earth. I don't need to own a car; I walk or use public transportation. The city of Somerville has an excellent program that allows me to recycle paper, cardboard, glass, plastic, and metal.

My friends and I share resources easily, as many of us live within a mile of each other. I'm a proud trash-picker; I've found toys, furniture, and books on the curb. I live in an apartment of a three-family house; I am not contributing to suburban sprawl! Okay, I don't use all-natural cleaning products, but I do feel appropriately guilty about it.

When out and about, I often pick up newspaper and food wrappers and drop them into a trash can. I think this action is powerful magic. It's a way of stating that I am determined to make a difference, no matter how small. Once, I saw a man on a bike throw a wrapper on the ground. Barely hesitating, I called after him, "Excuse me? You dropped something." He went back and picked it up, taking it with him. I couldn't believe I had the balls to do that. Must have been the Gods speaking through me.

On occasion, I will grit my teeth and "rough it" at a Pagan festival. When I go, I bring a carload of crap to be prepared for every possibility. I took my daughter to Rites of Spring in western Massachusetts this past year and decided I believed in hell. I'd been attending this wonderful gathering for over a decade, but take it from me: do not attempt to bring an almost-potty-trained three year old. Our luggage smelled like a New York City subway station. One of these days, I need to figure out how to attend a festival and sleep at a bed and breakfast . . . one with laundry facilities.

I believe that the divine is immanent everywhere, and that means *everywhere*. I love the beauty of untamed wilderness, but I also love the beauty of coffee shops, thrift stores, and dance clubs. If each person is the image of God, I live in the midst of a pantheon. I'm a city Pagan.

Somerville, Massachusetts

THE SEASONS

๛ Singing to the Deer
Patricia Monaghan

At solstice, the woods were bright in a snowy way, the sky pearl gray above the stately maples and gnarled burr oaks. An Alaskan marooned in the urban Midwest, it took me years to find this nearby patch of relatively undisturbed land where I can sense the power of wildness. Now I go there often, watching the seasons unfold their changeful unchanging patterns in the increasingly familiar forest.

I especially like to walk among the sleeping trees in the half-lit silence of winter dawns. The trail I follow winds and twists, new patches of mixed woodland appearing at every turn. That morning, I reached a point where the path turns sharply left to follow a small ravine. In spring, ephemeral ponds—lively with salamanders, loud with frogs—form in the creases of the forest there. But in frozen winter, I expected nothing beyond silence and wind.

So I did not see them at first, three deer beside three empty larches. When I made them out—gray-dun hides against a gray-dun world—they were motionless, white tails aloft like flags of distress. I stopped in my tracks, thinking how lucky I was to meet the animal my Celtic forebears called the spirit of wildness on that auspicious day.

I often encounter deer on my morning walks. The woods are close enough to roads and homes that we humans are no strangers to them. But like any animal of the suburban wild—squirrel or opossum or raccoon—the deer keep their distance. An instant after they see me, they bound silently away, their white-flag tails on high alert.

But this morning, the deer only stared at me across the ravine. To the left stood a tall stately doe; to the right, an older heavier one; in the center, one of the previous spring's fawns, all gangly adolescence. Huge soft ears held high, they cast dark liquid gazes at me. And did not run.

Desire burst in my heart: to speak to the deer, to tell them how beautiful they were, to thank them for bringing wildness to the edge of the vast city. To speak from my heart, my own little wild heart, to theirs. To celebrate the season with them.

But I stood silent, for I do not speak the language of deer. I stared silently at them, awaiting the inevitable flight. But moments stretched out like fingers of light from the rising sun, and the deer did not run away.

Then, for no reason I can easily explain, I began to sing, my voice loud in the silent forest. A plaintive minor-keyed medieval song sprang to my lips, a holiday carol I've known since girlhood. *Lo how a rose e'er blooming, from tender stem hath sprung. . . . It came a floweret bright, amidst the snows of winter, when half-spent was the night.*

I thought the sound of my voice would frighten the deer away, but I wanted to speak to them, and music seemed the only way.

Just as I expected, they began to move. But not swiftly. And not into the forest. Not away from me at all. No. One slow step at a time, the deer moved towards me.

When I started singing, they were perhaps fifty feet away. By the time I began the second verse, they were half that distance. By the time I finished the song, the deer stood just across the ravine. In the sudden silence at the song's end, three tails went suddenly up again, sounding a silent alert. So I began another song. Tails went down, ears moved slightly forward. Dawn light emblazoned lemon and melon stripes upon the snow as three deer listened to carol after carol after carol. A quarter-hour passed and still they did not move. I kept singing.

It was not the deer but me who ended our encounter. The sky had moved from pearl to sherbet to azure, and I had promises to keep. I thanked the deer for listening to my dawn chorus. The sound of my words shook them awake. Tails went up, forelegs tucked up, and in an instant they were gone.

In the silence, I stared into the gray forest. Only a few months earlier, standing below a high-massed mountain glacier I have known since childhood, now shrinking fast away, its ancient snows surging down to the gray sea in cold torrents, I had felt overwhelmed with hopelessness. Do we only take from nature, giving nothing in return? If so, what use are we? Why should the universe continue to provide for us, if we are such ungrateful children?

But there on the edge of a tiny ravine, hope washed over me like light. Perhaps there is a reason for our being. Perhaps what we give our lovely blue earth is song. Beauty. Art. Perhaps that is the reason we were created: to entertain the universe. Perhaps the great spirit is amused and touched, thrilled and delighted by our childlike creativity. Today we leave art to the professionals: to those with beautiful voices and firm bodies and exciting visions. But perhaps art is not frozen moments of perfection but the process of creation itself. Perhaps we were put here to pleasure the world, making art as spontaneously and joyfully as children drawing great yellow suns with wax crayons. Perhaps we should all be singing more, and dancing, and painting with bright colors, and chanting out poems. Perhaps we silly wonderful amateurs most please the universe when we act that way.

MacDonald Woods, a forest preserve in Glencoe, Illinois

ᥬ The Melting of the Ice
Diane

The room had been ready for months. We attended parental classes, completed a stack of paperwork, and our lives had been scrutinized by case workers. Still, when the call came, it was quite a shock.

It arrived unexpected on a cold January day during what was one of the worst winters in recent memory. The snow was being measured in feet, not inches. Even the brook near our house had fallen victim to the bitter temperatures; its joyful voice stilled, frozen into a shimmering ribbon of crystallized water.

As we carefully drove down the slick streets to the Department of Social Services office, we discussed what was happening in nervous but excited tones.

"I know you want to adopt a young child," said the voice of our social worker over the phone, "but I have an emergency situation. I have a five-year-old boy who was in a temporary foster home. That placement ended this morning. He is sitting in my office with his belongings. I remembered that you have an open room, and I admit this is highly unusual, but would you consider allowing him to stay with you for the weekend? By the way," she added almost as an afterthought, "he is available for adoption."

She told us a little of his history. In his young life, he had seen and experienced more than any child should. Due to abuse and neglect, Manuel* had been removed numerous times from his family. After the fifth attempt at reunification, the state decided that returning him would not be in his best interest. He then entered into, and became a victim of, the system that had been created to help him. Manuel became a

---

*All the names in this story have been changed to protect the privacy of the child and his new family.

nomad moving from one placement to another, carrying with him his few belongings in a plastic bag. We were home number fourteen.

Manuel ignored us as we entered the office. He appeared to be playing intently with building blocks, but his taut body language told us he was very conscious of our presence. The social worker called him over to meet us. He made a show of annoyance at being asked to leave his play but responded to her request. His head down, he went to stand beside her.

He was very small for his age, no more than forty inches tall. He looked tired. Under his eyes, dark rings showed against his light brown skin. He didn't smile, but reached a hand up to take hold of the social worker's fingers.

"This is Diane and Paul," she said, introducing him to us. "They will be taking care of you for a while."

Still looking at the ground, Manuel nodded his head, indicating that he understood. We knew that he had heard this before and expected to hear it again. We got down on our knees so that we were level with his height. For a moment, he lifted his eyes to meet ours. Within them we could see mistrust. There was also deep pain, the ache of a child who could not understand why he stood before strangers being asked to trust that they would protect him. But we could also see something else . . . perhaps hope.

As we made ready to leave, the social worker picked Manuel up to give him a hug good-bye. Suddenly, he grabbed hold of her tightly and began to sob. Our hearts ached as we realized that his social worker was the one consistent person in his life. Unable to convince him to let go, she carried Manuel to our car. Speaking reassurances that he would soon see her again, she gently placed him into our waiting car seat.

Manuel softly cried most of the way home. He displayed no emotion when we showed him his new room. He had been this route before. We were, to him, just another stop in his life. He collapsed on his bed, hiding from us in sleep.

As we watched him in his restless dreams, we realized that the Gods had just blessed us with a son. In our hearts, we could not tell this young boy that he had to leave.

But it would be hard to convince Manuel this was his last stop, that he had arrived home. To survive, he had created a wall around his fragile soul. If he allowed no one in, then he couldn't be hurt. But his tears told us that, despite his attempts to hide it, he felt intensely. We chose to embrace him with love, offer him protection and stability, and hoped that, in time, he would heal enough to reach out and learn to trust again.

Imbolc Eve arrived and we were unsure of what to do to celebrate the holiday. Normally, we would create a sacred circle and welcome the God and Goddess of the awakening Earth. But we had not yet told Manuel of our religious beliefs. He had already been asked to accept many major changes: new parents, new culture, new home, new life. We were concerned that a full Pagan ritual, with its concepts of animism and polytheism, would be confusing and frightening to a young boy whose only previous experience with religion was the Catholic Church. But Imbolc is one of my favorite Sabbats and I wanted to do something as a family to mark the turn of the seasonal wheel. We decided on simplicity.

I pulled out my large cast iron pot. Bundling Manuel in his winter coat, we headed outside and through the snow. We let the moonlight guide us to the spot, a pristine snowdrift. Paul and I filled the cauldron with snow while Manuel, shivering under his coat with his hands stuck deep in his pockets, silently watched us.

With our pot in hand, we followed our footsteps back to the house and into the warmth of our kitchen. Leaving our wet clothes on a hanger by the door, we dropped the pot of snow on the kitchen table. Manuel stood in a doorway watching as we took a tall, white taper and stuck it through the snow into the candlestick holder we had left on the bottom of the pot. We then packed the snow tightly around it.

As we lit the candle, Paul and I talked about how Imbolc represents the breaking of the back of winter, the return of the sun and the warmth of spring. The snow-filled cauldron symbolizes the frozen earth and the burning candle the sun. When flame and ice touch, the warmth of the candle transforms the frozen water—just as winter submits to spring. The look on our new son's face clearly said, "You two are out of your minds!"

Before he went to bed, Manuel stopped to take one more look at our candle. It burned brightly on our kitchen table, its glow reflecting off the walls and window panes, filling the room with a magical warmth. He looked at it with curiosity and, for a moment, he was an innocent, young child.

In the morning, we stumbled out of our beds to begin our day. I watched Manuel as he made his way into the kitchen, rubbing the sleep from his eyes. Suddenly, he stopped, his focus directed on the view outside our large bay window. He turned and looked at our pot still sitting on the table. The snow had melted; the candle having done its job was now extinguished by the water. He looked out the window again, then back to the pot, and again to the window. His eyes grew wide with surprise and a look of amazement appeared on his face. I walked over to stand beside him and gaze out the window. It was raining. I felt a small hand reach up and quietly find its way into mine. Hand in hand, we stood and watched the ice melt.

Somewhere in the United States

ᴥ Inanna on the Rocks
Barbara Ardinger, Ph.D.

Note: In the late 1980s, I belonged to a coven in Long Beach, California. Although some details have been changed, this is a true story. The cave is near San Clemente. I was so traumatized by this journey that I wrote the story in the third person to distance myself from it. But it's really me. I was really there.

It is Friday night, about 10:30. The first full moon after the spring equinox has already risen above the cliffs, and the coven has gathered on the beach. They are headed for a small cave a mile or so to the north under rocky cliffs that overlook the Pacific Ocean. Although this stretch of beach is under water twice a day, the tide is outward bound and the cave will not be flooded again until dawn.

One member of the group is a middle-aged woman. A self-described intellectual, she is out of shape and unaccustomed to physical exertion out of doors. Nevertheless, she starts out, smiling, with the younger men and women, who are wearing jeans and boots, their sweatshirts and jackets zipped and buttoned against the cold ocean wind.

Setting out in clusters of two or three, they walk north along the sand under the cliff. Snatches of happy conversation and laughter carry above the sounds of the waves.

As they leave the sandy part of the beach, however, the explorers become subdued. Their laughter begins to sound like the brittle gaiety that drives away fear. They are following a narrow path just at the foot of the cliff, and even though the moon above is extraordinarily bright, they are overshadowed. Everyone carries a candle as well as feathers, crystals, or other small gifts to be offered in the cave to the spirits of fire, water, air, and earth.

Almost immediately, the intellectual woman falls behind. Wearing tennis shoes, a flannel shirt, an old sweater, and a large hooded sweatshirt, she is already overwarm. Everyone assumed—but no one told her—that flashlights would be needed, so she is also apprehensive, for she does not see well in the dark and has never been out on an empty beach at midnight. She begins to wonder if the exertion will trigger a panic attack, which will lead to an asthma attack. It's happened before.

As the others move jauntily ahead (many of them know the way), she moves more slowly, hesitating before trying to navigate around the ankle-high, wave-washed stones. For her, the way becomes a struggle within a dozen steps and she begins to slip on the broken shells and other debris. "Oh," she says aloud each time her foot slides off a wet stone. She goes on with great deliberation.

Where the path is made of packed sand and broken shells, she can walk comfortably for two or three minutes. The sky is cloudy, the water black, and she feels that she must be going downhill. The waves seem tall, but she keeps reminding herself that the tide is going out. She sidesteps something that suddenly moves and cries out as a wave comes within inches of her shoe. The water washes over a stone and flows back out.

Boulders ahead, and they're knee-high. The so-called path is invisible, and the only smooth sand is right at the edge of the water. Considering her options, she decides that, as the boulders are dry and relatively flat, they offer the safest route. She steps over and around with elaborate care until she finds the path once more, now several feet to her right and under the cliff. The sandy part of the beach makes a sharp turn to the left, right into the ocean.

She can't see the rest of the coven! She stops, rubs an ankle, and realizes that she is sweating underneath all the clothes, although her face and hands are cold. She's alone on the beach, suddenly aware of the noise of the waves, aware, suddenly, that the waves are all she can hear. The group has already gone around the turn up ahead. She sees a flash of light. *They can't be too far away, can they? Why don't they notice that I'm no longer with them?*

She looks around—boulders behind her and before her, wet sand under her feet, the cliff rising straight up on one side, the ever-hungry ocean on the other side. For just a minute, she considers sitting down to rest. *No. I'm not too tired and I'm still breathing okay. I'll rest later.*

The cliff, which must be a hundred feet high now, seems more menacing, with its rocky outcroppings and shallow caves. Even under the full moon, she is walking a shadowed path. As the path disappears under the rocks again, she feels as though she's moving literally at a snail's pace, but while she repeatedly stumbles, she does not quite fall down. She notices that one of her shoes seems to be disintegrating.

Another left turn where the cliff meets the water, then a long, straight stretch. Voices ahead! So she's not the only human being on the beach after all. Longing to rest, she stops and looks apprehensively out to sea. "Blessed Mother," she prays aloud, "help me down this path." It can't be time for the tide to turn. Surely she won't be swamped by the waves. But why doesn't someone come back and help her? As she stands there, the voices fade into echoes that are drowned in the roaring waves.

Alone again. Well, here's a trace of the path, just where the cliff touches the tideline. Suddenly, it's darker, for the moon has become obscured by the blowing clouds. She has no way to judge how far she's come, no idea how far she has yet to go. The coven's leader said it was half an hour's walk to the cave, which is just beyond the end of the cliff. *Sure, half an hour for people who know where they're going. Who know how to walk on slippery rocks. Who can see in the dark.*

Well, just take it one step at a time. If she stops here, she has no idea where she is. *Well, yes, I'm somewhere on the western edge of the continent.* She has no idea how long she would have to wait till her friends found her on their way back. She pulls her sweatshirt off and ties it around her hips.

She's in the dark in a wet and rocky wilderness. Around the next curve, an empty stretch of sand. *I will* not *fall down!* The wind unexpectedly unties the scarf covering her hair and takes it away. *Where's the path?*

Another sharp turn. Far above—cliff and moon, both hostile. To her left, the ocean inexorably washes in and out, washing the path away, swallowing the earth. Aha, here's a tiny cave. It looks relatively clean and dry. She could rest here, wait until everyone else comes back. Spend time in private meditation.

How much time? And what if she's trapped here when the tide turns? How high does the water actually get? What if they don't come back this way? What if there's some other way out? What if a stranger comes and finds her alone? "No, no, no," she says aloud. "You can't meditate when you're filled with self-pity and foolish fears."

How can it be so dark under a full moon, so cold in the spring? It never gets this dark in the city. Never this silent. When did she cut her leg? Scrape her wrist? Where did she lose an earring? She could be at home, reading, writing, perhaps listening to music with candles burning. How did her precious amethyst point fall out of her pocket, and where? Why on earth did she say she could come along on this awful trek?

Before she knows it, she's around the next curve. *Where's the path gone now?* If she could see better, perhaps she could move with as much assurance as her young friends. When she finds the path again, it is still going downhill. She's apparently moving in the proper direction. *As if I have a choice.*

She looks up. Flashlights! Her friends are nearby! She can see their silhouettes above giant rocks at the very edge of the water. They're only a hundred feet ahead.

But the rocks are taller now, and sharper. *Take care*, she tells herself. *Crawl across this large, flattish one, slide between those two. Watch out—this one's unsteady. Long step now, climb up, slide down. Then up again. Jump across this rivulet, climb over one more rock.*

No one speaks a greeting to her. Haven't they even noticed her arrival? Some are gazing into the ocean, others sit with their eyes closed. Panting, she overhears someone saying that a few have already gone down into the cave. It's only a couple hours until the tide begins to turn. There will be time enough for ritual and renewal, time enough to get up again.

She catches her breath and massages her ankles. When did she lose her sweatshirt? She's exhausted and windblown and muddy up to her knees. She feels crippled and old and her dignity is long gone.

So where's this famous cave?

A young man before points it out. "You go down there," he says. "Slip through that narrow crevice in the cliff wall. Not to worry," he adds with a chuckle. "It's wider than it looks."

And, oh, yes, there's water in the bottom. "You have to carry your shoes and socks," he says.

"It's waist-deep in the middle. Walk close to the side. Hug the wall." Finally—a hand to help, a torch to show the way. "Hold your breath," he says. "Squeeze through that narrow opening, crawl into the cave. That's the only way out, too, unless you want to swim out to sea. I'll walk with you when we go back."

In front of her, a tall form rises out of the shadows in the cave. She recognizes the young woman who leads the coven. "You made it. That's wonderful for someone who can't see in the dark. Let's start our ritual of spring renewal now."

The cave in which they sit is egg-shaped, its walls and ceiling scoured smooth by the tides of a thousand years. And it's pink, a pink made golden by the light of the candles set around the perimeter. Someone has lit a driftwood fire in the center, and the wood burns blue and green, and gold. On the seaward side of the egg are three arches through which they can see the full moon reflected in the water.

"Springtime has come," the priestess says. "We're in a cave, underground. Like Persephone and Attis, like the flowers and the wheat, we can grow and return to the light."

Yes, the woman thinks. *It's Good Friday and we're in a cave.* She remembers her studies in comparative religion. *In a symbolic three days and nights, we can rise again. It's the beginning of Passover, and in a few minutes we will set forth together on our tribal, life-changing journey back up to the ordinary world.* Like Inanna rising into the world from the dark, frightening realm of Erishkegal, she and her friends will arise from this cave and be reborn into a new season of their lives.

Long Beach, California

ཀ Planting
Patricia Monaghan

Potential, they call it. Youth, they say, is full of potential. Spring, full of potential.

It sounds so hopeful. As though potential always means growth and bursting life, extravagant boom, fullness of fruit.

I am in the garden in soft rain. Dark soil clings to my skin. Rain slides like tears down my cheeks. My hair curls against temples and neck, tendrils in rain. The moon is new. It is time for planting.

From my pocket I take a white packet from which I pour a hundred seeds, tiny seeds that barely fill my palm. Into chevrons my hoe has grooved into the soil, I slowly pour these weightless bits of life. In a few weeks dark reddish green will appear. In a few months, those leaves will become my food. In a season, the plants will grow and die, as in my season I grow and will die.

Not all these seeds will sprout. Some will not survive the tearing open of their protective casing. Some will never raise shoulders, then heads, to the sun. Some will be tattered by hard rain, some betrayed by hail, some eaten by insects and birds, some thinned by my gardener's hand.

Potential: for death, for failure, as surely as for life and success.

So it is with me: Some selves that might have flowered were stillborn, some happinesses died in the struggle to endure, some talents never fruited. It is easy to grow hard, as though by failing to hope we can avoid inevitable pain. But plant a hundred seeds, and ten will grow. Plant ten, and one will grow. There is no reason not to be profligate with seed, as with hope.

So every season of my life I plant, and plant, and plant again. I do not stint on seed, those tiny miracles, those small promises. For some things survive. Some things endure. And that must be enough.

Chicago

ꙮ My First Beltane
Edmund

In the winter of 1968–1969, I was in as good a position as any would-be Wiccan in his midteens could hope to have reached. My surviving parent was what we would now, without hesitation, call a Pagan, devoted to a view of the natural world as animated by inherent divinity and represented by spirits ultimately derived from a mother goddess. This view was associated with a tendency to treat the literature of pagan Greece and Rome, and especially the works of Homer, Virgil, and Ovid, as a body of sacred texts. I liked and respected what my parent believed, but found it too passive, solitary, and theoretical for my needs. I wanted a paganism that was apparently rooted in Britain itself and that had allegedly survived until the present day and could still be practiced, and I had found it in the books of Margaret Murray, Sir James Frazer, and Gerald Gardner. They made me drunk with excitement, and at school my teachers and class-mates listened respectfully as I lectured them on the Old Reli-gion. Their respect was based largely on the fact that I treated the subject as purely a historical one, interesting and enter-taining but with no necessary relevance to the present. What they did not know was that I was determined to play an active part in a living Pagan group: and in England in the 1960s that could only mean a Wiccan one.

A coven of young Wiccans had been formed not far from my home district and, though I was technically too young for initiation, I was receiving some basic training and could look forward to taking my place in the circle when I turned eight-een. To encourage that process, and to fill in time, I had taken to hosting what we would now call open circles at each of the main seasonal festivals of modern Paganism. I lived on the border of Epping Forest, the largest area of old deciduous woodland in England, and my home was at the very tip of a tongue of settlement that poked out into the countryside. To the north and east was the forest, and to the west a large area of wild meadow grass thickly studded with trees and bushes. Local people had often held informal bonfire parties there, and so, at Halloween 1968 I coordinated a ceremony for a group of friends between two aged oak trees in a secluded part of the wasteland. It worked so well that my chums and I set about celebrating each festival in turn. The format was always the same: a fire for warmth and light, some rites taken from standard books on old seasonal customs such as those of Frazer and Christina Hole, some snatches of Wiccan liturgy that had already been published, honoring deities and spirits, eating and drinking, and games. A dozen people usually attended. My parent approved though did not participate and sportingly provided hot drinks when we came back to the house.

As we approached Beltane, the festival that had always excited me most, I planned something more ambitious: about twenty people, a bigger fire, which would need to be trenched inside a ditch to keep it safe and make it more sacred, a labyrinth constructed of brushwood, and an enclosing stone circle. Ours was not a stony landscape, but the concrete blocks of a ruined wall supplied substitute megaliths. It inspired me further that I had just become partnered with an unusually beautiful girlfriend, whom I could visualize all too easily as a Queen of the May. To get the site ready, half a dozen of my male friends turned up a week before the set date, and we soon had the ditch dug and the blocks in their circle.

We were getting the wood for the labyrinth when a gang of local children came across us—whom we had never seen there before—and began throwing stones. I wanted to conciliate them, but before I could act some of my mates lost their tempers and chased them off. We returned to work, and only half an hour later two police officers arrived, to say that a local resident had reported us for suspicious behavior. I explained carefully and politely that we were going to hold a bonfire party as local people had often done on that land and asked whether this infringed some regulation of which nobody had hitherto been aware. The policeman with the natty moustache puffed himself up and informed us all my words were lies and that our actual intention had been to start a brush fire. We would all be charged with conspiracy to cause arson. Our names and addresses were taken and we were ordered to disperse. Shortly afterward, somebody pushed over or broke all the blocks that we had set up as standing stones.

In view of all this, it was a considerable act of bravado that we decided to hold the Beltane festival exactly as we had designed to do, in the face of what we now took to be persecution. On May Eve, I went into the forest at moonrise to gather foliage and flowers with which to deck my home and to make crowns, as *The Golden Bough* told me that I should do. I then wrote a poem about it, imitating the style of Doreen Valiente. On the following evening the weather was warm and dry. My expected score of guests arrived, and at sunset we processed to the site between the old trees. We stacked the fire and lit it easily, with invocations to the Sun God and Earth Goddess. My male friends drew lots to choose the Beltane Carline, the person who (also according to Frazer's text) represented the human sacrifice in folk celebrations of the festival, and would have the honor and risk of making the first three leaps across the flames when they died down sufficiently. We completed the labyrinth, which was a true maze, with dead ends and a single twisting route through. The men were blindfolded one by one, hoping to earn a kiss by making their way to the woman standing in the center. A rope was fastened to the arm of each male and held by the lady in the middle, so that she had the option of guiding a wooer to success if she chose. My own girlfriend went first and duly led me to bliss. She then remained and did the same thing for other men, but I thought that simply a function of the divinity that she represented, and was proud of her and her radiant beauty. There followed fire-leaping, songs, and general merrymaking that lasted far into the night.

Within a few days, my immediate neighborhood was rife with stories of Satanists or lunatics holding diabolic rites in the wasteland; inspired, seemingly, just by the physical remains of our fire and maze and our attempt to make a circle of blocks. Nobody knew who had started them, just as nobody knew who had set the police on us earlier, but everybody was hearing them. My hitherto cooperative parent decided, reasonably enough, that henceforth any Pagan ceremonies in which I engaged had to be a long way from our home and neighborhood. No retribution was ever directed at us, and the police never carried out their threat to press charges, but somebody took a chainsaw to the two oak trees between which we had celebrated. Having stood for hundreds of years, their lives were now claimed in sacrifice to a moment of collective hysteria.

In addition, I had more personal problems resulting from the festival, as my girlfriend ditched me immediately after it. She had transferred her affections to one of my closest male friends, whom she had met in the labyrinth. I could not forgive him, and the rift between us fissured our social world. Nor was I ever initiated into a local Wiccan coven, for the one that I had wanted to join broke up before I reached the age for it, leaving no successors. The whole sequence of events left a lot of lessons to be learned; too many, and too big, for a teenager to digest easily. What I had to accept was my total defeat, and thereafter I postponed any further adventures in Paganism until I had left school and gone to work in London. On Midsummer Night, the next festival in the calendar, I went alone to the old ritual site and poured a libation in honor of its spirits and especially of those that had belonged to the innocent trees. Then I made myself drunk to vent my feelings and went away. It was closure.

My false friend invested so much attention in his affair with my ex-girlfriend that he began to neglect his studies and eventually dropped out of school and vanished into obscurity, to my huge private satisfaction. Long afterward, however, I learned that the two of them had got married, enduringly, and so for them, at least, our rites on that May evening had held real magic. For myself, however, there was only one permanent effect: that Beltane has never since been one of my favorite festivals.

Epping Forest, England

❧ Trials and Tribulations of a Pagan: A Midsummer's Bathing Vignette

Michael York, Ph.D.

The midsummer solstice has traditional associations with water. I believe it was Sir James Frazer who records a number of the European folk practices associated with bathing at the time of the summer solstice. In Lithuania, people traditionally roll in the dew at the time of the midsummer sunrise.

Consequently, I have long indulged in the Pagan practice of ritually bathing in rivers, lakes or other bodies of water—especially if and when considered sacred through indigenous or historic tradition. For midsummer's, this practice occurs at the time of sunrise. One problem has always been deciding which the proper day is, but I have followed European customs associated with the Feast of St. John the Baptist that occurs just after the actual summer solstice itself. When Julius Caesar reformed the lunisolar calendar in 46 B.C.E., because of frequent political maneuvering by the pontifices officially in charge of the calendar to extend the length of office for consuls in their favor, it was enormously out of sync with the seasons. In Caesar's reform, the solar year was taken to be exactly 365¼ days, and the vernal equinox was fixed to March 25—making midsummer's June 24. However, with the Julian reckoning, the calendrical year is slightly too long compared to the actual year, and the seasons appear to advance. When the computation for determining Easter was fixed in 325 C.E. to the first Sunday following the full moon after the vernal equinox, the equinox itself had already shifted from the 25th of March to the 21st of March. Pope Gregory XIII remedied the calendrical inaccuracy in 1582 by deleting the accumulated days and modifying subsequent intercalculation, but he kept to the 21st of March as the moment of the vernal equinox. As a result, in the

Gregorian calendar we use today, the summer solstice occurs around the 21st or 22nd of June.

Nevertheless, in the ecclesiastical calendar Midsummer is still June 24, rather than the slightly earlier solstitial turning point itself when the day no longer increases in length and is about to decrease. In practical terms, the sun is virtually at a standstill from the vantage of the earth, and the days of June 20, 21, 22, 23, 24 and 25 are all of comparatively equal length. Out of sheer habit if for no other ritually cogent reason, I have chosen invariably to bathe on the morning of June 24. My ritual ablution has ranged from the Oakland foothills in California to the Ganges River in Benares, India. I have had to use mucky swamps in Jelling of Jutland to the private expanse of a pristine Provençal lake. Describing our life together, based on our joint midsummer bathings and the feeling of being dragged along at "ungodly" hours in which "normal" people are still asleep and not standing naked next to cold Alpine lakes, my partner has wanted to title a proposed book *Madness at the Crack of Dawn*.

Since working in Britain, I have used both the Serpentine and, more regularly, the Thames River in London for this annual purification rite. Rising for the approximately 4:30 moment of sunrise, the city is wondrously quiet and unpeopled at that time. Even in London, I have experienced many magical moments, such as seeing a fox in Burton Court and also on the grounds of the Royal Hospital of Chelsea.

If and when I am in Bath for the solstice period, I will use the Avon River. A few days before the first occasion of bathing outside in the city of Aquae Sulis for midsummer's, I noticed some youths jumping into the river at the weir just below the Pultney Bridge. The water carried them down each level where they would then reappear before being swept down the next. *Yes!* I thought, *that is where I want to perform the midsummer ablution*.

The morning of June 24 arrived, but the weather had

decided to be typically English. On this occasion, I was solo and
wore my jogging shoes for traction as I climbed out along the
upper level of the weir. I was in my swim trunks and, because it
was so unseasonably cold, a t-shirt. But since I was about to
jump into the water, I did not wear my watch. Consequently, I
could only guess the moment the sun was reputedly at the horizon—the problem being complicated by the geographic fact
that Bath is like a bowl and surrounded by hills so that the
actual rise of the sun cannot be seen. In the bleak gray and
wintry coldness, I could just not make myself leap into the
water this moment rather than the next. Over and over again,
I kept telling myself, *Do it now!* But each time the body refused
to obey. One moment kept leading to another, and how long I
finally stood there at the head of the weir, I shall never really
know.

Eventually, I did indeed jump into the water. I knew I had to
do it, and I was only getting colder the longer I waited. Once
in, the river swiftly carried me through the aperture at the
bottom of the weir's horseshoe shape and plunged me deep
below the surface. This part was fun, and I forgot immediately
about the cold. Up I came only to be rushed through the next
level's aperture and down well below the river's surface yet
again. And after the third passing, I emerged at the base of the
weir and began to swim to the edge of the river to climb out.

But as I approached the bank, a policeman and policewoman
were waiting for me.

"What are you doing?" she asked sternly.

Now how does a Pagan in our rationalized and disenchanted
society answer that kind of question in a situation like this? My
mind raced through possible answers, but all were rejected as
unfathomably inappropriate. The policewoman asked a second
time.

Finally I replied, "I'm just having a midsummer's swim. I do
this every year."

The policeman, more empathically and almost blue in color, asked while shivering, "Isn't it cold?"

"It's not so bad once you are in the water," I answered.

"We had a call," the policewoman went on. "Someone thought there was a suicide attempt. May I see some identification?"

Climbing out of the water, naturally I did not have any ID with me. "I can produce my passport at home," I replied. And so they accompanied me to my building, but as soon as I pulled out my key and unlocked the street door, they said, "That's fine, that's all we have to see."

And so I completed my first ablution in the river Avon. It was only subsequently that I learned that people have, and have since that occasion, actually drowned in the weir due to undertows that trap them beneath the water's surface. On subsequent occasions, I have found a less prominent section of the river where I can climb down some steps to enter the water. A Pagan's life in our modern world is not necessarily an easy one.

Bath, England

ᕗ Samhain Snake Watchers
Flame RavenHawk

It was the afternoon of Samhain. I bustled back and forth between the kitchen, garage, and the fire pit area behind the house, getting set up for that evening's ritual. I was expecting company at this year's Circle, so I paid special attention to creating a space that felt welcoming: dead leaves were swept from the ring of stones that circled the cast iron fire pit, which cradled our central fire. Extra chairs were dragged out of the dusty garage, swept off, and set up around it. A painted lid placed on a cut willow tree stump became the altar. In anticipation of the piles of food it would soon hold for the feast, the picnic table was swept and covered in a festive cloth.

Remembering the previous year when even with a lively fire it was too cold to stay outside, I was grateful for the relatively mild temperatures. Here in the northeast woodlands of North America, the weather at the close of October can vary greatly from snow and freeze to balmy Indian summer. On this Samhain, however, the weather was perfect for an autumn evening around a warm fire. I soaked up the last of the late afternoon sunshine as I worked.

The path from the house to the backyard leads past an eight-foot hedge of forsythia bushes. All of their leaves had fallen, leaving the branches suitably skeletal for the season. After several trips to the fire pit and back, an unusual texture in the bare branches made me pause in midstep and take a closer look. High up in the branches of the hedge, about five feet above the ground, were two garter snakes intricately entwined with one another, motionless. Their two heads were facing the fire pit, so although they were motionless, they appeared to be watching my every move.

I froze and stood transfixed, locking gazes with the twin set of liquid black reptilian eyes. With my mind already half-dwelling within the spirit worlds, I instantly began to spin through the possible messages that these spirit sisters, the snakes, were trying to share with me.

My mind quickly darted to the Native American story of Snake Woman, whose shedding skin embodies the idea of growth, change, and rebirth. That was certainly a suitable message for the season. For millennia, snakes have served as symbols of wisdom. As the seasonal tide shifts, I seek the wisdom of my ancestors as the veil between the worlds thins. The snakes silently affirmed the energy of this time of year, so I saluted them for their watchfulness as I resumed my activity.

My rational mind then got busy trying to explain why two

snakes were nesting in bushes in late October, long past the first hard freeze of the season. Although it was a relatively mild day, I had expected that most cold-blooded creatures would have begun their winter rest by now.

The sun carved its shortened arc across the sky, and twilight fell. Still, the snakes remained watching, motionless. The altar and table were both lavishly laden with the fruits of the harvest. Carved pumpkins were placed out in the twilit yard at each of the quarters, to guard and beckon the directions. Candles were set out, and the altar was dressed with the tools that would be needed: sage to purify the space, water to cleanse it, and an athame to define it. Wood to feed the fire was stacked off to the side, and kindling was laid in the fire pit with care.

More trips from house to yard caused the contents of the picnic table to grow. I stepped back to admire the effect, when suddenly another nearby bush caught my eye. Three more snakes were in that bush, watching the sacred space from several feet farther away! Two were entwined in the forked branches several feet off the ground, and another snake was stretched out sinuously along another branch. All were facing the altar and fire pit. I circled the bush in renewed wonder at such a sight. My mind boggled at the motionless reality of snakes, many snakes, nesting in my bushes.

I now had five snakes staring inward, motionless. I stood between the fire pit and the altar, facing the two bushes that cradled the watching snakes. I realized with a little thrill of recognition that I was staring due north, where winter dwells. At once, the layered message of the watching snakes clicked into place.

The snakes were honoring our sacred space, guarding the gates of winter. Their presence was encouraging us to honor the wisdom of our ancestors and reminding us of the rebirth that comes from shedding the husks of our former selves. My skin tingled with the energy of their presence.

When my friends and family arrived for ritual that night, I

did not mention the snakes. Not everyone has lost his or her deep-rooted fears of creatures that slither and crawl, and I was concerned that some guests might feel uncomfortable with the unexpected company that had joined our Circle. As I guided our Circle through our Samhain celebration, I asked guests to write down what they needed to cast off with the old year, and we shed our woes into the fire. I passed along their message, without revealing the messenger. The temperatures fell with the setting sun. Although the fire pit warmed the people around it, the heat wouldn't have reached the bushes beyond. Even so, the snakes remained in the bushes watching the entire evening. Although it was too dark to see them clearly, a few guests spied them and gazed back in wonder.

The next day, when I returned to the fire pit to put everything away for the winter, the snakes were gone. They had guarded our passage through the gates of winter, leaving their wisdom behind them. I had been gifted with a potent Samhain message, and I carried it with me from the celebration into the new year that followed.

Upstate New York

5

SPIRIT

The God and Goddess in Our Lives

If everything in nature is connected through subtle but real energies, so, too, are we linked with the Goddess and the God. We must become more intimately familiar with this connection. We can't accomplish this by searching our bodies and asking, "Where's the Goddess? Where's the God?" They don't reside in any one part of us; They're simply within. They exist within our DNA. They're present in our souls. The Goddess and God are infused into every aspect of our beings.

—Scott Cunningham, *Living Wicca*

✎ Faces of God
Ember

My sisters, have you seen God?

I have seen God.

He is a man wearing a blood red skirt and feathers in His hair,

face painted in Life and Death.

He is an adolescent boy at 3AM feeding wood to the fire.

God is a man standing at the djun djun, silver hair around his

face like a mane, eyes closed, head thrown back.

God is turning cartwheels in the dirt.

I have seen God.

He is tall and lithe, stomping a graceful dance round the flames

with black dreds flying,

He is dancing with fans,

He is pounding a djembe with taped and bleeding hands,

His voice is hoarse with dust and ash, and He is singing.

I have seen God.

He is crying at the edge of the Circle,

He is dancing in ecstasy,

He is standing at dawn with hands upraised,

He is alive and breathing, singing,

Warrior lovers with fierce and golden hearts,

Alive, here now.

My sisters, have you seen God?

Las Vegas

❧ Solstice in Calgary

Starhawk

It is June 2003. We, the Pagan Cluster, an open group of people who bring earth-based spirituality into political actions, and thousands of other people have come to Calgary to protest the meeting of the World Trade Organization (WTO).* There is tension in the air generated by both the protestors and those who call this old city home. Previous meetings in Seattle and Genoa, and the subsequent protests to the economic and environmental damage the WTO is wreaking on the planet, have resulted in riots and violence between the protestors and the police. But conflict and fights for human rights are nothing new in Calgary.

At the Olympic Plaza, across from City Hall, stands a grouping of statues honoring the Famous Five: Emily Murphy, Henrietta Muir Edwards, Louise McKinney, Irene Parlby, and Nellie McClung. Five women who in the early 1920s won the landmark court case that officially established that women in Canada are legally, persons.

They sit, somewhat larger than life, caught in bronze, drinking tea. One lifts a glass, one peers forth earnestly, one stands and looks on, and another points as one lifts high a scroll proclaiming, "Women are persons!" They are older women, white, affluently dressed in a bronze rendition of the clothing of the 1920s, sitting in oversized chairs and drinking from giant teacups. Within their grouping, a plaque is inscribed bearing their names.

It is here we decided to do our impromptu Summer solstice ritual. A few of our organizer friends, mostly from the legal collective, just recently arrived, bringing the other members of our affinity group. This brings our count up to eleven. We

*For more information on the Pagan Cluster, go to www.pagancluster.org.

gather late, after the meetings and trainings are over, and spend time chatting among the statues who seem alive.

Finally, we make a circle, do a short grounding, and create a sacred space from within the statues who seem to be observing us, raising their cups in a silent toast. We call in the directions, the moon, and the sun. I make an offering of Waters of the World to the spirits of the land, asking for permission to do our ritual here. The opera house is letting out across the street, and a few individuals stop and stare. A couple of homeless people wander by, and a group of teenage boys stand and laugh. A bearded homeless man who looks like a worn-out version of an ancient prophet wanders to the edge of the circle. As I ask the spirits for help and support in the action, the prophet beams at us, raising a hand in benediction. I am thinking about fairy tales where the gods appear as beggars. I know that our call has been answered.

We have decided to work two pieces of linked magic. The first is to create a vortex, a drain for the fear we feel swirling around us here in the center of Calgary. Our intent is to siphon off the fear that is being dumped on the city daily, the warnings about protestors being terrorists, the cautions by the police to people who would rent to us that their houses will be bombed if they do, the instructions to all teachers and school personnel not to talk to us, and the whole usual boring campaign of criminalization that is being used to justify the crackdown on all of our rights and freedoms.

The second is to form a counterforce to the drain. We need to create a wand or opposite pole, something that can draw in and ground positive forces, hope, vision, courage, justice, love of liberty, and truth.

We begin chanting the wordless A-O-O-A chant that opens the gates between the worlds. Charles, one of the collective, steps out of the circle to walk the edge to guard us and our possessions as we slip quickly into trance.

The vortex opens up immediately. It's like a giant whirlpool, flowing both clockwise, like water down a drain, and counter-clockwise, the direction of releasing. It's sucking fear out of us, out of the city, out of the rest of the world. I suddenly become aware of how much fear we walk through every day, how it clouds our vision and slows our steps, like walking through a heavy, gray, toxic snowfall. And what it would be like to be fear-less, weightless, dancing in a world of clarity, doing what we needed and wanted to do without the clutching sense of dread. Earlier in the night, during our direct action training, we were discussing tear gas, pepper spray, rubber bullets, tasers, cattle prods, and all the other weapons that might be used against us. "Remember, they are all weapons of fear," Charles had said. If we truly drain the fear, if we don't respond out of fear, all the weapons are disarmed.

"If you are fearless, you are invincible," I hear. I am thinking of the ride to Nablus a few weeks back when I was in Palestine with the International Solidarity Movement, which supports nonviolent resistance to the Occupation in the Occupied Ter-ritories of Palestine. We were making our way to Balata, a besieged Palestinian refugee camp, to be peace witnesses and try to safeguard the human rights of the people there. We were talking about what level of risk we were willing to take. "I'm willing to die," Neta had said. We'd had a long talk the night before, about her month in Yasser Arafat's besieged compound in Ramallah, with little food or water. She was there with other internationals committed to peace—sitting with Arafat's own security forces armed with Kalashnikovs—prepared to fight a war. Neta had been telling me about one of her friends, how much he loved and enjoyed life, and how completely he was ready to die. They all were: they faced the daily, moment-to-moment reality of their imminent death. Her face was glowing and her eyes shined as she described how they fed the wounded first and shared the food they had and the love they felt for each other.

"And after enough time expecting to die," Neta said, "you start to want to run out and meet it. To grab a rifle and go out under fire and just say, 'Okay, kill me.'"

Caoimhe, another friend who was also there, hated it. She felt trapped in a place that she was not supposed to be, unable to get out and be with her own close friends who were being massacred in Jenin. She was far, far more cynical about what was going on, insisting that Arafat and his close guard were eating well upstairs.

The others in our group in the van to Nablus agreed that we are willing to risk our lives, that we have accepted the possibility that we could die in this work. "But I'd be really, really pissed!" I said. "I am willing to give my life for the cause, but I would need a lot, lot, lot of convincing that my death would be anywhere near as valuable as my life. Or yours, Neta, or yours or yours."

All of this is swirling in my mind as the vortex grows, and I think about suicide bombers, who are so fearless because they seek death that they become unstoppable. And how much trickier it is to become fearless while seeking life. Yet, that is what I believe we are called to do. I am still in a state of awe, gratitude, and wonder just from the kids in the training—some of them totally new to any form of protest, and scared, and some of them veterans of Quebec City or even Genoa who are back, again and again, as if some cosmic hand has tapped them and said, "You! I want you as one of my agents of transformation."

The chant swells and ebbs and I think about the pole, the wand of the ancient wizard I saw in a dream. He was teaching a group of us how to use a wizard's staff. It had to be thick, wide, he warned us, not a skinny little branch that would break under pressure. "If you think this is powerful when it's not activated," he'd said, "when it's awakened it can move mountains!"

We need some mountains moved, desperately. "Where I'm going, I can't take a staff," I had said to him in the dream, thinking about actions and jails.

"You can use mine, as an inner image," he said.

I picture it rising out of the vortex. It becomes a pillar of fire, that becomes the trunk of a tree, its roots a web of fire in the core of the earth, its branches reaching up beyond the highest heavens, alive to draw down sunlight and moonlight, alive with squirrels and birds and animals. I look around the circle. We are all having the same visions.

I sense movement behind me. Two homeless people are standing there, an aboriginal man and a slight, old woman with short gray hair who is holding Charles's hand and dancing to the music. Suddenly, I feel that she should come into the center and dance. She steps into the circle and Charles moves to gently guide her away but I shake my head and he lets her go. She begins to dance.

She is completely, utterly drunk but her dance is clear, graceful, and beautiful, an uncensored movement of the energies we are raising, a spontaneous ballet. Her face is still, enraptured, her hands and arms become precise, expressive; her feet keep the rhythm as her hips sway. I am thinking of a ritual long ago when I took on the aspect of the Baba Yaga, the ugly old hag witch of Russian fairy tales, who told us, "Once I had a beautiful face!" I think that it has been a long time since anyone has seen this woman's beauty, and I am silently cheering for her, because she has become the hag who when embraced becomes the beautiful Goddess of the land, the Crone, the ancient, unloved, broken, hurting, drunk, and battered Earth herself, taking visible form for us, drinking in our attention, admiration, and love.

When the chant ends, and the dance is over, she throws herself into Laura's arms. "It's been so long," she sighs. "So long since I've been loved."

She tells us she is going to change her life. I am old and wise enough to know this may or may not last, that the woman in her finite, human life may or may not take this love and go the tremendous distance she would need to go to heal. She has become, for a moment, the Goddess in visible form for us. That is the promise, after all, of the Pagan gods, that they will actually manifest if we have eyes to see them. We have witnessed a true miracle.

We ground the energy. I look up and catch the eye of the statue of one of the Famous Five who was a pillar of the Women's Christian Temperance Union. I tell the others and we all laugh.

So here we are, in staid, conservative Calgary, with a vortex established, the gates between the worlds propped open, the military massing, and the action gathering, on the longest day of the year.

Calgary, Canada

ᨘ Spirals
Eve LeFey

There are many theories about the significance of spirals found etched in the pre-Christian megaliths—those giant mystical standing stones that mark sacred sites and burial mounds—of ancient Ireland. Some say the sets of two spirals that connect to each other like a swirling yin-yang symbol represent the sun, one in winter, and one in summer. Others say they represent the male-female duality of nature. Perhaps the spirals are the mathematical pattern etched by the earth's course around the sun in a year, and the spirals etched on the doorway of Newgrange, an ancient passage tomb in county Meath, Ireland, indicate the solstice. Indeed, this theory is backed up by the natural occurrence of the sun beaming directly into an otherwise dark chamber on the very hour of the winter solstice. It's also been said that the spirals have religious or mythological significance—that the triple spiral, for instance, is the Maiden, Mother, and Crone aspects of the Goddess. There's even a biological theory: each spiral in a triskele (three spirals connected in the center) represents a trimester in a pregnancy. I personally think there's truth to all of these—after all, a symbol as old and rich as a spiral must have had many meanings for many people over the centuries, and so how is any *one* person to define a symbol? For me, however, the spiral has a very different significance.

The day was unusually sunny and warm—the tour guide at the visitor's center who was to take us to Newgrange told us we were very lucky to have come when we did as the weather was lovely and it was still pretourist season. We thanked him as though he were responsible for these phenomena. We were wide-eyed and ready for mystery as he led us down a trail to the ancient burial mound. The air smelled clear, green, and blue. A light breeze tickled my skin, but I let the lambswool wrap I had bought on Inis Maan remain open, and its soft fringes fluttered freely. I silently regretted not bringing my little travel harp with me that day. I wanted to hear what its strings had to say about this marvelous place.

I felt my mind drifting back to New York, and scolded it. *I'm on vacation,* I told myself, closing my eyes and inhaling the clean East Irish wind. *Not the time to worry now.* But the mind can often be a stubborn child, and it stomped its foot and forced me to listen. *No!* It said. *You have bills to pay! How are you going to pay your bills if you spend all your time playing music? It's time to be an adult! To be responsible!*

We crossed a little wooden bridge that draped itself casually over the River Boyne. I tried to reason with my brain. *But I'm on vacation,* I pleaded again. *And I can't give up music! It would be like giving up my voice.* I looked over the bridge and saw the sunlight dancing on the water like silver fairies. I wanted to stop, to write a song for the river. But my friend, anxious to get to our destination, urged me on and I followed.

The spirals of Newgrange greeted us, spotlit by the sun, and the stone doorway whispered ancient secrets in a language that could not be heard, only felt. The ancient rocks were cold to the touch, and the interior buzzed with energy. I tried to concentrate on what the tour guide was saying, but my attention kept drifting inward. The voice in my head started to sound like the creditor that had been leaving messages for me every week back home. The chamber started to become too close, dark, and uncomfortable. The tour guide's voice became a slow, warped drone. Feeling trapped, I closed my eyes to keep from panicking. *Be an adult, Eve. It's time to grow up! Get a real job. Work isn't supposed to be fun, that's why they call it work!*

When after what seemed like forever we were given permission to go outside and explore a bit, I walked around the monolith and touched the stones. I put my ear to them to hear what they had to say. I closed my eyes and let my fingertips grope along the etched spirals as though they were messages written in Braille. I asked the spirals questions. Questions about my path, about my purpose on Earth, about my career choices, about my dreams and whether they would come true. I silently poured my deepest desires into the stones, my loves, my passions, my fears. I begged of them to tell me their secrets, to give me just one precious tidbit of their ancient and vast wisdom. The stones, however, said nothing.

I sighed, feeling slightly disappointed and more than a little ridiculous, and wandered away from my friend and the rest of our tour group, who were meditating or discussing mythology with the guide. I wandered back down the path. Back to the bridge.

Leaning over the side of the bridge, I once again let my eyes drink the sunlight sparkling on the river. I watched the movement of the current under the bridge and was pleasantly surprised to see a familiar symbol right there in front of me: spirals! Dozens of them. They swirled toward and against each other, deosil and widdershins, just like they did in the etchings on the stones. Then they would spiral away and be replaced by new spirals that would move just a little differently than their predecessors. I watched, amused, as the spirals danced for me and it wasn't long before I felt my eyes blur a little, my brain slipping into that place in between consciousness and dream. I feel the sensation of my body being pulled toward the water.

Deep, deep into the river I sank. I could feel the water filling me, blending with my blood, carrying me to another place, moving to my rhythm. The sun shining through the water sent a beam of light down to the depths below, and from behind that beam appeared Boyne, the goddess of the River that is named for her. She wore a gown that matched the water's blue, with trim the color of the sun's silver-white reflection. Her hair was a silky mass of spiral currents in motion, her skin translucent and lovely like a clear pool. Her voice was tinkly like the high treble of a zen desk fountain. She smiled as she spoke, and her expression held wisdom, maternal love, and maidenly wonder all at once. "You are a maker of music," she said. "And you are a teller of stories. Follow your passions and do not judge yourself so harshly. When you let go of fear and are true to yourself, the rest will come. You must learn to trust your own heart. Remember to love yourself as we do. And know that we read every word and we hear every note." She gently pushed me upward, and like a child on a swing I rose back to the surface of the river.

As I walked back toward the monolith, I thought of all those old Irish stories where the faery/goddess/otherworld-creature gives the human a stone or a feather or some other token. When the people in the stories woke up, they still had the gift in their hand, so they knew it wasn't "just a dream." I glared at my empty palm, sighed, and started looking for my group. When I got to the ancient structure once more, they weren't there so I turned around, crossed the bridge, went up the trail, and back to the visitor's center where we started. My friend came running up to me. "Where the hell have you been?" she squealed. "We've been looking for you for an hour!"

"I was on the bridge, meditating." I said.

"We crossed that bridge a dozen times and we didn't see you. Where were you really?"

I thought for a moment, remembering the stories and said with a smile, "With a goddess, I suppose. In the Other World."

My friend (a non-Pagan) rolled her eyes and said, "Come on, I'm starving. Let's go get some fish and chips." So we did.

As for my token, which I only discovered upon reflection, I wear it proudly on my back, right over the chakra at the base of my spine, in the form of a tattoo—a triple spiral with Celtic knotwork around it. Whenever I feel fear or doubt, or I forget what my purpose here on Earth is, I look in the mirror, and I see the gift the goddess Boyne gave me. I feel it tingling at the root of my body, always in motion, a current in my soul. And I remember.

Brooklyn, New York

ᕫ Initiation of the Little Witch That Couldn't
Rowan HawkMoon

Last spring, at Beltane, I received initiation at Circle Sanctuary with Selena Fox. The ritual was everything an initiation should be: transformative and heartfelt. There has only been one other ritual that for me resonated deeper or was more empowering. It was a circle held at the dark of the moon, the eve before my formal initiation rite.

The months prior to my initiation were very stressful. Initiation is a very serious and important step, one that engenders much introspection and reflection. I had been struggling for some time with the issue of personal and magical power, and I questioned whether or not I had any. I doubted that, by merely concentrating, I could manifest and move energy to affect magical change.

One of my friends recently said of me, "She shimmers." But to myself, the image gazing out of the mirror most certainly does not shine.

One of the keys to working magic is to still the mind until the intent is the only focus. But meditation didn't come easy to me. My brain constantly swirled around with ideas and questions.

Connecting with the Elements was also very difficult . . . except for the element Air. Air is associated with the mind, thought, and clear vision. As a computer systems analyst, I spend most of my work day in my head, problem solving. Yes, in that way, Air was an old friend.

Nor did I feel "touched" by the Goddess. Everyone around me had these wondrous stories of personal interaction with the Goddess; seeing Her at the foot of their bed during a serious illness, hearing Her voice, being filled with Her presence. I had experienced none of this. At one point, feeling sorry for myself and discouraged, I referred to myself as the "little witch that couldn't."

One of my favorite chants goes, "She changes everything She touches, and everything She touches changes." Little did I know that I, too, was in for some changes.

In the past few years, I have been blessed with many magical people in my life. But the greatest and most important of these is my spirit sister, Holly. Where she is the full moon, I am the dark. Her totem, the great horned owl, is the nighttime equivalent of my totem, the red-tailed hawk. We finish each other's sentences, use the same quirky word at exactly the same moment, and are connected with a bond that defies logic and explanation.

As my initiation loomed on the calendar horizon, I voiced

my concerns to Holly. I told her that I felt disconnected from the Goddess, magic, and even the world around me. I felt as though I had a big feather pillow wrapped around my head. I couldn't meditate, the right words for my dedication oath eluded me, and I didn't feel any particular Goddess calling me to Her service. I wanted to be ready spiritually and emotionally for this important rite but no matter how hard I worked to prepare for it, instead of feeling closer to the Goddesss, I felt further away. I even told her that I felt like a poseur, a fraud, an impostor and that I was considering canceling my initiation.

First, she slapped me upside my head with a dose of reality. She reminded me that the Goddess works in her own time, that She is about inspiration, about planting seeds and waiting for them to sprout. She told me to remember things happen as they are meant to. Impatience just doesn't work with the Goddess.

Holly suggested I was, perhaps, making too big a deal over initiation. She stressed initiation was not an epiphany, just a semipublic affirmation of what I was already doing: walking the Path and following the Goddess. She then reminded me I had *The Goddess Oracle** and suggested I draw a card to see what message it revealed.

That night I unboxed the cards and sat with them on my lap. I read through the accompanying book while studying the pictures in the deck. Each goddess in the deck has a beautiful picture and poem associated with her. Some include simple rituals or meditations. I cleared my mind as best I could and started shuffling through the cards. I didn't formulate a specific problem or pose a specific question. I figured She would know what I needed.

The card I chose was Lilith, who "appears to tell you to take back your power." I read her poem and her story and

---

*Amy Sophia Marashinsky, *The Goddess Oracle* (Rockport, Mass: Element, 1997); illustrations (copyright) Hrana Janto, 1997.

contemplated the possible significances it held. I journaled my thoughts and impressions: "I do not see the power within me— I do not see the shimmering. And because I do not see it, I do not believe that it exists . . . maybe I do not see it because to see it means I would have to acknowledge it and then use it."

I put Lilith's picture in a frame and placed it where I could see it first thing in the morning and the last thing at night. Words from her Goddess oracle lesson kept coming to mind, "The way to wholeness for you now lies in acknowledging that you're not connecting with your power, then coming to terms with and accepting your power."

In *The Goddess Oracle*, the Lilith card includes an unbinding ritual: A cord is tied around the body part that symbolically corresponds with the area you wish to strengthen. For example, low self-esteem could be seen as the inability to walk in power. To represent this, you might tie a cord around one or both of your ankles. If you have trouble speaking your truth, you might tie the cord around your neck. The bindings are tied on at the full moon to be contemplated on as the moon wanes. The bindings are removed at the new moon and, with the release, there is a reclaiming of the lost power.

Holly, who was teaching me how to spin wool, suggested that I spin my bindings. That felt perfect, especially since the wool I would be spinning was shorn from her sheep. At the full moon, I spun the fiber with intention. I put into the twist of the yarn all of my doubts and negativity. While I worked I chanted. Sometimes I said, "No more doubts, no more fears." Other times, I repeated the opening lines of Lilith's poem, "I dance my life for myself, I am whole, I am complete."

When the binding cord was completed, I tied a piece around each of my wrists and my left ankle in a simple ritual. I wore my bindings for two weeks. Whenever I felt the cord around my ankle, I would silently affirm that I walk in power, that I am not inferior to others. Whenever I saw the cord around my left wrist, I would tell myself that I will accept power in whatever form it may manifest itself. The binding on my right wrist reminded me that I will use this power in positive and beneficial ways.

The dark moon was the night before my Initiation. I planned to cut my bonds at Holly's stone circle on her farm. I am somewhat of an overachiever and a perfectionist. Usually, my rituals are perfectly scripted and choreographed. Before the start of the ceremony, each Quarter call and invocation is written and polished in advance. If there are other participants, they know where to stand and what to say. But this time it didn't feel right to sit and write things in advance.

The night of my unbinding was overcast but no storms were predicted. I walked out to the circle while Holly went to make sure the motion-sensor lights were turned off as the movement of a passing animal could trigger it and we didn't want the floodlights to go on unexpectedly.

As I approached the circle, I saw a flash of light out of the corner of my eye. I assumed it was just Holly turning off the inside lights. I stood in the middle of the circle with my heart beating fast and my body trembling with excitement and anticipation. When Holly joined me at the circle, I told her I didn't know exactly what I was going to do, but she should just jump in when she felt it was right. Again, there was a brief flash of light.

I called to the Guardians of the directions, and the wind started to pick up. I called to the spirit of the Elements, and thunder started to roll. I called to my ancestors. I called to the spirit of the wise and powerful ones who have gone before. I called to the spirit of the wise and powerful ones yet to be. Lightning started to flash. I called to the dark moon. I called to the spirit of this land on which I stand and the animals who dwell on it.

As I turned slowly in the circle with my arms upraised, I called to every deity I could think of, regardless of pantheon.

I called to the Green Man, Pan, Thor, Odin, Zeus, and Poseidon. I called to Kore, Persephone, Diana, and Demeter. I called to Yemaya, Oya, Kuan Yin, Amaterasu, White Buffalo woman, Spider woman, and Ixchel. I called to Cerridwen, Kali, the Morrigan, Bast, Hestia, Inanna, Shakti, Pele, and Tara. I called to Lilith, who enlightens me. I called to Brigid, who inspires me, to Isis, who mothers me, and to Hecate, who guides my path. I called to Gaia, who is all around all of us. I asked all of them to join our circle and to attend to and witness the rebirth of their daughter.

With each completed turn of my body, the lightning flashed more frequently and more intensely. Long, jagged fingers lit up the dark sky. The thunder rolled and rumbled around us and I needed to shout to be heard above it. The wind raced through the trees and their branches danced above our heads. A light mist filled the air, but rain had not started to fall. Gaia's voice, the wind chime in Her namesake tree, sang in the background. In the lightning flashes I could see Holly's face—awestruck, joyous, amazed, and shining with the light of the Goddess. I knew I must look the same to her. I had not expected, nor was I prepared for this level of response to our ritual.

In a loud voice, I proclaimed that I had come here to claim my power; that the cords I wore symbolized my hesitancy, my fear, and my doubts; and that tonight with this ritual I released, relinquished, and banished the emotions that held me back.

As Holly cut each cord, I named what I was releasing and the power I was reclaiming. She cut the cord on my ankle and I released all doubts and acknowledged and accepted that I walk in strength. She cut the cord on my left wrist, and I released all misgivings in accepting that I am a daughter of the Goddess and that as such I hold divine feminine power within me. She cut the cord on my right wrist and I released all fear of using my abilities and asked the Goddess to walk with me and guide me and to help me to fully use my potential.

We placed the cut bindings in a metal cauldron and burned

them. At the end of the ritual, I thanked all the deities and the Elements and the Watchtowers. The lightning stopped, the thunder faded away, and the wind died down.

Holly took my face in her hands and said, "And now it begins." As we left the circle, the rain finally started to fall, picking up in intensity. We went inside. The rain continued for a long while.

Watertown, Wisconsin

ᐑ How I Ignored Common Sense and Backed into the Morrigan
Grey Cat

For a long, long time, my only real connection with deity was the Great Cosmic two-by-four* wielded by an unknown figure I call Nudge. It was a pretty one-sided relationship; she indicated what she thought I should do and I cussed a bit and did it. This all changed at a Pagan Unity Festival (PUF) a couple years ago. Isaac Bonewits, the founder and past Archdruid of the Ar n'Draoicht Fein (ADF),† had volunteered to provide the main ritual when prior arrangements fell through. Since I had some experience in the ADF ritual forms, I offered to help and he accepted my offer.

I printed out all the information on Isaac's Web site on ritual, made sure I knew and understood it, and went to PUF feeling confident I could hold up my end of things. Isaac

---

*A popular idiom dealing with the rather clear hints from a deity when he or she feels you aren't paying attention. It comes from the old story about hitting a mule with a two-by-four to get his attention.

†For more information on Pagan Unity Festival, see www.paganunityfestival. org; for more information on Isaac Bonewits, see www.neopagan.net; for more information on Ar n'Draoicht Fein, see www.adf.org.

designs each ritual with feedback from probable participants during workshops leading up to the ritual. I don't remember which male deity Isaac decided to invoked but the female chosen was the Morrigan, warrior Goddess of the Irish, a deity I've always admired but not studied with any great dedication (I don't generally work with the Celtic pantheon). The morning of the ritual my voice was showing a lot of strain due to talking outdoors on damp evenings. Friends started worrying about whether or not I'd be able to take a leading role in the ritual with this much trouble with my voice. I assured everyone that it wouldn't be a problem. Meanwhile, I'm wondering why I'm so sure it will all go all right because I'm sounding like a boy breaking from soprano to bass.

So I go on through that damp and not very warm Saturday feeling totally confident about the ritual although, despite my understanding of it, I'd certainly never helped lead an ADF ritual before and my voice was getting worse and worse. As part of this, in conformation with normal ADF practice, it would be necessary for me to summon the Goddess in the name of my Irish ancestress, Mary O'Brian—and this somehow wasn't entirely comfortable for me. I was beginning to get the feeling that this wouldn't be a routine evening.

For example, ADF rituals are frequently long, with this one lasting around two and a half hours—almost two hours longer than I design. Still, no one was bored, and my voice was holding out with no problems other than the time some smoke from the ritual fire wreathed my head.

The usual pattern of an ADF ritual is to invoke deity and then to make offerings of some sort to them, generally through one of the bardic gifts—a song, poem, performance, a painting, or a drawing—as well as through such things as incense, lighted candles, and so on. My gift was my yearly reaffirmation of my third-degree oath, which is presented in the form of a brag, the words taken from a number of sources. In American folklore, the keelboatmen on the Mississippi would introduce themselves with a brag, such as, "I'm the son of an alligator and a water moccasin and I can whop any five men." Technically, the keelboatman was making a promise rather than relating actual history. This literary device is also found in some Celtic stories. There were an unusually large number of people making offerings and miraculously, none of the poems were embarrassing.

The power in the ritual area was entirely visible and I was extremely relieved to note that the young woman supporting the world tree, the conduit directing the power to the Gods, was handling it without strain.

The divination portion of the ritual, which is there to bring the messages of the Gods to those present, was amazing. The individual who did the divination is remarkable at any time, but what she was getting was quite out of the ordinary and not applicable to me. Though I don't remember the specifics, I do recall her prediction of two babies!

Almost from the beginning of the ceremony, I was beginning to realize that the Morrigan had, so to speak, claimed me as her own. How did I know? Well, I didn't get a vision, hear a voice, or anything quite that clear; it was something I simply knew, just as you know where your hand is. I have since thought that it's probable that the Morrigan has been *my* Goddess all along and what happened that night was primarily her showing me her face. In most ways, this hasn't made enormous changes in my life. For the first time, I felt inclined to have a small shrine (some people call it an altar) set up. Actually, it's on the top shelf of my computer hutch. I got a new pentacle with a crow on it (crows represent the Morrigan). I'm less likely to simply invoke the "Goddess." I now know why I see crows so often and from time to time I have a group (a murder of crows) around my house.

In another way, working with the Morrigan has made an

enormous change. I'm genetically predisposed to depression. Particularly since my back quit working right, I've been fighting large quantities of that mental condition. I began to feel a lot better once I learned that hydrocodone pain medication was causing my depression to be much worse, but I've actually lived with it for so long that when it suddenly went away, it's been a bit difficult to adjust to. For one thing, I never knew I was a moody person. When your moods are either lousy or worse, you don't get much practice coping. It is my impression that the Morrigan considered depression an efficiency problem and simply made it go away; certainly, she has made no effort to help me cope with the changes of being un-depressed! However, my observations have tended to indicate that none of our Pagan deities will help with a problem you can handle yourself.

It's a little difficult for a practical person such as myself to talk about having a meeting with an entity out of mythology. I don't think of myself as a visionary sort of person and I've always tended to listen to stories about this sort of thing with a certain amount of skepticism. I don't think, actually, I'll give up that skepticism; we all know of well-publicized occasions when some individual has been convinced he or she received a message from his or her deity of choice and has proceeded to follow those instructions to the detriment of others. I remain skeptical of my own experience. However, call it intuition, communication with deity, or release of inborn power of the human mind—I listen but make my own decisions. As a Wiccan teacher, I emphasize to my students that ours is foremost a religion of personal responsibility. No deity can relieve me of it and, therefore, all my actions must be based on my own choices. My actions are my own responsibility regardless of what the source may seem to be or actually is.

Pagan Unity Festival, Nashville

❧ Self-Dedication
Marilyn R. Pukkila

On the morning of the Vernal Equinox of 1999, in the stone circle known as Castlerigg just outside of Keswick in the Lake District in England, I dedicated myself to the Goddess Persephone. I had known Persephone since I was ten; I can still hear the voice of my mother's mother reading me Her story from Ingrid d'Aulaire and Edgar Parin d'Aulaire's *Book of Greek Myths*. Her abduction by Hades that ends with her seasonal descent and return from the Underworld is the heart of the Elysian mysteries. Many years later, with the help of a guide, I lived through Her story and found some surprising new twists.

It was pouring rain, it being spring in the Lake District, and there were people coming and going. I had had only about three hours of sleep the night before and was still jet-lagged and worried about all the driving I had to do that day. Other than the pendant I would use as a talisman for my dedication, I brought no tools. I had decided to commit myself to Persephone as restorer of balance. As I spoke words of dedication to myself and to All Those Who were present, I heard in my heart, "Sometimes it is necessary to go to extremes to restore balance."

Still, I did wonder if the dedication "took." I arrived home in Maine from England at midnight, to find water pouring through the ceiling of my study. The storm had blown the flashing off the roof, and it had been raining in for about three hours. I had visited several sacred springs on that trip to England; I really hadn't wanted to find one in my study!

This event (which a friend later described as "being psychologically raped by the weather") was the final stone in an emotional cairn that had been building slowly but steadily over the preceding nine (yes, nine!) months. I found myself in the depths of a full-blown depression (a Persephone event if ever there was one). After two weeks, I began to realize that my chief needs were to grieve my losses, my mother's increasing dementia and the sale of my childhood home, and to recover my trust in a universe of uncertainty, so I decided to seek counseling.

As I spoke to my counselor, she sorted through all of my losses, seed by seed. She then centered on the one that I thought I had released long ago and had only mentioned as an afterthought. "I want you to bring in your violin sometime," she said. The resulting wave of emotion just about drowned me then and there. I started playing when I was ten years old. Then, at the age of thirty-three, I developed tendonitis, which stopped my violin playing in its tracks. Nine years later, I wasn't sure if I could bring myself to open the case. I certainly didn't know if I could play again, though I'd been treating the tendonitis for years and had seen improvement if not complete healing.

But my counselor was right. More right than she could have known. A few weeks later, I opened up the case and began to play. Just long tones at first, and then I started the "Ashokan Farewell," a piece made famous by Ken Burns's *Civil War* series. I'd never played it before, or seen the music; there were parts of it I couldn't hear in my head, but my fingers knew the notes as though they'd written them. I played and played, and then I set down my violin and wept. A part of me that had been lost for years was reborn beyond my dreams, or even my conscious desires.

And, as so often happens, She came bearing other gifts, not just the one I'd lost. She brought me a new understanding: While it is the womb of the Woman that gives birth, it is the tomb/womb of the Crone that gives rebirth. Truly, Persephone had returned and restored my balance.

Waterville, Maine

ॐ Under the Protection of Ma Kali
Black Lotus

I am a Gardnerian Witch who often works with the Hindu pantheon.

For many years, I was employed at a Welfare Center in New York City. As you can imagine, working with clients who often view the civil servant behind the protective screen as the enemy who controls their economic fate can be very stressful. I received several threats on my life from clients. In response, I put a framed postcard of Kali, the goddess of change and transformation on my desk—I felt I needed Her protection.

I was serving a client at the window when Ms. Ruiz, a supervisor visiting from another floor noticed the image. She stared angrily at the picture, her mouth pressed in disapproval, her eyes wide in shock and disgust. She stood for a second, holding her breath, before growling loudly, "What is SHE doing here? She's demonic! Look, she's stomping on and killing her husband, and she's wearing the heads of her previous husbands around her neck. Ugh!" She slammed the picture facedown on my desk and stormed out of the room.

After helping the client, I quietly returned to my desk relieved the glass frame was still intact. "I gather Ms. Ruiz was upset with my picture of Ma Kali?" I said to another coworker.

She replied affirmatively.

"Oh, well—Kali has that effect sometimes," I explained. "She frightens away demonic beings."

We both exploded in mutually contagious giggles.

They say a Christian missionary in India once approached a Kali worshipper and asked how she could feel devotion to such a gory and outré image. The Hindu picked up the missionary's crucifix, examined the image of the tortured, dying Jesus, and asked how he could wear such an icon and ask her that question.

New York City

❧ Birthing Death
Caroline Tully

I have given birth twice, but I only have one living child. Before going through the process myself, I had assumed that pregnancy and birth were uncomplicated, Goddess-given activities that women just "did." I'd read all about Great Mother Goddesses, fertility cults, and women's mysteries—and lots of my friends had children—so surely reproduction was as easy as falling off a log.

Jasper was conceived sometime near Yule 1999 and born two weeks before Mabon 2000. Being our first child, we were pretty excited, so we marked the stages of his gestation at each of our Sabbat rites. The pregnancy seemed to be progressing along fine and I planned to have a natural birth at a nearby hospital. The day before my due date, however, I was diagnosed with preeclampsia—high blood pressure, swollen feet and hands, and protein in the urine. This meant the end of the "natural" birth. Labor was induced immediately. I recall during the labor just hoping I would get through the process alive and in the end, after a forceps delivery, I was lucky enough to be presented with a chubby, healthy baby boy.

But the drama didn't stop there! Next, my uterus refused to contract, so the midwives literally had to pummel it, expelling lots of clotted blood each time, until it started to shrink. The midwives estimated I lost 1.6 liters of blood at delivery, which apparently is quite a lot (the human body contains 5.6 liters). In my rather dazed state, it began to dawn on me just how easy it would be to die giving birth. My blood pressure, which had been skyrocketing during labor, now became dangerously low, and as the nurses bustled around trying to revive me with oxygen, I mentally withdrew into myself—I'd really had enough of the whole birthing thing by that point. It was during this weird time that I had a vision of the Goddess Kali, the Hindu Goddess of death and annihilation.

Kali appeared in vivid Technicolor, rather like a slide image projected on the far wall of the delivery room. Adorned with a skirt of severed arms, a necklace of freshly cut heads, earrings made from children's corpses, and wearing serpentine bracelets, she was dancing at the end of the world under a blood-red sky. This was hardly the nurturing, fecund image of deity that I associated with childbirth, but then my labor had not exactly been straightforward and assured of success. Two of Kali's four arms held a sword and a severed head, while the other two made the gestures of dispelling fear and offering boons—was she going to behead me or grant me life?

Without speaking, the Goddess conveyed an understanding about blood equaling life—the bloody uterine chalice, the precious liquid passed from parent to child, the river of generation spewing out of the cosmic cauldron, the potent elixir of perpetuity—I was a link in the chain of existence, a bead on the necklace of rebirth, and a skull adorning Kali's gruesome garland. I saw my body as a vessel: I had given lifeblood, provided nourishment, and enabled a new being to incarnate. Kali showed me death but granted me life.

After the birth drama was over and I lay in a hospital bed with my new baby, the Goddess Artemis appeared. Hovering transparently in midair, she oscillated back and forth between her human guise and the form of a big brown bear. Wordlessly, she expressed her nature as being the one who grants or withholds success in childbirth, the Goddess who allows mothers to live but who also kills them. I suppose she had come to see the result of letting me live, making sure I knew who to thank. I was aware that in the ancient world, one of Artemis's roles was to oversee the transition from girlhood to motherhood and although I was far from being a young girl, I was nevertheless going through a rite of passage specifically sacred to her. I was

both bemused and pleased to be having another Goddess
epiphany.

I became pregnant with my second baby around Lammas 2002.
I felt very clever and mused about being an alchemical instru-
ment mixing male and female essences together to create
something new—I was the cucurbit! The first two months were
characterized by a vile morning sickness, but after the beginning of the third month the nausea ceased and not long afterward I thought I detected movement—always comforting to a
pregnant woman—but no sooner had I started to expect the
movement than it seemed to stop.

My confidence waned but I put it down to paranoia. One
night, however, I had a vivid nightmare: In the dream, I went
into the bathroom and, after going to the toilet, began pulling
on a large red membrane, which seemed to be emerging from
my vagina. It came right out and panicking, I called my partner.
He held up the sheetlike membrane and turned it around; as
he did so we saw that stuck to the other side was a little white
skeleton. My heart sank, this was an ill omen for sure. After
waking, I chose to ignore the dream, but the apparent lack of
fetal movement did bug me.

At almost five months' gestation, I noticed an extremely
heavy secretion of mucus, which is not entirely unusual in pregnancy, but this seemed abnormal. At my next hospital appoint-
ment, I was assured that there was nothing to worry about, but
I still felt concerned. The midwife also had trouble finding the
fetal heartbeat, eventually detecting it very low down on my
abdomen, which seemed strange to me. She didn't think it was
a problem, however, and after talking with her for a while I was
reassured that the baby was alive and the heartbeat sounded
normal. I went home feeling slightly more confident.

The next day I planned to do some leisurely book reading.
In the past few weeks, I had developed an intense interest in
Goddess figurines from Ice Age art, specifically the Venus of

Willendorf, who had started to appear to me regularly in visions, and I hoped that this might indicate some sort of connection or favor that boded well for my pregnancy. I intended spending the day looking at photographs of various figurines, gazing at and meditating on their ample forms. Before getting down to it, I took a toilet break and it was then that I felt a strange pressure in my pelvic floor. Just on a whim, I stood up and inserted one finger into my vagina—imagine my horror when I actually felt something bulging downward from my uterus. I checked again, confirming my worst fears, something was definitely wrong, so my partner and I rushed to the hospital.

My cervix was dilating and I would miscarry unless I had a cervical stitch. All that mucus had been the cervical plug that keeps the womb sterile during pregnancy—it had fallen out. There was a chance that a cervical stitch, like a drawstring, might hold the womb closed, but it wasn't guaranteed. If the cervix continued to open, I would have to give birth to a baby who would die. (My baby was only twenty weeks old; the earliest a premature baby can be saved is twenty-three weeks.) For the rest of the night, I lay prone on the bed, hoping fervently that my cervix would stay shut.

A morning ultrasound revealed that the baby was descending into the birth canal; it was too late for the stitch. The worst part was that he was alive, vigorous, and perfectly healthy, but didn't stand a chance outside the womb. I was grief-stricken; it was so unjust, so wrong. I felt totally abandoned by the Goddess. Was this some sort of horrible punishment? Hadn't I appreciated the gift of pregnancy enough? There was no alternative but to push him out. It didn't take long, a few strenuous pushes and I felt a jellylike mass emerge from my vagina. I knew it was the baby in his amniotic bag, but I felt like I had given birth to a frog, a bird, or a bat. He was a lovely looking baby, but he died after about half an hour. We didn't name him, it just didn't seem appropriate at the time.

I felt cheated, robbed, bitter, bewildered, and sadder than I have ever been—definitely the worst experience in my life.

For the next two months, I was desperate to begin another pregnancy. Then, all of a sudden, the motherhood hormones dried up, disappeared, and a strange new "me" emerged. Cynical and morbid, I immersed myself in thoughts about the Underworld, spiritualism, poison, murder, and black magick. I was furious at the Venus of Willendorf—she could go to Tartarus!!! Who did she think she was, appearing to me in the weeks before my miscarriage like that? Why had she been hovering semitransparently in front of my eyes all that time? Wasn't she supposed to help pregnant women? Why had she been so awful to me?

As time passed, I began to realize that perhaps I simply had not read the signs properly: I hadn't sought to clarify my apparent rapport with the Venus via divination, to get another angle on what her appearances possibly meant, and had blithely coasted along, believing that she was a benevolent manifestation of the Great Mother. I now realize that I had been relying on popular assumptions about what this particular Ice Age figurine actually represents, when in fact we don't really know much about her at all. We don't know whether she was a Mother Goddess, a fertility idol, or an Ice Age pin-up girl—she may even have had something to do with limiting fertility because historically hunter-gatherer groups have been more concerned with keeping their population down to a level that their environment could support, rather than increasing their numbers exponentially. Whatever she is, I probably should have realized from my previous experiences with the liminal Goddesses Kali and Artemis that deities can take as well as give. If the Venus is a Great Mother, maybe she was simply taking the baby back, facilitating a reverse birth into the world of spirit? I am reconciled with her now and, in hindsight, I think she was doing me a favor.

Melbourne, Australia

❧ Bitchin' at the God

Lexa Roséan

There were three things that marked me deeply in childhood: reading, writing, and retail. I loved the first two, but retail was the bane of my existence as well as the source of my material sustenance. It was the family business. As soon as I was old enough, I was recruited into the family pharmaceutical business. I unpacked cartons of merchandise, took inventories, and wasted my teenage years behind a cash register. I took care of cranky sick customers clamoring for their Colace, colostomy bags, crutches, and Kleenex. I stocked all the shelves with a smile. An inward smile, for all the while my paychecks were goin' in to a savings account and it would one day be my ticket out.

Ten years later, I found myself in New York City writing poetry and plays and reading about the Sumerian/Babylonian deities while cultivating my spiritual path of Wicca. Of course, none of this paid the rent. So, I found a cool job that many a young witchlet might hex for: working in the hippest occult shop in New York City. At first, I was honored to be a member of the Pagan elite. Occult shop employees are engaged in service to the Goddess and the Pagan community. Plus, they buy all their magickal supplies wholesale! Unfortunately, the occult shop is also a hornet's nest for dysfunctional neurotic souls. A spooky place!

I began my apprenticeship, while working on a play about Lilith, the rockin' Goddess of feminism who was exorcised from the Bible. I was studying with my High Priestess (the owner of the shop) and earning my first Wiccan degree. I read, I wrote, I learned a lot, and I made some money, which sustained me as a playwright. I finished the play and eventually it was produced in a downtown theater. These were the years of bliss. It was the year of my second-degree initiation that things began to spiral downward. My High Priestess sold out her share of the shop and left. I should have departed with her, but like Persephone, I seemed to be stuck in the underworld.

In the blink of an eye, another ten years passed. I woke up one morning and realized, to my horror, that I was, once again, stuck in retail! I was writing down ISBN numbers of books instead of reading them. I'd stopped going to circles because I was too busy doing inventory during the Sabbats. The magic was gone. I was wasting my twenties sitting behind a cash register, staring warily at the cranky customers clamoring for their cauldrons, candles, Cernunnos statues, and Kava Kava. I was stocking shelves, grinning, and bearing it. There was no inward smile, because it is impossible to bank paychecks in the money pit of Manhattan. I was no longer helping people. I was burned out and unhappy. And worst of all, I had stopped writing. I was too tired by the time I came home from work.

I began to bitch at the god. Hermes, or Mercury specifically, who is the god of communication and writing. I would wake up cursing him and scratch angry talismanic messages into orange candles for him to remove my writer's block. It worked. I began writing again. The beginning pages of what would become a novel. Still, my thoughts and time were interrupted, taken up by the shop. I cut back my hours, which helped some. I contemplated quitting, but the truth was I only knew how to do two things: write and work in an occult shop, and I guess I still had the skills to deal drugs. Rarely is it wise to quit a job without having another job lined up. One morning, I woke up happy because it was my day off. I was planning to write. Uninterrupted.

The phone rang. Someone was out sick and my boss wanted me to come in to work. Arggh!! I was angry. Hot piping mad, but needing those extra dollars, I put down my pen and dragged my ass out the door, cursing all the way. If the gods can be angry, why can't we? I eye the orange candle burning at my desk and take a swipe at it. Damn that Hermes for not coming through. As a Wiccan, I was taught to approach the Craft with "perfect love and perfect trust," but all that had just flown out the window! What kind of fool would trust Hermes anyway?! After all, he is the god of trickery and deception. As I knocked the candle to the floor, I felt the powerful energy of my anger. The glass holder broke and with it, I felt an incredible release. The flame on the candle was still lit. I lifted it up and placed it in a dish in the sink. I suppose, as god of commerce, Hermes had been doing his best to get me those extra hours in the shop. So, I swept up the glass and headed out the door. With one last look back at the candle flame, I told Mercury that he had one last chance to open my path. Or else I would abandon the worship of him. Irreverent in my anger, I headed toward the shop.

It was a regular Circus Maximus at work. A psychic ER of sorts with all kinds of energies flying about. The manager, pulling out her hair and screeching at the top of her lungs, because the customers had purchased *too many* books and now she had to order them all over again. The Warlock (wannabe psychotherapist) in the back had reduced a customer to tears, dragging her through dialog about how all her former boyfriends were as deadbeat as her dad, instead of selling her the love healing potion she had asked for. The old Pagan beatnik sleaze hanging out on the stoop, seducing a young zealot and whispering real close in her ear that she could get her incense cheaper up the block. A lunatic returning candles because they had melted. Upon further questioning, it was revealed that they had melted after the wicks were ignited. The terribly off-key voice of a new High Priestess bouncing off the walls and singing an Isis, Astarte, and Diana chant that would make even the hounds of Hecate cover their ears and moan. The unwaning ring of the phones and some poor soul waiting patiently in this madness for an ounce of Heal All. It was business as usual.

One of my coworkers finally answered the phone. He began

to cackle and barked into the receiver, "We don't write books, we sell them!" He was about to slam down the receiver. My ears pricked up and my hands moved with Mercurial speed. I grabbed the phone out of his hand and quickly introduced myself as a writer and an initiated Witch.

The voice on the other end of that line belonged to the woman who was to become my literary agent. I wrote that book for her. In fact, I've written six books and am now working on the seventh and eighth. That day changed my life. It was May 15. No coincidence that this is the date of the ancient festival of Mercury. The god came through for me: He helped me open my path with a telephone! (So completely and absurdly a magickal tool of Mercury.) Today, I no longer work in retail. I make my living as a writer. I circle with the people of my choosing instead of "the shop crew" or coven by circumstance. I feel more involved in the Pagan community and the teachings of the Craft than ever. I smile inwardly and outwardly, because I am happy with what I do and I am overwhelmed when I think of all the people I am able to touch through my writing. No more cranky over-the-cash-register encounters at the Pagan Duane Reade. I'm bitchin', I'm witchin', and finally I'm walkin' my own path with the god.

New York City

❧ Baby Santera in the Wildwoods
Menoukha Case

I had a lot of fun as the year turned to 2003, facing the possibility of dying twice in the wildwoods of Massachusetts (yes, we still have wildwoods). I'm here to tell the tale. Except for a visceral moment, I wasn't afraid; the prospect was consummately peaceful. Let me tell you how it happened:

I'm a squatter/caretaker—a squaretaker—at a nature conservancy. I moved in one day and they let me stay. Each year, on Christmas morning, the middle-aged son and daughter-in-law of the very old man who donated the land to the conservancy appear and take a ritual ice-skating spin across the frozen pond; otherwise, no one comes here much. My job is to cut up trees that fall across the road, scythe the grass around the log cabin the old man built for his father during World War II, and rechink the cabin from time to time to keep the wind out. I live in the cabin and have an office in town.

It has been one hell of a winter. Deep and continual snowfall since Christmas Eve has elevated me. I can bite tasty branches I couldn't reach on tiptoes with my fingertips this fall. It is a snowy blowy day and I'm bundled to these same cold teeth. I have a pickax and bucket in hand to chop a hole in the ice and fetch water from the pond.

Stepping through snowdrifty remains of the world as I know it, I sink through crunchy snow and, uh oh, what's this? One of my feet continues to sink through hidden and thin ice. Instant fear motivates a step backward with my other foot to extricate myself, but my sodden submerged leg is incredibly heavy, and I wrench my other knee trying to drag it out. All to no avail. I wonder, shivering: Will my body remain here on one leg while my spirit slowly takes flight, awaiting the visual echo of the great blue heron's return in the spring?

I eventually succeed in dragging myself out on my back, crawling to the house, and removing my boot. When I take off the poor drenched thing, several quarts of icy water splash onto the floor and spread, turning the orange rug red with relief. I can wiggle my toes. Good. I have a fire going and plenty of firewood nearby, so I don't freeze to death: I don't die once.

But there is the matter of this hot and swollen, painfully throbbing knee. It's now nightfall, and I'm hopping from the woodstove to the bed, keeping the place good and warm. Though the hopping hurts, I'm not certain what I can do. This is the wildwoods. No electricity, no running water, no gas lines, and, more to the point, no phone (as if anyone could get to the cabin), and there's no way I can hike out in this shape. I still have a full five gallons of water, but only a quarter-cup of lentils in the cupboard.

I consider that perhaps if I eat all the lentils at once, I'll be propelled up the half-mile hill to civilization in a mighty blast. Instead, I pray on my good knee: I offer all I have in the house to the altar (staples like honey, rum, molasses, smoke, and dear water) and clean the knee in front of Obaluaiye* and he answers me more quietly than silence: yes. When I rise, the pain is gone. My gait is a bit stiff, but Obaluaiye himself has a limp. Very simply, I can walk to the kitchen and cook those lentils. But can I trust the miraculously healed knee to get me through the icy gulf before an increasing weakness overcomes me? I eat small and then smaller portions of lentils. When I can't stand another bean, I layer plastic bags beneath snow-pants and sweaters and snowshoe out of the cabin. Weak with hunger, I snowshoe the half-mile from the cabin to the car and escape death for the second time this week. Maferefun Orisha!

At my office, I find a voice mail message from my friend Joan. I call to tell her about my two brushes with death. She begs me to get out of the cabin, move into my office, and only visit the wilderness in daylight and on clear days at that. A country person herself, she grew up in the woods, hiking and hunting, and she says I'm underestimating the difficulties, the danger. She's afraid I'll have another slip and really die this time—or be eaten by a coyote pack who are hungering because of a harsh winter. She says I've been warned three times: the jeep stopped working, the battery charger stopped working, and now this plunge and injury. Which, amazingly, doesn't hurt

*Obaluaiye (also called Babaluaiye) is the mysterious and quiet Yoruba West African deity of diseases, Earth-balancing justice, and healing. In Nigeria, his temples are outside the village, away from people. In Diaspora, he lives in our houses, and his awesome power requires a peaceful home and the utmost respect.

anymore. Joan convinces me to ask the Orishas what they want me to do. Du-uh, why didn't I think of that?

So, I ask and they say they want us out of there, for the most part. Curiously, Obaluaiye will stay to "hold the space." In light of his healing my knee, this encourages me to maintain a relationship with the cabin. From now on, on every nonsnowing day, I will hike my lovely intact body over to the cabin and bring out those Orishas who choose to leave. I can also, since I'm there, make a fire, hang out, read, and meditate.

Well and good. But on the last trip, with my Osun-laden backpack carefully propped upright and waiting, I get a fifth sign. I'm ready to leave and I'm adjusting the woodstove when the dampers go off thread and adamantly stick open. Now there's no way to make a slow overnight fire. I try tin foil around the vents to block the air and it works, but not enough to hold an all nighter. I guess when Obaluaiye says he'll hold the space I should understand that he doesn't need my help. And that he likes being alone. That's why he's called "Hidden Man."

Great Barrington, Massachusetts

༄ Leprechauns in the City
Mary Grace Farley

I saw a leprechaun in the subway today. To be specific, at the Broadway N train station in Astoria. (No, I had not been hitting the Guinness.) He was about 5'6", maybe forty-nine years old, slim, neat and clean, with dark hair, a goatee, fierce gray eyes, and an angry expression. He was wearing a striped green-and-white Cat in the Hat–style top hat, a green riding coat with tails, green football pants, and green Converse high tops. He also had on green glitter cat-eye glasses.

At first I thought, *Oh, look at that guy dressed up like a leprechaun.* Then I met his fierce gray eyes and realized that he *was* a leprechaun, no messing around. A little girl saw him, too, and whispered to her mother that he was a clown. He glared at the girl and she started to cry. No Lucky Charms giggles here. He swiped his transit card, stalked up the stairs, and headed to Manhattan. I followed at a respectful distance, but lost him on the train.

As I made my way through the parade's unavoidable tumult, his image stayed with me, mocked by the little green men smiling from countless cardboard pub signs touting green beer and corned beef. What would bring a self-respecting leprechaun to New York City for St. Patrick's Day? What could he possibly be here to do?

I am not a big fan of St. Patrick's Day. I watch drunken suburbanites in green plastic hats vomiting into the gutters in "celebration" of my cultural and ethnic heritage, and I wish them the luck of the Irish (occupation, famine, sunburn, etc.). Green steam comes out of my ears when I think that my tax dollars are being spent to police and clean up after the biggest religious parades of the year in New York City—one that uses public dollars but excludes gay citizens. To my way of thinking, there is nothing valid or meaningful about it, nothing truly Irish. But I think this year might be . . . unusual.

Later, in the Village, I thought I saw another leprechaun. This time, I ran after him. He turned out to be a tall, fierce black drag queen in a green Lycra bodystocking, in his cups at 4:00 P.M. This gave me pause, but I asked anyway, "Excuse me . . . please, are you a real leprechaun?"

He stared deep into my eyes and said, basso profundo, "No, baby, I'm really Tinkerbell—but it's Leprechaun Day, so *kiss* me, I'm Iiiiirishhhh," ending with two big snaps up and regally presenting his hand. I bowed, kissed his ring, and watched him go.

I felt I'd somehow been told why a leprechaun would come to New York City on St. Patrick's Day, but it wasn't until later, on the edge of sleep, that I understood. The leprechaun had to come to the parade, like it or not. It was Leprechaun Day. His image was everywhere, people dressed up in green like him, we invoked him, acknowledged and honored him. Where else could he get that these days? When else are his stories told, songs sung, and toasts drunk? Where else do we gather by the thousands to clap, sing, and ululate in the streets as he passes by? Admittedly, we do all this in an unfortunate and cockeyed way, provoking the rage I saw on his face, but the force of it, the enormous rush of energy . . . how could he resist?

I was right about St. Patrick's Day, and wrong. It's not wise to dismiss the whole ritual just because we're not doing it right, or even because most of the people performing the ritual know not what they do. I realize now that the chaotic joy, the musicality, the expansiveness, even the ferocity of the celebration are deeply Celtic.

Next year, I may join the hordes on the magical isle as they paint their faces and charge howling onto Fifth Avenue to bagpipe and drum. I may do it in stealth, I may do it in protest, but I know that once I do, it will never be the same again. I will honor the little green man for what he truly is, and give him what he came for. Perhaps in time, the others will truly remember him, remember themselves as a tribe that needs and respects him, and he will be rescued from cereal-box purgatory, honored properly all the year long. Sooner or later, the leprechaun may have reason to smile.

New York City

≪ What's in a Name
FoolCat

Once, long ago, when I was a young man (I'm older now, if not much wiser), I attended a large gathering in upstate New

York. I had just gotten married. When I wed, my beloved and I thought it fair that rather than she taking my last name, or I taking hers, we would create a new last name; a name that we would both share.

So there I was at this festival, at the main dance, having a truly enlightening time (remember that enlightenment also means removing the weights). I felt connected to the singers and dancers on the stage and to all the other wonderful people surrounding me. While in this open state, I heard a now familiar voice speak to me in the back of my mind. It told me how fitting it would be, as I had changed my last name, to also change my Magical name.

The name I had previously chosen for myself was too obscure, too arrogant. (I took the name Triton—a minor sea god.) Instead, the voice said I should take a name that was simpler. A name that still spoke of a connection to the ocean, but was more common. A name that reflected my hippy, counterculture leanings, but less pretentious.

Wave, the voice whispered.

That would be perfect! Wave would definitely be my new name. How inspired. How right. It was a precious gift, given directly from the Gods themselves. I felt so blessed! Wave *would* be my new name!

Then I remembered my recently chosen *last* name. You see, my wife and I had agreed to take the name of a species of feline; cats being something that we both greatly loved. Lynx was our new last name. So, put together my new last name with the name I had just been given by divine message was: Wave Lynx! Of all the terrible, awful puns to perpetrate!

Again I heard that voice in my head, *laughing uproariously!*

So, take heart. The Gods *do* have a sense of humor, even if they occasionally make us the butt of their joke.

Machias, Maine

⮂ Out of the Waves

Penny Novack

My life has moved through the Elements in an orderly widder-shins progression—which is reasonable, the usual result of entropy. Working my way through Water, I settled on first one manifestation and then another, trying myself against the ambiance of each. When I found the picture of Yemayah, it came to me that I knew where Her altar should be: on the West wall of the house, of course—above the kitchen sink. No. On the sink.

I realized, almost by accident, that I had been building Her altar for about a year. There were the little fish hanging from the cupboard over the sink, swimming in air. There was the large starfish, the huge fish-shaped clear dish hanging in a net strung across the back wall, and the seashells on the space behind the sink.

How amazing. Gods seem to pick the strangest places to call home. She wanted to be set up there at the New Moon and for about a year, perhaps a year and a half, we had our monthly meetings. Everything needed came to me, such as the silver-backed antique mirror and the colors of cloth to drape Her grotto. It was like being in love. And, for a while, She told me things.

For instance, once I gushed, "You are so beautiful."

To which She replied, "Of course, I am Beauty."

I was stunned. "You are Beauty? You are the nature of what is beautiful?"

"Everything is Beautiful," She told me. "I created everything and it is all beautiful."

Hoping She wouldn't be insulted, I said, "Everything doesn't look beautiful to me."

I could feel her amusement, "That is because you cannot see it as I do. I made everything and all is beautiful."

I considered all the Goddesses I've studied over the years.

"All the Goddesses I have known were beautiful, but I thought that was just a side effect."

She was tired of the conversation and only would say, "Beauty is the meaning of Creation."

I was, I admit, stunned. My concept of Creation had not really covered this. An anthropomorphic Persona to say such a thing boggled my mind. But . . . it is foolish to refuse the gifts of the Gods—perhaps particularly foolish to refuse Their wisdom. The Crone has been telling me for years that I'm funny and I've had to admit I have more in common with the Fool in the Tarot than I can refute.

Almost a year later, I attended the Witches Halloween Ball (held locally and sponsored by the area's only Pagan supply store). As I danced to the music of a Yoruba rite–inspired reggae band named Gaia Roots, I found myself trancing out to the music of a Yoruban drum paeon to the goddess Yemayah. It was the last time She spoke to me.

She danced before me in an ocean of energy. Waterlike but also firelike, She flickered between shapes of sinuous musical energy and that of a Feminine Power, vigorously flinging bits of iridescent drops of essence about.

"I Dance and as I Dance, drops fly from my finger tips and the entire universe is made by my Dancing. You are an iridescent drop of Myself Dancing My Dance. How can you not be beautiful?"

It will always daze and humble me to remember. Perhaps something so vivid is reason to question my sanity and yet, I did learn new things, new visions. And I am grateful. She told me true, I believe. When I learn to truly see, I will know that everything is beautiful.

The Berkshires, Massachusetts

CONTRIBUTORS

Margot Adler is the author of *Drawing Down the Moon* (1979), the classic study of Goddess spirituality and contemporary Paganism, and *Heretic's Heart: A Journey through Spirit and Revolution*. She is a correspondent for National Public Radio (NPR), and her reports air on NPR's award-winning shows *All Things Considered, Morning Edition,* and *Weekend Edition.* She hosts *Justice Talking,* a new radio show on the subject of the U.S. Constitution, which is produced by the Annenberg Center for Public Policy of the University of Pennsylvania. She also lectures widely on Paganism and Earth traditions. She has been a Wiccan priestess for more than twenty-five years.

Amara (Natalie J. Case) is an eclectic Shamanic Witch. She currently resides in northern California, where she is working on founding a tradition dedicated to the Morrigan. Amara has also published a short chapbook of poetry and has placed poems in several anthologies.

Anonymous. Not all people whose stories appear in this anthology felt comfortable revealing their legal or full names. In many corners of the world, Witches and Pagans face harassment and persecution for practicing their beliefs. Loss of employment, housing, and even the removal of children from a family are still risks. For those who needed to be Anonymous, I thank you for having the courage to share your stories. May the day come when we can all stand proud in the light.

Barbara Ardinger, Ph.D., is the author of *Finding New Goddesses* (2003), *Quicksilver Moon: A Novel* (2003), *Goddess Meditations* (1998), and *Practicing the Presence of the Goddess* (2000). Her day job is freelance editing for people who don't want to embarrass themselves in print. She works with authors of nonfiction books on spiritual, metaphysical, and other topics and she also edits novels. She lives in southern California and can be reached at www.barbaraardinger. com.

Susan G. Curewitz Arthen is a member of the Glenshire Order of Witches. She lives in a hilltown in western Massachusetts and has not missed a Rites of Spring since 1981. For more information about EarthSpirit and Rites of Spring, visit www.earthspirit.com.

Bob Barraco is a Witch with a diverse background, including traditional Wicca, Third Road Faerie, Native American Shamanism, and Buddhism. He is also a tattoo artist living in central New York.

Peter Bishop is the former High Priest of Stepshild Coven and a member of Mount Toby Meeting of Friends. He lives in Northampton, Massachusetts, with his wife, daughter, and two (at last count) dogs.

Black Lotus (Len Rosenberg) is a devotee of Ammachi of Kerala. He teaches Shakta Hinduism, astrology, mantra, and the magical uses of incenses and gems. As a Protean/Gardnerian High Priest, he coleads Children of Memory Coven with Alexei Kondratiev in New York City. He can be reached at kalipadma@juno.com.

Menoukha Case is a fairly newly made Santera of Obatala, an astrologer, a diviner, a student, a teacher, an artist, and a writer.

Cat Chapin-Bishop has been a Wiccan High Priestess since 1989, and a Quaker-Pagan since 2001. A lifelong New Englander, she currently lives with her daughter, husband, and two dogs among the landspirits of the Connecticut River Valley. Her Pagan writings have appeared in *The Pomegranate, Enchanté, Moonrise, Harvest,* and *The Covenant of the Goddess Newsletter.* Cat also maintains the Lady's Spindle/Pagan handspinner's listserve.

T. Thorn Coyle, author of *Evolutionary Witchcraft* (2004), is an Anderson Feri tradition Priestess who teaches internationally. Please visit www.thorncoyle.com for information on her CDs, DVD, writing, and workshops.

Francesca De Grandis is a grassroots spiritual activist, humorist, and the author of *Be a Goddess!* (1998), *Goddess Initiation* (2001), the humor book *The Modern Goddess' Guide to Life: How to Be Absolutely Divine on a Daily Basis* (2004), and *Be a Teen Goddess! Magical Charms, Spells, and Wiccan Wisdom for the Wild Ride of Life* (2005). Francesca provides spiritual counseling by phone to people all over the world. She also teaches Goddess Spirituality through international teleseminars—classes by telephone. Contact her at (814) 337-2490.

Edmund is one of the names of a well-known British Pagan who has worked as a High Priest in both the Gardnerian and Alexandrian Wiccan traditions and is also a Druid. He has a special interest in the history of Paganism and of related areas such as magic and folklore.

Ember is a Pagan girl and hippie-chick from Las Vegas, Nevada. She has been involved in Earth-based spiritual community for thirteen years and is currently practicing with Desert Moon Circle. Ember discovered Fire Circle technology at her first festival, Firedance, in August 2000, and has since become involved on many levels with the Firedance event, local drum and dance events, and the Las Vegas Earth-based community. She can be reached at tandy71@yahoo.com.

Douglas Ezzy, Ph.D., is a senior lecturer in Sociology at the University of Tasmania, Australia. He is interested in trying to discover what sort of Paganism makes sense for a fifth-generation Tasmanian with European ancestry who prefers the company of Tasmanian rivers, trees, and mountains. His academic books include *Narrating Unemployment* (2001), *Practicing the Witch's Craft* (2003), and *Researching Paganisms* (2004), edited with Jenny Blain and Graham Harvey. He also wonders what matters to wombats.

Mary Grace Farley followed her personal rainbow from New York City to the green hills of western Massachusetts and feels very, very lucky to be there. Learn more about her bodywork practice at www.gracebodywork.com.

FoolCat, who was until his divorce called Wave Lynx, is a High Priest in the Protean tradition. He lives in Machias, Maine, with his beloved second wife, Rhea. FoolCat has a stream of consciousness like a white water rabbit and is currently working on his own sense of humor to mirror that of the Gods.

Thom Fowler is a San Francisco–based culture and lifestyle writer, a Witch of the Third Road tradition and a student of Francesca De Grandis. More of his work and random tours through his brain and out into the cosmos can be found at www.thomfowler.com.

Autumn Amber Fox (Christine Highfill) is a Witch and a member of Circle Sanctuary Community. She was initiated into the Circle Craft tradition by Selena Fox on Samhain 2002. Her stories and poems have appeared in *Circle Magazine*. Now that her two sons have grown, Autumn lives with her husky-coonhound dog, Cernunnos, and two cats, Grim Reaper and Calliope, in Rockford, Illinois.

G~ walks the Third Road tradition and is a longtime eclectic solitary. An unabashed spiritual sensualist, she revels in the nuances of the Divine from the smallest feather to the greatest storm and believes that belly laughter and loving yourself are the strongest magic.

Grey Cat is the author of *Deepening Witchcraft: Advancing Skills and Knowledge* (2002), which is listed as one of the modern classics in *PanGaia Magazine*'s Pagan Bookshelf, and of chapters in the first two volumes of *Witchcraft Today* (1992, 1993) and coauthor of *American Indian Ceremonies: Walking the Good Red Road* (1990). She is the founder of the NorthWind tradition of American Wicca and lives and teaches in Tennessee "under the supervision of her feline associates."

Judy Harrow is the High Priestess of Proteus Coven and the chair of the Pastoral Counseling program at Cherry Hill Seminary. She is also the President of the New Jersey Association for Spiritual, Ethical, and Religious Values in Counseling. She has written two books, *Wicca Covens* (1999) and *Spiritual Mentoring* (2002), edited and contributed to the anthology *Devoted to You* (2003), and coordinated the fiftieth anniversary reissue of *Witchcraft Today* by Gerald Gardner (2004).

Rowan Hawkmoon is a semisolitary eclectic Pagan who lived through the 1960s (disproving the phrase "if you remember the 1960s you weren't really there"). She is blessed with a spirit sister, loves animals, and wants to run away and be the "crazy herb lady who lives in the forest" when she grows up. She hates writing bios because she isn't through remembering who she is.

Holly Heart Free is a fifty-seven-year-old Crone who lives on a farm in southeastern Wisconsin. An Earth practitioner, she is especially thankful for the animals on her land who daily reaffirm her life and decisions and teach her the most important lessons of all.

Tree Higgins is an Asatru Pagan, performance artist, poet, and activist with a magic heart. She spends most of her time on the open road and in forests where she is frequently found in deep conversation with other trees. She has self-published a chapbook of poems *A Pagan Heart*.

Ellen Evert Hopman is the author of *Tree Medicine, Tree Magic* (1991), *A Druid's Herbal* (1995), *Walking the World in Wonder: A Children's Herbal* (2000), and coauthor, with Lawrence Bond, of *Being a Pagan* (2002). She is a Druid Priestess of the Order of the Whiteoak (Ord Na Darach Gile). Ellen lives in an oak forest in western Massachusets. She is the companion human to two cats, Tir and Nemetona. She can be reached at saille333.home.mindspring.com/willow.html.

Jennifer Hunter is the author of *21st Century Wicca: A Young Witch's Guide to Living a Magical Life* (1997), *Wicca for Lovers: Spells and Rituals for Romance and Seduction* (2001), and *Rites of Pleasure: Sexuality in Wicca and Neo-Paganism* (2004). At the time of this writing, she is working on a book about Jewish Paganism. She is self-employed as a writer and editor, and lives in Somerville, Massachusetts with her four-year-old daughter.

Angela Huston is a third-degree Priestess and Witch in both the Gardnerian and Georgian traditions. She is the High Priestess of RavenCroft, a Gardnerian coven. Angela lives in the Appalachians with her husband, Bill, her cats, Mr. Sphinx and Ophelia, her dog, Sage, her lovebird, Pyxis, and her horse, Opal. She is a full-time nurse in the emergency care setting.

Dana Kramer-Rolls holds a doctorate in Folklore and History of Religions. Her stories have appeared in Marion Zimmer Bradley's *Sword and Sorceress* anthologies and she was a major contributor to *The Encyclopedia of Modern Witchcraft and Neo-Paganism* (2002). Her newest book, *The Way of the Cat* (2004), talks about our cats as our teachers, and opens the door to interspecies communication and respect.

Lady Rhea is the author of *The Enchanted Candle* (2004). She has been in the occult store business all of her working life. Lady Rhea owns and operates Magickal Realms in Bronx, New York, with her partner Lady Zoradia, where she is also a professional Tarot reader. Lady Rhea is the cofounder of the Minoan Sisterhood which merged with its counterpart, the Minoan Brotherhood to form the Minoan Fellowship. She works with Orishas and saints, as well as Wicca and a host of other pantheons.

K. A. Laity, Ph.D., is a medievalist at the University of Houston-Downtown, where she teaches early British literature, creative writing, and film. An eclectic for many years, she studies historical magic in Anglo-Saxon and Old Norse cultures. Her novel *Pelzmantel: A Medieval Tale* (2003) adapts a Grimm tale to a medieval

Scandinavian setting and offers a showcase of actual charms, healing, and herbal magic from the period. Her work has appeared in *The Beltane Papers, Circle, NewWitch, The Seeker Journal, New World Finn*, and *The Pagan's Muse* (2003).

Frederic Lamond is a life long pantheist. He was initiated in February 1957 into Gardnerian Witchcraft (now called Wicca). He is also a member of the Fellowship of Isis and the Church of All Worlds, the Children of Artemis and is on the Council of the Pagan Federation. Besides many articles in Wiccan and other Pagan publications, he is the author of *The Divine Struggle* (1990), *Religion without Beliefs* (1997), and *50 Years of Wicca: A Critical Personal Retrospective* (2004).

Eve LeFey is a freelance writer, musician and composer. She coauthored *The Enchanted Candle* (2004) with Lady Rhea. A second-degree Priestess with the Coven of Eleuthia, she lives in Brooklyn, New York, with her two furry feline familiars, Anna and Lord Byron.

Carl McColman is the author of several Pagan and Pagan-friendly books, including *The Well-Read Witch: Essential Books for Your Magickal Library* (2001) and *Before You Cast a Spell: Understanding the Power of Magic* (2003). He lives in Stone Mountain, Georgia, and can be found at www.carlmccolman.com.

Patricia Monaghan is one of the leaders of the contemporary Earth spirituality movement. She has spent more than twenty years researching and writing about alternative spiritual visions of the earth. She is a writer and an award-winning poet whose work has been set to music and is performed around the world. Much of her work explores the role of feminine power in our world, in an inclusive and multicultural way. She is a winner of a 2004 Pushcart Prize for literature, and has an essay included in *Best American Spiritual Writing, 2004*. Her newest book, *The Red-Haired Girl from the Bog: The Landscape of Celtic Myth and Spirit* (2003), explores the way that Irish mythology expresses the power of the Irish land.

Her other books include *Meditation: The Complete Guide* (1999), *The Goddess Companion: Daily Meditation on the Feminine Spirit* (1999), and *Wild Girls: The Path of the Young Goddess* (new edition, 2004).

M. Macha NightMare is the author of *Pagan Pride: Honoring the Craft and Culture of Earth and Goddess* (2004), *Witchcraft and the Web: Weaving Pagan Traditions Online* (2001), and, with Starhawk, *The Pagan Book of Living and Dying: Practical Rituals, Prayers, Blessings, and Meditations on Crossing Over* (1997). An all-round Pagan webweaver, she teaches on the broomstick circuit and currently chairs the Public Ministry Department at Cherry Hill Seminary. She can be found at www.machanightmare.com.

Penny Novack was born on Summer Solstice 1941. She is a mother, grandmother, and friend to many. Her spiritual philosophy is often self-described as "Judeao-Pagan Taoist," and she is best known for her Erisian humor and sentimental relationships with trees and other living things. An Initiated Witch since 1969 in an eclectic American tradition, Penny was one of the early organizers of the Pagan Way (1971). She is a poet, philosopher, environmentalist, crone in training, and a determined partaker of the philosophy that "life is for living."

Oriethyia has lived and taught women's magic for many years. She resides in upstate New York.

David L. Oringderff, Ph.D., is a veteran of over thirty-five years in military and civilian law enforcement and intelligence work. In the 1970s, he worked as a Patrol Officer, Criminal Investigator, and Chief of Police in northern Texas. In 1981, he was awarded a direct commission in the U.S. Army and recalled to active duty. He retired in 1995 as a Major in the Military Intelligence Branch. Dr. Oringderff is a Subject Matter Expert consultant to the Department of Defense Armed Forces Chaplains Board on Alternative Religions, Sects, and Cults. He has appeared on *ABC World News Tonight, Good Morning America, NBC Dateline, VRT Television* (Belgium), *ZDF Television* (Germany), and national and international print media including *Time, Texas Monthly,* and *US News and World Report.*

Marilyn R. Pukkila is a Quaker Wiccan in the Reclaiming Tradition and an ordained Priestess in the Fellowship of Isis through the Temple of the Feminine Divine in Bangor, Maine. She works as a librarian at Colby College, where she teaches courses on contemporary Witchcraft, women in myth and fairy tale, and J. R. R. Tolkien.

Flame RavenHawk is a writer who has been teaching Shamanic Wicca for over a decade. Professionally, she teaches reading in a public high school, and her hobbies include yoga, drumming (Middle Eastern Doumbek), poetry, gardening, and cultural anthropology. A collection of her articles and writings can be found at her Web site, www.flamesfirepit.org, a site for teaching and exploration of Shamanic Wicca and Pagan philosophy.

Lexa Roséan is the author of *The Supermarket Sorceress* (1996), *Sexy Hexes* (1997), *Enchanted Evenings* (1998), *Easy Enchantments* (2002), *PowerSpells* (2001), *ZodiacSpells* (2002), and *Tarot Power* (2004). Visit her Web site www.lexarosean.com.

Victoria Slind-Flor, in her mundane life, writes for a publication dedicated to technology and intellectual-property law. She is a Pagan who is exploring the religious and cultural roots of her mixed Norwegian and Saami heritage, and she also makes Goddess-themed fabric art.

Kathi Somers is an Initiate and Priestess of the Third Road tradition, mother and grandmother, sex goddess, and crone.

Spellweaver continues to live in the "Happy Pioneer Valley," where she participates in various community events, including Morris dancing, mead making, and singing to the stars every chance she gets.

Starhawk, a committed global justice activist and organizer, is the author or coauthor of nine books, including *The Spiral Dance* (1979; reprinted 1999), *The Fifth Sacred Thing* (1994), and *Webs of Power: Notes from the Global Uprising* (2002). She is a veteran of progressive movements, from antiwar to antinukes, is a highly influential voice in the revival of the Goddess religion, and has brought many innovative techniques of spirituality and magic to her political work. She works with the RANT collective, which offers training and organizing support for peace and global justice movements, and with Reclaiming, which offers training in Earth-based ritual, healing, and community building, and teaches Earth Activist Trainings, which combines permaculture design and organizing skills.

Susan Taplinger is a freelance editor and writer living on the cusp of New York City. She has studied and practiced a variety of spiritual paths, both Eastern and Western, for over twenty-five years. She is currently a consulting editor for a weekly direct-marketing column and a passionate baseball fan.

Caroline Tully is an Australian Witch with a penchant for Hellenic Reconstructionism. She is a feature writer and reviewer for several Pagan publications, including Australia's *Witchcraft Magazine,* and contributed a chapter on the Southern Hemisphere sabbats in *Practising the Witch's Craft: Real Magic under a Southern Sky* (2003).

Wren Walker is the co-founder/chairperson of The Witches' Voice, Inc. (www.witchvox.com) and she is the author of many of the basic documents posted on the Witches' Voice site. Speaking as a life-long Pagan and civil rights activist, she has been interviewed on numerous radio programs, television shows and many major newspapers. Wren currently provides a news clipping service called, "Wren's Nest" which focuses on religious and spiritual articles of interest to Pagans (www.witchvox.com/xwrensnest.html). She shares a home with The Witches' Voice co-founder and husband, Fritz Jung and their three kitties, Ruby, Djinn-Jinn, and Lei-Lu.

Brook Willowbark was raised in a small New England town and educated in Berkeley, California. This nurse has returned to her roots to build her own energy-efficient home on a hundred acres.

John Yohalem was the publisher, editor, lead writer, and coroner for the now-defunct *Enchanté: The Journal for the Urbane Pagan*. He may bring out a compendium of its best bits under the title *Black Magic: Its Cause and Cure*, but then again, he may not. For extreme and orgiastic Pagan ritual, he goes to the opera. This makes it necessary for him to live in New York, despite his better judgment and bad feet.

Michael York, Ph.D., is a professor of Cultural Astronomy and Astrology at Bath Spa University, England. His most recent publications are *Pagan Theology: Paganism As a World Religion* (2004) and *Historical Dictionary of New Age Movements* (2004).

Oberon Zell-Ravenheart has been active in the Pagan community for over forty years and has been involved in the founding of several major groups and alliances and in the publication of the legendary journal *Green Egg* (1968–1975; 1988–1996). In 1970, he formulated and published the thealogy of deep ecology, which he called the Gaea Thesis, antedating James Lovelock's similar Gaia (*sic*) Hypothesis. Oberon is the primary artist of *The Mythic Images Collection*, producing museum-quality replicas and beautiful original altar figurines of Gods, Goddesses, and mythological creatures. His first book is *Grimoire for the Apprentice Wizard* (2004).

∾ About the Editor

Laura Wildman is the author of *What's Your Wicca I.Q.?* (2002) and *Wiccan Meditations* (2002). She is a Third Degree Gardnerian Witch trained in the Protean tradition, and High Priestess of Apple and Oak Coven. Laura is the Administrative Dean and an instructor at Cherry Hill Seminary, a Pagan seminary located in Bethel, Vermont (www.cherryhillseminary.org). She lectures, offers classes, and has published articles on Wicca and the Tarot. Laura is active in Weaver's, a local chapter of Covenant of the Goddess (www.cog.org). She is a co-founder of New Moon, a Pagan Networking Organization in New York, and has helped to organize hundreds of rituals and workshops. In 1993 Laura became a legally recognized Wiccan clergy in her state of Massachusetts. In this role, she has had the honor of performing over one hundred wedding and handfasting ceremonies. She lives with her loving husband, Tom, and their three wonderful children, and considers every day a gift to be savored.